# THE DEATH OF
# COMMUNAL LIBERTY

# The Death of Communal Liberty

A HISTORY OF FREEDOM
IN A SWISS
MOUNTAIN CANTON

Benjamin R. Barber

PRINCETON UNIVERSITY PRESS
PRINCETON, NEW JERSEY

Library of Congress Cataloging in Publication
Data will be found on
the last printed page of this book.

This book has been composed in Linotype Baskerville

Printed in the United States of America
by Princeton University Press, Princeton, New Jersey

To Hans K. Maeder

*who has devoted his life to man's freedom*

# Contents

# Illustrations

# Maps

# Acknowledgments

THIS study has been fitfully in the making for nearly ten years—a somber fact which, if justice were done, would compel me to acknowledge what now amounts to my entire intellectual heritage. The few debts I enumerate here must serve, then, to represent a far larger debt that by its nature cannot be specified.

In Switzerland I have had the benefit of conversations with and the patient counsel of Dr. Rudolf Jenny, the cantonal archivist of Graubünden, and Professor Erich Gruner, Director of the Research Institute for the History and Sociology of Swiss Politics at the University of Bern. Professor Peter Liver of the University of Bern, a native of Graubünden and a prolific commentator on its history, was helpful in early stages of my research. Informal conversations with Dr. Joachim Wolff, Professor Jakob Amstutz, National Assemblyman Paul Raschein, and Miss Erika Weibel provided a vital foil for my evolving ideas about Swiss life and politics. Dr. Raymond Riedi, with his unflappable expertise and his many small kindnesses, made what ought to have been a grueling ordeal in the cantonal library of Graubünden an ongoing pleasure. Above all, in Switzerland, I owe a profound debt to the late Hans Casparis, founder and long-time director of the Albert Schweitzer College in Churwalden, and to his wife Thérèse Casparis. They introduced me gently to Swiss life when I was barely seventeen, and later made it possible for me to spend several years teaching at Albert Schweitzer College when as a doctoral candidate I worked on preliminary drafts of this study.

In England and the United States, I have been fortunate

ix

to have had responses to various facets of my work on Switzerland from Michael Oakeshott and Ralph Miliband, both formerly of the London School of Economics and Political Science, from John H. Van de Graaff of Yale University, from Herbert J. Spiro and Henry Abraham of the University of Pennsylvania, and from Carl J. Friedrich, Judith N. Shklar, and James Luther Adams of Harvard University. Louis Hartz of Harvard University played a very special role in the making of this book. As a dissertation director, his critical acumen leavened always with a catalyzing enthusiasm brought me through the first stages of the work; as a friend and critic his subsequent encouragement led me to revising, redrafting, and finally a complete reworking of the study without which it probably never would have turned into a finished project.

The Research Councils of Rutgers University and the University of Pennsylvania have facilitated my recent work with timely summer research grants. For typing of the manuscript I regrettably have no one to thank but myself—a dismal innovation I do not urge colleagues to emulate.

To my wife Naomi I owe a debt too personal to be put into words, too deep to be repaid by publication of this book. She alone knows how large that debt is.

# A Note on Names and Translation

MOST of the sources utilized in this study are German-Swiss or French-Swiss; consequently, a great deal of translation has been required not only of passages cited in the texts and notes but also of key concepts and terms. Special difficulties have arisen in trying to find English equivalents for archaic German terms that are embedded in an experience easily misconceived when re-presented in an Anglo-American political-legal vocabulary reflecting our own experience. I have therefore tried to include a parenthetic reference to original German terms following their initial translation, and to employ their English equivalents fairly consistently, although style has at times forced compromise in this practice. Unless otherwise noted, all translations from German or French sources are my own. I have aimed at conveying meaning rather than at literalness, hopefully not at the expense of accuracy.

The region of Switzerland that serves as the focus of this study presents certain additional difficulties. The modern canton is called Graubünden, a derivative from the name *Grauer Bund* or Gray League. Although it is frequently referred to in American and English studies by its French name *Grisons*, there is no good reason to imitate that practice. On the other hand, the region has historically been known under several different names. During its Roman and Carolingian periods it was called Upper Raetia *(Oberraetia)*, *Churraetia*, or simply Raetia, distinguishing it from the Western regions of modern Switzerland then known as Helvetia. From 1524 to 1800, Raetia became an independent Republic, and was known as the Republic of the Three

Leagues (*Freistaat der Drei Bünde* or *Dreibündenstaat*). Historians looking back on the period often speak of Old Free Raetia (*alt Frei Raetia*). I have restricted use of the term Raetian Republic or simply republic to the period of independence, but have otherwise employed both Raetia and Graubünden interchangeably in speaking of historical Graubünden, Graubünden alone in referring to the modern canton. As qualifying adjectival forms I have used Raetian and Bündner interchangeably.

# PART I : Introduction

Hail thee, lasting freedom; thou land,
        simple and true;
  Thy free spirit, rest on thee contented people.
Through modesty thou are rich, in austerity
        of morals, great.
  Raw, thy courage, as glaciers—and cold
        when danger strikes.
Firm as mountain crags, powerful as the
        thundering Rhinefall;
  Worthy of thy nature, worthy of thy fathers,
        And free.
      —Johann Gaudenz von Salis-Seewis
      *Elegy to my Raetian Fatherland*

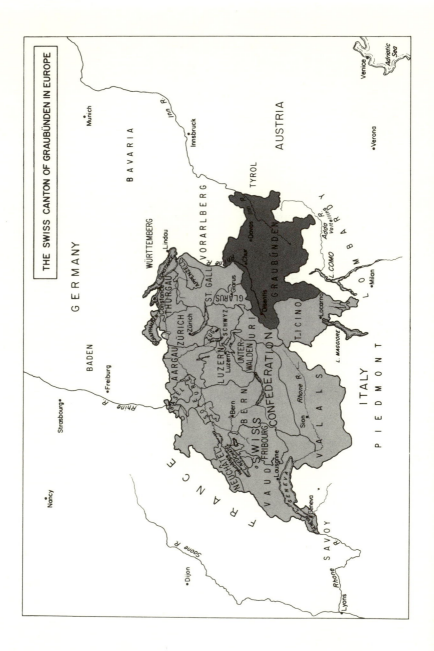

THE SWISS CANTON OF GRAUBÜNDEN IN EUROPE

# CHAPTER I

# Political Theory and Swiss Practice

## THE POLITICAL THEORY OF FREEDOM

THE apparent pluralism and professed heterogeneity of current political thought sometimes lead us to forget its stunning parochialism. Many of our political ideas and most of our political practices have been distilled from an Anglo-American tradition that is as insular as it is fertile, as narrow as it is long, as dogmatic as it is convincing. This tradition takes its theoretic orientation from the psychological hedonism and atomistic individualism of Thomas Hobbes, and relies on terms like power and interest to get at the political. It has been conditioned by the history of constitutionalism, limited government, and natural rights it helped to make. It informs almost everything written today about notions of freedom, democracy, and popular sovereignty. It does not so much offer answers as dictate the framework within which questions can be formulated and posed. It does not, for example, always insist that men must choose private rights over public obligations, but it does suggest that the two are necessarily incompatible. It may not deny that freedom can be construed as something more than the mere absence of constraints, but it will be certain that such constructions tend inevitably to totalitarianism. It is a tradition the spokesmen of which represent a noble lineage from Hobbes, down through Locke, Hume, Bentham, and John Stuart Mill, to Bertrand Russell and Isaiah Berlin. Although it has had to compete with philosophical rivals as vigorous as romanticism, Hegelianism and phenomenology, its place in Anglo-American popular thinking and political practice has always seemed untouchable. As a re-

3

sult, whatever inroads fashionable European ideologies like historicism or existentialism may make in academic and literary consciousness, liberal constitutionalism as it has been shaped by British empiricism and American pragmatism continues to dominate the way we think about and practice politics. This is particularly true of two paramount political ideas to which we have already alluded: freedom and democracy. Both notions have had a normal form in our thought; deviations from the norm have generally been understood as aberrant or even pathological. Thus, freedom has generally been associated with a physical-mechanistic model exemplified by Hobbes' well-known definition of liberty as "the absence of external impediments of motion."[1] Any number of sources can be cited that confirm the preeminence of the Hobbesian view. To the eighteenth-century *philosophe* Helvetius, "the free man is a man who is not in irons, nor imprisoned, nor terrorized like a slave by fear of punishment."[2] Isaiah Berlin concludes that "the fundamental sense of freedom is freedom from chains, from imprisonment, from enslavement by others. The rest is extension of this sense, or else metaphor."[3] In political terms, freedom as the absence of constraints connotes limited or minimal government. "Perfect liberty is equivalent to total absence of government," writes Bernard Bosanquet,[4] echo-

[1] Thomas Hobbes, *Leviathan*, ed. Michael Oakeshott (Oxford, 1960), Part II, Chapter 21.

[2] Cited by Oscar and Mary Handlin, *The Dimensions of Liberty* (New York, 1966), p. 9.

[3] Isaiah Berlin, *Four Essays on Freedom* (Oxford, 1969), p. lvi. For a full discussion of the theoretical and psychological implications of the physical-mechanistic model of freedom, see Benjamin R. Barber, *Superman and Common Men: Freedom, Anarchy, and the Revolution* (New York, 1971), pp. 40–73; this discussion will provide interested readers with a full account of the author's views on freedom as an abstract construct. Its availability is partly responsible for the brevity of the philosophical discussion here.

[4] Bernard Bosanquet, *The Philosophical Theory of the State* (London, 1951), p. 125. John Laird's approach is similar: "*Nihil obstat* is

ing a sentiment with which even Lenin can feel comfortable. "While the state exists," insisted Lenin in *State and Revolution*, "there is no freedom. When there is freedom, there will be no state."[5]

Democracy likewise has been interpreted within the confines of our liberal constitutionalism to mean a system of government founded on popular sovereignty as a fundamental check on political power. The focus has been on controls over and limits on government rather than on public participation in government, on civil rights rather than on civic virtue. Democracy has had for us an instrumentalist flavor. It has preferred to treat public actions as a means to achieving private ends and defending personal rights, where it might have conceived of participation as an end in itself. It has insisted on equality of participation without regard to quality of participation, and has thus acquiesced in the gradual displacement of participation by representation.[6] Where democracy in its classical form meant quite literally rule by the *demos*, by the *plebes*, by the people themselves, it now often seems to mean little more than elite rule sanctioned (through the device of representation) by the people. Competing elites vie for the support of a public, whose popular sovereignty is reduced

---

the whole meaning of [freedom] and is wholly that." *On Human Freedom* (London, 1947), p. 13.

[5] V. I. Lenin, *State and Revolution* (New York, 1932), p. 79.

[6] "Among political theorists and political sociologists the widely accepted theory of democracy (so widely accepted that one might call it the orthodox doctrine) is one in which the concept of participation has only the most minimal role. Indeed, not only has it a minimal role but a prominent feature of recent theories of democracy is the emphasis placed on the dangers inherent in wide popular participation in politics." Carole Pateman, *Participation and Democratic Theory* (Cambridge, 1970), p. 1. This focus on the stability of democracy is particularly evident in what might be called the "Princeton approach." See, for example, Gabriel Almond and Sidney Verba, *The Civic Culture* (Princeton, N. J. 1963).

to the pathetic right to participate in choosing the tyrants who will rule it.[7]

Such partial and rather singular views about freedom and democracy are, in philosophical terms, patently something less than inviolate. Classical political thought regarded democracy with considerable skepticism, as the inherently unstable type *ochlocracy*, unreasoned rule by a populace that was intrinsically passionate; it regarded freedom hardly at all, at least not in the political context. More recently, liberal constitutionalism has had to treat with a rival tradition whose meandering way has been marked by Rousseau, Kant, Hegel, and a diverging group of later neo-Rousseaueans, neo-Kantians, and neo-Hegelians whose only common denominator has been a distaste for liberalism and dissatisfaction with the notions of freedom and democracy it has generated. In other words, there is no lack of theoretical challenges to the tradition of politics so firmly entrenched in the Anglo-American consciousness, and it is not a philosophical battle that we propose to join here. That battle has been and continues to be fought and fought well.[8] But even the most successful theoretical advocacy of alternatives to liberal constitutionalism must confront that tradition's ever-present embodiment in Western political life and in the historical process of modernization that has finally been made almost synonymous with liberal constitutional "Westernization."[9] It must contend,

[7] This approximates Joseph Schumpeter's elitist definition of democracy in *Capitalism, Socialism and Democracy* (London, 1943).

[8] See, for example, Christian Bay, *The Structure of Freedom* (New York, 1965); Franz Neumann, *The Democratic and Authoritarian State* (Glencoe, Ill., 1957); Stuart Hampshire, *Thought and Action* (New York, 1967); Erich Fromm, *Escape from Freedom* (New York, 1941); Hannah Arendt, *Between Past and Future* (New York, 1961); and Bernard Crick, "Freedom as Politics," in P. Laslett and W. G. Runciman, eds., *Philosophy, Politics and Society*, Third Series (Oxford, 1969), pp. 194–214.

[9] Lucian W. Pye thus notes that his concept of "modernization

moreover, with liberalism's most disquieting charge: that democracy disenthralled from the confines of liberalism is predisposed to totalitarianism,[10] and that liberty when extended to encompass more than the passive absence of external constraints on action mutates into the most perverse tyranny; that, in other words, however sound alternatives to the liberal constitutional tradition may seem in conceptual terms, their manifestation in political life inevitably reveals them not only as deficient but also as profoundly dangerous and ineluctably pathological.[11]

To combat the authority of actual political life, of a tradition that for all of its inadequacies has been a practical success for several centuries across two continents, requires something more than the rehearsal of adversary arguments in the abstract. We need instead the weight of arguments embedded in their own historical traditions, carrying the authority of an actual political experience. If the parochialism of our political thought issues from the potency of our political experience rather than the insularity of the philosophical traditions that inform that experience, what is required to counteract its influence is an alternative experience, not an alternative philosophy.

This book is an attempt to challenge liberal constitutionalism as a philosophy and as a political way of life—to uncover its limitations and to explain certain of its failures—through a sympathetic examination of the political life of an alpine people over the last 1,500 years. The multiethnic people of the once independent Republic of Raetia—now the Swiss canton of Graubünden—have experienced

---

. . . might also be called Westernization, or simply advancement and progress"; *Aspects of Political Development* (Boston, 1966), p. 8.

10 A full discussion of this charge in the context of recent political theory can be found in Benjamin R. Barber, "Conceptual Foundations of Totalitarianism," in Benjamin R. Barber, C. J. Friedrich, and M. Curtis, eds., *Totalitarianism in Perspective: Three Views* (New York, 1969).

11 This is the position of Isaiah Berlin in *Two Concepts of Liberty* (Oxford, 1958).

7

within their mountain communities a form of direct self-government far older than liberal democracy, and completely unassimilable by its categories. Their understanding of the relationship of freedom and communal politics has refused to obey the definitional rules laid down by liberal philosophers. More significantly still, they have pursued their alternative vision of liberty and democracy without either slipping into totalitarianism or being reduced to knavery.[12] Their experience thus becomes a potent vehicle for the reevaluation of liberal democratic thought and a perspective from which the parochialism of Anglo-American political traditions is thrown into sharp relief. In this sense our study is truly comparative, for as Harry Eckstein has said in a study of democracy in Norway, the attempt to "compare a case with a body of theory pertinent to it" is comparative in the richest sense.[13]

Not that this account of Swiss political experience can pretend to establish decisively the philosophical validity of alternative views of liberty and democracy. At best it can suggest the alternatives while disestablishing the claims to exclusivity of constitutional liberals. Switzerland's past may not precisely prove Rousseau's notion of moral freedom, but it seems to indicate conclusively that the predictions made by liberals about its consequences are false. Beyond this, however, there are neither pretensions of nor aspirations toward social scientific "objectivity." By the very nature of our concerns, our approach must remain nonsystematic, impressionistic, and be guided by a normative focus and an engaged passion, which the social scientist, though he will not evade them in his own work, will feel obliged to con-

[12] We would have to expect this, if we were to take seriously the analysis of Karl Popper in *The Open Society and Its Enemies* (London, 1945); or J. L. Talmon in *The Origins of Totalitarian Democracy* (New York, 1960).

[13] Harry Eckstein, *Division and Cohesion in Democracy: A Study of Norway* (Princeton, 1966), p. ix.

8

temn. Its ideal is the strategy that has been described by Christian Bay as building "not only a bridge but a multi-lane freeway [to cover] the gulf between factual knowledge and normative study," and that has been so successfully employed by Louis Hartz.[14]

Our normative concerns, then, must guide our inquiries into Swiss life, but Swiss life and the political notions that issue out of it must in turn take precedence over theory. The point is not to compel the Swiss to conform to the theoretical infrastructure precipitated by liberal democratic thought, but precisely to utilize their unique history to precipitate its own theory with which liberal thought can then be compared. Consequently, it does not seem prudent now to anticipate our study with a passive display of philosophical wares whose viability is at the very heart of the questions we need to raise. We will deal with theory, in transit as it were, only to the extent the materials themselves seem unable to speak for themselves. No grand theories will be propounded, no novel ideas proposed. Our task, rather, will be to convey, as unobtrusively as possible, the Swiss vision of political reality that, while it evolved within the familiar framework of Western political history, is strikingly inhospitable to the familiar predilections of Western political theory—at least in its liberal variations.

## THE POLITICAL PRACTICE OF GRAUBÜNDEN

"In the mountains: freedom!" exclaimed Schiller in tribute to the nation whose founding legend *Wilhelm Tell* he enshrined in verse. "Free, the Swiss?" mocked Goethe in response: "These well-to-do burghers in their closed-in cities? Free, those poor devils on their crags and cliffs? Yes,

---

[14] Christian Bay, *The Structure of Freedom* (New York, 1965), p. xvi. Louis Hartz in *The Liberal Tradition in America* (New York, 1955) has done as much to revise our notions of comparative methodology as it has to modify our understanding of American liberalism.

they once freed themselves from a tyrant . . . but now they sit behind their walls, imprisoned by their customs and their laws, their pettiness and their philistinism. And there, up in the mountains, where they also affect to speak of freedom, but are trapped like marmots by six months of snow!"[15] In fact, Switzerland has been subjected to a variety of searching inquiries—on nationalism, neutralism, federalism, and pluralism, for example.[16] But its most frequent and controversial role has been as an exemplar or as a counterexamplar of freedom and democracy. Gibbon preferred the "liberty of the Swiss" to all other subjects (exemplar), while Count Keyserling concluded that despite its "self-appointed role as the land of freedom in all of Europe, Switzerland is in truth the most narrow and constricted" (counterexamplar).[17]

Reviled or eulogized, the Swiss Confederation presents a unique profile that sharply distinguishes it from other European lands. It has known some form of republican independence since 1291 when the little forest cantons of Uri, Schwyz, and Unterwalden broke away from Hapsburg Austria; it has remained neutral in every major European war since the beginning of the sixteenth century. It possesses the most decentralized governmental structure in the Western world—its twenty-two constituent cantons retaining considerably more power than its federal apparatus; its 3,000 communes remaining more autonomous than the cantons themselves; its executive branch constituted by a

[15] Goethe, *Briefe aus der Schweiz*, Section 1, in *Goethes Sämtliche Werke*, vol. 27 (Berlin-Leipzig, n.d.).

[16] For example: on nationalism, Hans Kohn, *Nationalism and Liberty: The Swiss Example* (London, 1956); on neutralism, William B. Lloyd, *Waging Peace: The Swiss Experience* (Washington, D. C., 1958); on federalism, David Lasserre, *Schicksalsstunde des Föderalismus* (Zürich, 1964); on pluralism, Kenneth D. McRae, *Switzerland: Example of Cultural Coexistence* (Toronto, 1964).

[17] Count Hermann Keyserling, *Das Spectrum Europas* (Heidelberg, 1928), p. 308.

collegial cabinet of seven ministers among whom the honorific presidency rotates annually. As a consequence, Switzerland's experience of freedom and democracy has shaped its political ideas and political institutions in ways that Anglo-American political thought has a difficult time conceptualizing. For it, freedom and political community have represented antagonistic parameters of an essentially anarchistic scale moving from individualism (freedom) to statism (political community, thus nonfreedom); in Switzerland freedom has been understandable only within the context of community. For it, autonomy has suggested a private right that defines the prepolitical individual; in Switzerland it has been a collective right that defines the self-governing community. The symbol of Swiss freedom has thus been the *Landesgemeinden*—the cantonal assemblies through which direct participation was assured, and ongoing self-government guaranteed—rather than a bill of rights or a declaration of freedoms. For Anglo-American political thought, democracy has been a servant of equality and an instrument of private and group interests; in Switzerland it has slighted equality (women received the vote only in 1971) in pursuit of a quality participation that would lend to citizenship a sense of public virtue and collective responsibility unknown to representative, pluralist democracies. For it, rationalization has been synonymous with centralization, which in turn has become integral to notions of progress; in Switzerland the spirit of localism (so-called *Kantönligeist*) has been regarded as an indispensable requisite of democracy and thus, as incompatible with progress only inasmuch as it can be established that progress is inherently undemocratic.

Indeed, the decentralization of Switzerland presents us with a paradox: in attracting us to the land as a fit subject for study, it repels our attentions with the reality that, by the very nature of its diversity and decentralization, it does not exist. That is to say, generalizations about Switzerland inevitably run up against Switzerland's integral diversity, and there they flounder. Switzerland's twenty-two cantons, in at least some cases, have differed more from each other in their historical experiences than they have from neighboring European countries. For centuries the Swiss Confederation was little more than a loosely knit permanent alliance of semisovereign states, and even today it draws together four national cultures (German, French, Italian, and Romansh), two periodically warring Christian confessions, and a range of life-styles encompassing the isolated alpine cowherd and the cosmopolitan Zürich banker. Diversity is Switzerland's essence, drawing our interest, yet defeating our inquiries. In Hermann Weilenmann's words,

> there is hardly a single country which, in so confined a space, is so diversified as Switzerland, hardly a people so un-unitary as the Swiss, hardly a state with fewer competences or less power than the Swiss Confederation. Neither national nor historical frontiers, nor any other objective characteristic such as language, have helped to mould these individuals into a people; neither dynastic authority nor centralized government have helped to create from the valleys and towns a common fatherland, from the welter of communes a common state.[18]

The common solution to this overwhelming diversity has been to focus on regions or single cantons of Switzerland and hope that they will provide conclusions about the country at large.[19] The success of this strategy depends largely on the appropriateness of the example chosen. To think that the history of Geneva—an urban, French-speaking, aristo-

[18] Hermann Weilenmann, *Pax Helvetica: oder die Demokratie der Kleinen Gruppen* (Zürich, 1951), p. 11.

[19] This is the strategy, for example, of Marc Bridel, ed., *La democratie directe dans les communes suisse* (Zürich, 1952), and of Urs Dietschi, *Das Volksveto in der Schweiz* (Olten, 1926) both of which are executed as a series of essays on individual communes.

12

cratic town annexed by Switzerland only in recent centuries
—may illuminate the nature of Swiss politics can, for example, only result in a major distortion of the Swiss experience. What is needed is a "little Switzerland" that retains much of the diversity of the larger country while reducing its scale and diffuseness to manageable proportions. The canton of Graubünden, once the independent Republic of the Three Leagues, has already suggested itself to many observers as an ideal surrogate. As the historian Bonjour has noted, "the inhabitants [of Graubünden] long exhibited by their diversity, variety, independence and isolation, as well as by their forms of government, a Switzerland in miniature."[20] Even in the eighteenth century it was clear to the German historian Zschokke that "of all the Republics associated with the Swiss Confederation, none is richer in the lessons of freedom than the Three Leagues of free Raetia."[21]

Graubünden, in fact, has often been dubbed *die kleine Schweiz* (little Switzerland). It is the largest of the Swiss cantons, encompassing roughly one-sixth of the total area of Switzerland (over 7,000 square kilometers of Switzerland's 41,000 square kilometers), although also the least dense (with a population of over 150,000). Its history has followed an independent course for over 1,500 years, converging with Switzerland's only in 1800. It is especially Swiss in its diversity. Most cantons have had culturally homogeneous histories despite the heterogeneity of the country they together constitute. But Graubünden has had a mixed population of Germans, Raeto-Romansh, and Italians throughout its history, saddling it with problems of diversity no less troublesome than those of Switzerland as a whole. Again, where Switzerland is divided by religion—

[20] E. Bonjour, H. S. Offler and G. R. Potter, *A Short History of Switzerland* (Oxford, 1955), p. 109.
[21] Heinrich Zschokke, *Geschichte der Freistaates der drei Bünde* (Zürich, 1817), p. v.

13

individual cantons tend to be either Catholic or Protestant
—Graubünden, on the other hand, has had to tolerate a
population which, since the Reformation, has been almost
evenly divided between Catholics and Protestants. In many
regions, these differences have segmented even the citizenry
of single villages. Graubünden's religious complexion has
been further complicated by the presence at its capital,
Chur, of a Roman Catholic bishopric since the fifth century.

If Graubünden has almost seemed to parody Switzerland's
rich diversity, it has also typified Switzerland's putative
geographical character. It is not merely mountainous, but
strewn with inhabitable valleys, making possible that diversified, decentralized, pastoral life often regarded as definitive of Switzerland. Its economy is also pastoral rather than
agrarian, service-oriented rather than industrial, in the
typical Swiss fashion. Its history, like Switzerland's, has been
closely bound up with the rest of Europe's, for its passes
and its centrality have made it a strategic key to central
European politics.

Graubünden, then, presents us with a panorama of variations almost as multifarious and diversified as Switzerland
itself, but on a scale which permits focused inquiry. It is
particularly fertile as a source of ideas about freedom and
democracy. As early as the seventh century, it had developed
institutions in its higher alpine communities with some of
the features of self-government. It later resisted both the
external pressures of the Carolingian and subsequent German empires and the internal pressures of local ecclesiastical and secular lords and established itself as a republic well
before the major European countries had solidified their
national monarchies. "Nowhere," writes the historian F. G.
Baker, "through the whole range of history, is it possible to
find a country where the democratic principle was more
thoroughly applied than in the case of the little Graubünden Republic, or where the good and bad results of that

principle have been more thoroughly demonstrated."[22] But Graubünden's history as a republic was not merely democratic: it was democratic in a particular way not easily accounted for by the conceptual perspective of Anglo-American political thought. As a local historian recognized a long time ago, "the general, world-historical significance of Graubünden's history lies in the originality of its political development: if there has even been a community founded in accord with Rousseau's ideas . . . it is Graubünden. . . ."[23] Graubünden's experience with democracy has been inseparable from its experience with community, and as a model of integral community, no region of Switzerland can equal it, for "Graubünden is the classical land of communal freedom. In no other canton of Switzerland, has the autonomous commune played so vital a role."[24]

Graubünden, then, is not offered as a paradigm, either in its historical embodiment as a republic or in its present dilemmas as a direct democracy struggling against modernity. R. C. Brooks goes much too far when he enthusiastically asserts that "to all other democracies of the world the Helvetic example presents a measure of instruction of such scope and richness that their admiration must go forth without stint or limit to so staunch, courageous and labori-

[22] F. Grenfell Baker, *The Model Republic* (New York, 1892), p. 308.

[23] Johannes C. Muoth, "Aus den alten Besatzungsprotokollen der Gerichtsgemeinde Ilanz-Grub," *Bündner Monatsblatt*, July-September 1897, p. 153.

[24] A. Meuli, "Die Entstehung der autonomen Gemeinden im Oberengadin," *Jahresbuch der Historisch-Antiquarischen Gesellschaft Graubünden*, 1901, p. 5. In a similar vein, R. C. Brooks observes caustically that "Traditionally, Graubünden, which is rather proud of itself as the birth-place of the referendum, deserves first-place for the independence, sometimes referred to as pig-headedness, of the village hampdens. Town meetings in the 222 communes of that canton possess the widest powers of home rule." *Civic Training in Switzerland* (Chicago, 1930), pp. 129–130.

ous, so matter-of-fact and yet so idealistic a people."[25] No social scientist schooled in the limitations of comparative methodology is needed to tell us that Raetia's experience of democracy and freedom must be regarded as suggestive rather than exemplary, as productive of alternative ideas and contrasting political categories rather than of firm predictions or decisive refutations. Rousseau himself, an invisible presence throughout our study, warned "great nations" not "to apply to themselves what was meant for small Republics."[26] James Bryce, an early admirer of the Swiss experience, likewise cautions against a vulgar reading of his conclusions about Switzerland: "Where an institution has succeeded with one particular people and in one set of economic conditions, the presumption that it will suit another people living under different conditions is a weak

[25] Brooks, *Civic Training*, p. 432. William Rappard devoted a long career to foisting Swiss institutions on an unsuspecting world. In *Pennsylvania and Switzerland: The Origins of the Swiss Constitution* (Philadelphia, 1941), he abandons all caution: "Don't tell me what our old politicians have told us for centuries past and what our new-baked grand-masters are repeating today: that we should and can learn nothing from [Switzerland] because we Swiss are a very special people, because our country is entirely different from other countries . . . men and passions are everywhere about alike . . ." (pp. 97–98). We are especially loath to generalize too liberally on the basis of specialized sources with which we have only a novice's acquaintance. Max Weber's caveat is particularly pertinent: "It is quite obvious that anyone forced to rely . . . on the use and evaluation of monumental documentary and literary sources, has to rely on a specialist literature which is often highly controversial, and the merits of which he is unable to judge accurately. Such a writer must make modest claims for the value of his work" *The Protestant Ethic and the Rise of Capitalism*, trans. Talcott Parsons (New York, 1958), p. 28. This warning would seem to apply with particular force to Graubünden, whose history and institutions are mired in controversy, uncertainty, and scholarly debate.

[26] From the Third Dialogue, cited by Bertrand de Jouvenal, "Rousseau's Theory of the Forms of Government," in M. Cranston and R. S. Peters, eds., *Hobbes and Rousseau* (Garden City, N.Y., 1972), p. 487.

16

presumption, and affords slight basis for prediction."[27] Nothing we learn from the remarkable history of liberty in Graubünden can be used to deny definitively the lessons of American or English history, nothing revealed by its unique political life taken as a certain remedy for the deficiencies of our own. Yet almost every discovery we make in confronting it acts as a foil to familiar ideas and as a challenge to liberal shibboleths. Without disregarding the immediacy and historical validity of the liberal democratic tradition, the Graubünden experience sets that tradition within a perspective that allows critical evaluation. Without ignoring the seeming inevitability of political centralization in modern industrial society, it raises normative questions about its desirability. It can no more subsume Anglo-American practice than it can be subsumed by Anglo-American theory.

The organization of this study is primarily historical, in part because it is a work of historical sociology, but mainly because the unfolding of liberty in Raetia can be broken into a number of historical periods that enable us to ask several distinctive kinds of questions about freedom in the Alps. Part II of the study is altogether historical: a straightforward, unembellished account of events and men that provides the factual foundation upon which all subsequent analysis is based. Some readers may want to pass over it initially, satisfied that it is there to set the scene when analysis appears to outrun historical realities in latter chapters. Part III raises a set of relational questions concerning the impact of geography (Chapter IV), feudalism (Chapter V), independence and foreign affairs (Chapter VI), and dem-

[27] James Bryce, *Modern Democracies*, 2 vols. (New York, 1921), I, p. 447. Simon de Ploige takes a similar tack: "No one imagines that [Switzerland's democratic institutions] could be transplanted to a new soil. Nowhere else could we find the conditions universally regarded as essential to the proper working of direct legislation." *The Referendum in Switzerland* (London, 1898), p. 25.

17

ocratic institutions (Chapter VII) on the gradual emergence of notions of freedom, community, and political participation in Raetia prior to and during its history as the free Republic of the Three Leagues *(alt frei Raetia)*. Part IV treats the political commune and direct democracy in the modern canton of Graubünden as they have been affected by federalism and political centralization (Chapter VIII) and by industrial and social modernization and economic interdependence with Switzerland and Europe (Chapter IX). Chapter IX, in particular, moves somewhat beyond the borders of Graubünden to raise more general questions about the nature of political community and democracy in a Switzerland increasingly committed to cosmopolitanism and full affluence—whatever the cost in terms of traditional values.

The motif that ties together these diversified forms of inquiry over fifteen centuries is one of an enduring struggle to preserve the special freedom that came to characterize the self-governing alpine community—a struggle that pitted a handful of uniquely autonomous villages against feudalism, ecclesiastic tyranny, empire, corruption, foreign aggressors, confederal integration, centralizing federalism, and finally against modernity itself as expressed in the aspirations of materialistic consumer capitalism in its most centralized, egalitarian form.

# PART II: The History of Raetia

There is one theme I should prefer to all others:
"The History of the Liberty of the Swiss."

—Gibbon

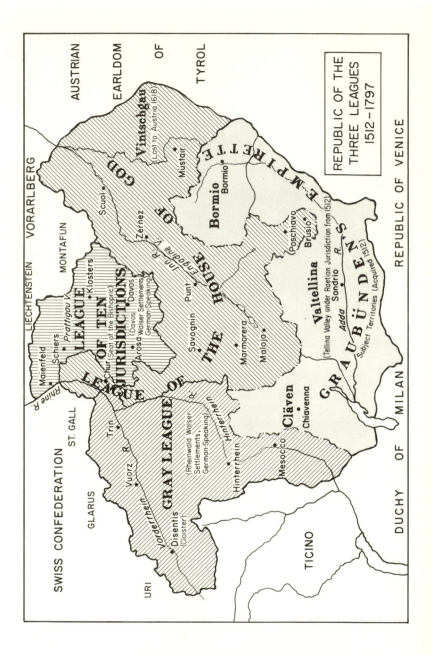

SWISS CONFEDERATION

AUSTRIAN EARLDOM OF TYROL

REPUBLIC OF THE THREE LEAGUES
1512-1797

VORARLBERG

LIECHTENSTEIN

ST. GALL

GLARUS

URI

TICINO

DUCHY OF MILAN

REPUBLIC OF VENICE

MONTAFUN

Maienfeld
Schiers
Prattigau V.
Klosters

LEAGUE OF TEN JURISDICTIONS

Chur (Seat of the Bishopric)

Arosa Walser Settlements, German-Speaking

Davos

Scuol

Zernez

Vintschgau
(Lost to Austria 1618)

Müstair

Bormio
Bormio

GOD OF HOUSE THE OF

Engadine V.

Inn R.

Punt

Savognin

Trin

Vuorz R.

Vorderrhein R.

Disentis
(Cloister)

GRAY LEAGUE OF

(Rheinwald Walser Settlements, German-Speaking)

Hinterrhein

Hinterrhein R.

Marmorera

Maloja

Mesocco

Cläven
Chiavenna

Poschiavo
Brusio

Valtellina

Adda R.

Sondrio

GRAUBÜNDEN

R. S.

(Teltina Valley under Raetian Jurisdiction from 1512)

Subject Territories (Acquired 1512)

CHAPTER II

# Raetia to 1524—the Formative Years

HISTORY has a certain tiresome fascination of its own. Names and dates accumulate, epochs fall away, and we are finally drawn into the least interesting records of man's past. Nevertheless, that fascination has overwhelming limitations and the details into which we must now enter are hardly significant, let alone entertaining, for us unless they can be regarded as a background against which the more vital dilemmas of Raetia's political experience can be viewed with proper contrast. Raetia's chronological history, like just about every country's, unfolds as a succession of kingships and wars, of constitutions and usurpations, of personal heroics and anonymous calamities, and of unending struggle for emancipation; it is distinctive only in the perspective of our concern with pure democracy and with the requisites of collective freedom. As related here, it is old-fashioned history *in extremis*—unleavened by economic profile, biographical anecdote, or sociological theory. We have held these catalysts in reserve for the crucial analytic sections that follow.

## PRE-ROMAN AND ROMAN RAETIA

Graubünden has interacted with and to some degree shared the history of its better-known neighbor Helvetia;[1]

[1] Indigenous histories of Switzerland abound. Three of the best known, focusing in the customary German public law fashion on constitutions, institutions and events, are Karl Dändliker, *Geschichte der Schweiz*, 3 vols. (Zürich, 1893), J. Dieaurer, *Geschichte der Schweizerischen Eidgenossenschaft*, 5 vols. (Gotha, 1920–1924), and Gottfried Guggenbühl, *Geschichte der Schweizerischen Eidgenossenschaft*, 2 vols.

21

it has also been profoundly influenced by larger European affairs. Yet from its earliest beginnings in the late Stone Age, it has had a distinctly independent history very much its own. Well before the Roman conquest of Europe north of Italy, unrelated tribes populated Helvetia and Raetia— the Helvetii being predominately Celtic, the Raetii being a branch of the Veneti of Ilyrian origin.[2] Roman conquest came a half century apart to the two countries, Helvetia falling in 58 B.C., the more warlike Raetia succumbing only in 15 B.C. to the sons of Augustus. The two regions subsequently fell under different provincial jurisdiction within the empire, and suffered very different fates at the hands of the Goths, the Franks, and eventually the ruling houses of the Holy Roman Empire of the German Nation. Their destinies converge only after hundreds of years of independence for each, with Napoleon's compulsory unification of "modern" Switzerland.

Little is known about pre-Roman Raetia. There is some evidence of a primitive pastoral economy founded on rudi-

---

(Zürich, 1948). The first comprehensive Swiss history, a romantic and wildly unreliable account, was Johannes von Müller, *Der Geschichten Schweizerischer Eidgenossenschaft*, 5 vols. (Leipzig, 1815). The best English history is the Oxford *Short History of Switzerland* by E. Bonjour, H. S. Offler, and G. R. Potter (Oxford, 1952), although *The Model Republic* by F. Grenfell Baker (New York, 1895) devotes more space to Raetia.

By far the best comprehensive history of Raetia is Friedrich Pieth, *Bündnergeschichte* (Chur, 1945). Earlier works include Peter C. Planta, *Geschichte von Graubünden* (Bern, 1913), Fritz Jecklin et al., *Bündnergeschichte in Elf Vorträgen* (Chur, 1902), and Johannes A. von Sprecher, *Kulturgeschichte der Drei Bünde*, new ed. by Rudolf Jenny (Chur, 1951); the latter includes the most comprehensive bibliography of Raetian historiography presently available.

[2] The question of the origin of the Raetii has not been satisfactorily settled. Peter C. Planta suggests Etruscan origins in "Die Vorrömische Zeit," in Jecklin et al., *Bündnergeschichte*, while more recent archaeological evidence suggesting a Celtic background is discussed by Pieth, *Bündnergeschichte*, pp. 8–9.

mentary dairy-farming, and even of vineyards and honey production; but according to the Romans the Raetii were "wild and cruel people, reflecting the raw character of their habitat."[3]

Roman Raetia, following the occupation, was considerably larger than modern Graubünden and included not only the Rhône river valley to the west (the Valais) but also most of the region lying between the Rhine headwaters and the Danube—its capital being Augustus Vindelicorum (Augsburg). In creating Raetia, the Romans hoped to provide a defensive perimeter stretching to the Danube against the hostile tribes to the north. Nevertheless, by the end of the first century the Valais had been separated from it; by the reign of Diocletian it had been subdivided into two civil districts: Raetia Prima in the south, with its capital at Curia Rhaetiorum (Chur)—a slightly larger area than modern Graubünden—and Raetia Secunda in the north, encompassing Swabia and Bavaria.

Roman settlement appears to have been more limited in Raetia Prima than in Helvetia or Raetia Secunda, possibly because the major military roads had been constructed over the Brenner pass to the east, and the Simplon to the west. The Septimer, Julier, and Splügen passes remained relatively insignificant. Nevertheless, by the fifth century Raetia Prima, known more and more as Churraetia, appears to have been extensively Romanized—the predominant language having become a provincial Latin, which has survived in its original form into the present day as Raeto-Romansh. It even seems likely that Roman citizenship had been extended to the Raetians under Caracalla.

However, Rome's major bequest to Raetia was neither citizenship (which had depreciated to the point of worthlessness) nor language, but Christianity. A bishop appears in Martigny (in Valais) in 381, and a bishop of Chur is mentioned in documents dating to 451, which suggests the pres-

[3] *Ibid.*, p. 10.

ence of a bishopric well before that time. Initially, the coming of Christianity made few inroads against the animistic cults that prevailed among the mountain men, but its political effects were immediate and with the coming of the Franks to Raetia decisive.

## OSTROGOTHS AND FRANKS

In ironic tribute to the power of culture and the impotence of administration, at least once upon a time, the successful rooting of Roman culture north of Italy coincided with the collapse of Roman government there. The Alemmanians, having paid scant heed to the Roman frontiers of the Helvetic and Raetian provinces, even when they were defended, were able in 451 to seize Helvetia outright. Before the mountainous bulwarks of Raetia, however, they drew up short. While Helvetia was being radically Germanized, Raetia remained almost purely Romanic in language and culture well into the ninth century. By 476 Rome had fallen to the rampaging Ostrogoths under Theodoric. Shortly thereafter, the Alemmanians seized Raetia Secunda, leaving ancient Graubünden hanging precariously between Goths and Alemmanians.

The energetic Goths, sweeping back up through north Italy at the end of the fifth century, finally secured Raetia for themselves—the first in a long succession of interventions that were to jeopardize the autonomy of the Raetian people right up to the Napoleonic occupation during the latter part of the French Revolution. In retrospect, the Raetians were probably better off with the Goths than they might have been with the Alemmanians, for the Goths neither settled in Churraetia nor tampered with the prevailing system of Roman administration and taxation, and their relatively civilized forty years of overlordship left few traces. In 535 the Goths bestowed Raetia on the Franks in return for their aid against Constantine who was busily campaigning to win back the western empire from his sanctuary in the east. Although the Franks were battlefield victors over the Goths in earlier Rhineland struggles, were more capable of intervention, and were thus more disposed to an active hegemony, their preoccupation with holding together their diffuse, disintegrating empire led them to tolerate traditional Raetian arrangements. Hence, though Raetia was regarded as a Frankish church-state, authority continued to be exercised in a relatively autonomous manner by the bishop of Chur even after the conversion of the Frankish kings to Christianity. Moreover, the bishopric was itself under the control of a domestic aristocracy made up of powerful families like the Viktoriden. There was even a degree of popular participation in the election of both bishop and civil governor (the Roman-style *praeses*), through the participation of the city council (*curia* or *Stadtrat*), and some have suggested that public acclamation permitted even more extensive participation.[4] However, the Viktoriden and other oligarchic families continued to dominate the politics of Raetia throughout the sixth and seventh centuries, and what we need to note about Graubünden under the Merovingians is not popular rule, but autonomous rule. The Viktoriden were a local Raetian family, not Frankish provincial governors or vassals. Raetia was thus unique in the empire—already displaying that remarkable penchant for self-sufficiency and autonomous government that make its later history so intriguing for those pursuing alternative visions of political freedom and democracy.

## The Carolingians

The extended period of semiautonomy enjoyed by Raetia under the indifferent and increasingly ineffectual Merovin-

[4] J. Danuser, *Die staatlichen Hoheitsrechte des Kantons Graubünden gegenüber dem Bistum Chur* (Chur, 1897).

gian kings came to an end with Charlemagne. His prede-
cessor, Pippin the Short, had already begun to take Raetian
noblemen into his service as vassals. Under Charlemagne
the imperial grip was tightened. A code of law was promulgated under the seal of Bishop Remedius (the *capitula
Remedii*) that diluted the previously all-Roman *lex curiensis* with Germanic law.[5] Since the *lex curiensis* had itself
been introduced only toward the end of the eighth century,
the *capitula* represented an obvious heightening of Frankish interest in Raetia. Although Charlemagne magnani-
mously permitted Bishop Remedius to retain the form of
both temporal and spiritual authority in Graubünden,
Remedius's death in 806 meant the end of Raetia's precarious autonomy. During the brief ecclesiastic interregnum,
Charlemagne abruptly imposed the full Frankish administrative organization on Churraetia.

The Carolingian constitution provided for the division
of the empire into very large military districts (*Gaue*) and
lesser earldoms (*Grafschaften*) around which a loyal feudal
establishment could be created. By maintaining his own
vassal hierarchy, Charlemagne hoped to undermine the
status of local landholders who, under the Merovingians,
had become so disproportionately influential. Under the
new order Raetia was divided into two earldoms: Upper
Raetia, old Raetia south of the Landquart with its capital
at Chur; and Lower Raetia in the hills and along the
Rhine valley north of the Landquart. The two earldoms remained formally in the duchy of Raetia, but their histories
diverge—Upper Raetia becoming, for all practical purposes,
the Raetia known to later history.

However, the administrative restructuring of old Raetia
was the least important consequence of Carolingian intervention in Raetia's domestic life. Just as the coming of the

---

[5] P. Mutzner gives a full account of both codes in *Beiträge zur
Rechtsgeschichte Graubündens im Mittelalter, Seperatabdruck aus der
Zeitschrift für Schweizerisches Recht*, Neue Folge, vol. 2.

Romans eight centuries earlier had meant cultural and political Romanization of primitive Raetia, so the coming of the Carolingian earls and their followers signified the beginning of the cultural and political Germanization of Romanic Raetia. Politically, the most salient effect of the new order was the secularization of civil authority, the rights of the bishop being fully supplanted by the prerogatives of the emperor's new vassals. The startled bishop found himself transformed overnight from an omnipotent lord into a mere servant of God and the church. Nor were the temporal rewards of spiritual service any longer available to him, for all of the holdings in property of the bishopric and its 230 dependent churches and several autonomous cloisters were sequestered—expropriated—by the emperor's representatives, who had found a warrant for plunder in the traditional imperial title to proprietorship over all land throughout the empire.

The reorganization of the empire also had the effect of abolishing the old Roman city council (*curia*) of Chur, thus terminating such vestiges of popular participation in administration as had survived the Viktoriden aristocracy. Election of the bishop fell completely to offices of the church and remained there despite a formal confirmation of public participation by King Lothair in 843. At the same time, the bishopric was severed from the Milanese archdiocese and grafted onto the archdiocese at Mainz—one more expression of the new, northward, Germanic orientation of Churraetia after the ninth century.

These political innovations, although they did not prove permanent, temporarily interrupted Raetia's gradual evolution toward regional autonomy. Only in the mountain common association (*Markgenossenschaften*), where ancient usage and geographical remoteness had protected small communities of men from external influences, and where egalitarianism had continued to flourish, did the seeds of Graubünden's later experience with collective freedom and self-sufficiency persist in their centuries-long incubation. For the rest, Raetia appeared under the Carolingians as one more earldom contributing to the centripetal integrity of the reborn empire.

Carolingian rule also had a marked cultural impact on Raetia. The new vassal hierarchy, Germanic in background, could hardly depend on the local Romanic population in exercising its authority; the earls brought with them followers, retainers, servants, and craftsmen who quickly spread the German language and Germanic customs. In 765 there was hardly a single German official to be found in all of Raetia. By 830 more than one-half of officialdom was German. Yet despite these critical demographic shifts, and notwithstanding the increasingly pervasive influence of Germanic law, Raetia did not undergo total cultural metamorphosis. Particularly in the mountains, Romansh flourished and the Romanic outlook survived. (In 1960 nearly 30 percent of the population of modern Graubünden still spoke Romansh as their native tongue.) Alone in Europe, Raetia preserved enclaves where men carried on a natural evolution untouched by the tribes, empires, and cultural cataclysms that were remaking the continent. But, meanwhile, the more vulnerable institutions of Raetia were undergoing still one more set of changes as the keepers of the empire once again revised their strategy in trying to hold together their unwieldy kingdom.

## THE RESTORATION OF THE CHURRAETIAN BISHOPRIC

Within thirty years of the death of Charlemagne, his successors increasingly had doubts about the fealty of the vassal hierarchy that they had created. Saracens, Danes, and Magyars threatened the empire from without, disloyalties jeopardized it from within. Following the Treaty of Verdun in 843 by which Charlemagne's three grandsons had partitioned the empire among themselves, Raetia became part of the Eastern Kingdom. Unlike Lothair's Middle Kingdom, which did not survive his heirless decease in 875, the Eastern Kingdom, after the death of the last Carolingian there and under the forceful suzerainty of the Saxon kings in the tenth century, achieved greater glory. But it did so only by creating an elective system of kingship that dangerously inverted the usual feudal relationship.

Realliance with the church appeared a prudent way to reinforce centralism in this period of centrifugal disintegration. The great medieval principle *omnium Christianorum una respublica est* became the source of a practical policy of gifts and grants of immunity to regional ecclesiastical powers, many of whom had only recently been dispossessed by the Carolingians. As early as 831, a tentative grant of immunity (*Reichsunmittelbarkeit*) had been offered to the bishop of Chur, releasing him from certain obligations due the king's local vassals and placing him directly under the purview of the king.[6] By 849 and from that time on, Raetian bishops had exclusively German names. In the tenth century following the death of the last Carolingian in the Eastern Kingdom in 911, Raetia was incorporated into the duchy of Swabia. Swabia, Franconia, Bavaria, Thuringia, and Saxony together comprised the Eastern Kingdom. Efforts to secure the allegiance of the church were intensified. The Saxon kings, spurred on doubtlessly by their apocalyptic expectations of the year 1000, became ever more generous and transferred land at a rate that under Otto I fully restored the bishopric to its pre-Carolingian eminence. To Otto this beneficence was only an insignificant stratagem in the reconquest of Lom-

---

[6] The granting of immunities, so-called *Reichsunmittelbarkeit*, can be traced to the sixth century, when Theodoric freed the Christian clergy of all "public obligations." The history of imperial immunity is a history of the changing relations of the empire and the church. Its impact on Raetia is assessed by William Plattner in *Die Entstehung des Freistaates der Drei Bünden und sein Verhältnis zur alten Eidgenossenschaft* (Davos, 1895), Chapter 3.

bardy that eventually led to the restoration of the empire under the name Holy Roman Empire of the German Nation. But for Raetia the return of land to the church signified a crucial reemergence of ecclesiastic omnipotence. The vaunted earls, rendered ever more powerless by these transfers of jurisdiction and property to the revivified bishopric, gradually died out. Hardly a trace of them can be found in the written sources of the eleventh century.[7]

The power and wealth of the church inexorably grew: in 1170 Frederich I named the bishop of Chur a prince of the empire (*Reichsfürst*), conferring upon him extensive jurisdictional prerogatives over nonecclesiastic affairs. Only the imperial advocacy (*Reichsvogtei*) remained beyond his grasp. The Raetian noble house of Vaz retained control of this office throughout the twelfth and thirteenth centuries. Because the advocacy encompassed powers of a bailiff over all the king's lands, it was coveted by the church. In 1299 a bishop was finally able to purchase the title, which gave him direct jurisdiction over most of the area that later was to become the League of the House of God.

The rise of the bishopric to hegemony in Churraetia coincided with and was thus enhanced not only by the decline of the empire that affected to use it but also by the dying out of the competing noble houses of Raetia. The empire's relationship with the universal Catholic Church had been undermined, and was eventually to be destroyed, by the long struggle over lay investiture that followed the ascension of Gregory VII to the Holy See in 1073. The erosion of imperial influence in Raetia was underscored in 1122 when election of the bishop was transferred from the German king to the cathedral chapter (*Domkapitel*)—an integral office of the bishop's court (*Bischofshof*) in Chur.

---

[7] Peter Tuor argued that the later earldom of Laax represents vestiges of the old Carolingian earldom of Upper Raetia in *Die Freien von Laax: Ein Beitrag zur Verfassungs- und Standesgeschichte* (Chur, 1903), but his view is highly controversial.

The Saxon and early Salian emperors, in their ultimately futile struggle to build a truly unitary empire, had emancipated the church from the jurisdiction of untrustworthy and ambitious local vassals, but now Rome had emancipated the church from the emperor himself. Elsewhere this new ecclesiastic independence was being employed to forge new alliances, often with disillusioned former vassals of the empire. In Churraetia the bishopric moved toward real autonomy, for only a declining secular aristocracy and a remote system of common associations stood between it and total hegemony. The nobility was too disorganized, too faint-hearted, and too close to extinction to compete effectively, while the mountain common associations were not yet ready to make a fight—hardly yet conscious of the need to assert themselves.

## THE RAETIAN NOBILITY

If the noble houses of Raetia could not permanently obstruct the bishopric's road to political dominance, they could and did impede its progress. Like the church, they too had been able to exploit the erosion of the Carolingian constitution; like the bishop, they had maneuvered to supplant the authority of the disowned earls with their own. The bishopric held sovereign jurisdiction over the old Churer *Hundred (Cent)*, but not over the rest of Raetia. Almost exclusively Germanic in origin, the Raetian nobility had acquired their estates through vassalage in the early empire, or through the exploitation of imperial office; occasionally, nobles had simply resorted to seizure under some appointive office such as bailiff for a cloister. However, by the twelfth century, Raetian noblemen had dropped the Germanic titles that advertised their former dependence on imperial patronage in favor of the provocative generic name free lord *(Freiherr)*. As in the case of the church, the powers they now enjoyed were their own.

31

The most prominent among the leading families of
Raetia were the free lords of Vaz (from whom the bishopric
ultimately bought the imperial advocacy), whose holdings
encompassed much of the area of the later League of Ten
Jurisdictions, as well as territory along the Rhine. The
free lords of Rhäzüns also controlled alodial holdings along
the Rhine, with a stronghold at the junction of the two
major Rhine tributaries (the Vorderrhein and Hinterrhein). The free lords of Belmont, perhaps the third strongest family in Raetia, controlled much of the Upper Rhine
valley above Rhäzüns. Scores of lesser families held diminutive fiefs elsewhere in Raetia, along with such semiautonomous cloisters as Cäzis and Churwalden; for the most part,
however, these depended on the good will and military
capabilities of the larger houses. With this diversity, castles
sprang up like mountain wildflowers, dotting the crags of
Raetia with a profuseness that cannot be matched anywhere else in Europe.[8] The bishopric confronted a web
of feudal relations so diffuse that despite its own imposing
primacy and the relative weakness of its feudal competition
it could not quite achieve that overwhelming preeminence
it sought. In the manner of irksome wasps, the secular
houses of Raetia stung the bishopric repeatedly and then
went off to die—slowing its progress toward hegemony just
enough to permit other forces to enter the contest. By the
fifteenth century, most of the leading families were dying
or dead. The lords of Vaz disappeared in 1337, the lords
of Belmont in 1380, the lords of Toggenburg in 1436, the
lords of Rhäzüns in 1458, and the lords of Werdenberg-Sar-
gans in 1505—all well before the formal constituting of the
later Republic of the Three Leagues in 1524. But they had
persisted and contested long enough. Although the bishop
of Chur remained the largest property holder in Raetia and

[8] One powerful bishop, Hartmann, was lord of no fewer than
thirty-six castles in the year 1410 according to Johannes C. Muoth, ed.,
*Codex Diplomaticus*, vol. 6 (Chur, 1898). Ruins can be seen in almost
every valley of modern Graubünden.

the most powerful lord of the region, the way had been prepared for new developments that, while predicated on the partial unification and quasi-independence won by the bishop of Chur, led not toward theocracy but toward republicanism, not toward centralized Caesaropapism but toward confederal democracy. Towns with restive populations of free mountainmen began to assert themselves; even larger towns like Chur and Disentis developed identities unrelated to the church that stood at their centers (the bishopric in Chur, the abbacy in Disentis). In the mountains, villages and communes that for centuries had fostered an insular self-sufficiency became aware of the need to partake in the larger struggle for local rule if their own autonomy was to survive. With the aid of the expiring nobility, they combined to guide all of Raetia toward a status of independent republicanism that two centuries earlier would have seemed unthinkable and that by themselves they never could have achieved.

## The Period of Leagues and Alliances

The bishop's opportunity had come and gone. In a century-long collaboration, the communes of Raetia, with the leadership of prominent noble families, had seized the initiative. At the beginning of the thirteenth century, Raetia was a country divided into almost as many feudal estates as there were mountain valleys—a number of small, dependent entities over which the bishop of Chur seemed an obvious and irresistible master. At the beginning of the sixteenth, it comprised three viable confederal leagues, the constituents of which were neither church estates nor worldly fiefs but free communes that would soon put an end irrevocably to the dreams of hegemony of the Churraetian bishopric. In its three-century journey to independence, Raetia traversed historical ground increasingly unique in its political character and ever more separate from events in the larger Germany to which it nominally belonged.

33

Of the three leagues that eventually constituted as the Republic of the Three Leagues, the League of the House of God (*Gotteshausbund*) was both first and most exemplary of the forces at play in fourteenth- and fifteenth-century Raetia. It gradually evolved as a response to pressures within and outside the region most directly under the jurisdiction of the bishop of Chur: the city of Chur, the so-called four villages, much of the Domleschg and Schams valleys, and the Poschiavo and Münster valleys in their entirety. The external threat was Hapsburg Austria. Following the death of the last Hohenstaufen in 1273, the Hapsburgs had successfully claimed the imperial title. It was a frustration for them and a misfortune for much of central Europe that the title no longer carried its indigenous authority. An emperor could exercise only as much power as he could bring with him from his own feudal realm. Consequently, the Hapsburgs embarked on a long quest for the kind of security that could only be purchased with limitless power. The loss of Helvetia following the death of the forceful Rudolf of Hapsburg in 1299 and the temporary loss of the imperial crown itself during the same period underscored the need for an extended hegemony. The case of Helvetia—traditional Switzerland of the William Tell era—was particularly galling, because three minuscule "forest cantons" with diminutive peasant populations had made alliances among themselves to defy the empire, defending their audacity with a vigor that astounded Europe and allowed them a permanent and growing place in European affairs as the Helvetic Confederation.[9]

---

[9] In 1291 the three peasant communities lying on Lake Luzern—Uri, Schwyz, and Unterwalden—allied themselves and successfully overthrew Austrian overlordship that had lasted for several centuries. In the next century, the young Confederation accepted Luzern, Zug, Zürich, and Glarus into membership, followed later by six more cantons or *Orte*. By 1513 the Confederation had thirteen members—a

34

However, losses in Helvetia were immediately compensated for by the acquisition of full sovereign jurisdiction in the Tyrol and Vorarlberg, and extensive influence in the north Italian plain. Raetia, more proximate geographically than Helvetia, the home of a potentially friendly bishopric, and in control of all of the most vital eastern alpine passes, became Austria's prime target in the next several centuries: indeed, it did not again free itself of Austria's unwanted attentions until Napoleon forced it into the Swiss Confederation 500 years later.

Austrian strategy was quickly adapted to the special circumstances of the struggling Churraetian bishopric. The bishop who only recently had used the struggle between Rome and the empire both to liberate himself of jurisdictional interference by the emperor and to consolidate his own jurisdictional autonomy within Raetia now turned back to the empire for aid and succor in dealing with the irksome encroachments of the Raetian nobility and the obstinate self-sufficiency of the free communes. The unsavory marriage of convenience that ensued on the heels of this propitious convergence of interests presented intolerable threats to the region immediately under the bishop's control. By the 1360's the threat reached crisis proportions. A bishop of foreign origin, Peter of Bohemia, already much mistrusted for his Austrian liaisons, was discovered in an apparent conspiracy to introduce direct Austrian rule into

---

figure that remained stable until Napoleon reorganized Switzerland in 1800.

This early period of Swiss history is surrounded by romantic legend and controversy. Müller gives the romantic vision, immortalized by Schiller in *Wilhelm Tell*, in *Der Geschichten*, vol. 1, pp. 600–648, while a version shaped by the Higher Criticism of the nineteenth century can be discovered in Dändliker, *Geschichte*, vol. 1, pp. 343–428. Recent historiography has once again begun to pay more attention to the legends and "myths," which turn out to be supported by a remarkable amount of archeological and documentary evidence.

the old Churer Hundred where the church's landholdings were concentrated. Representatives of the city of Chur, of the cathedral chapter of the bishops' court (*Domkapitel*), which was constituted independently of the bishop and could operate as a check upon him, and of free communes from as far away as the Oberhalbstein and Domleschg valleys met for the express purpose of curtailing the bishop's power and treating the financial indebtedness into which his corrupt rule had brought them. The discussions resulted in the formation of an emergency community (*Notgemeinschaft*) authorized to administer the bishop's estates until the end of Peter's reign, Peter himself having abandoned Chur for more convivial places well before his resignation in 1368.[10]

This emergency community, convened as an *ad hoc* assembly to resolve a crisis, continued to meet from time to time, accumulating precedents for conflict resolution and constructive collaboration that soon made it a permanent structure. Around it, the mature League of the House of God eventually developed, a source of increasing irritation to the Hapsburgs. Subsequent bishops, at least those gifted with some vision of Raetia's future, came to understand that without the support of the emergency community's constitutents they could not rule at all. One of the most corrupt, Bishop Hartmann, who spent almost thirty years (1388–1416) feuding alternately with the Raetian nobility and the Austrian Court that hoped to use him, inadvertently enhanced the status and power of the incipient league, for it finally became his only ally. And while he was growing weary, the league was growing bold.

[10] The text of the agreement can be found in Theodor Mohr, ed., *Codex Diplomaticus*, vol. 3, no. 134. The history of the League of the House of God is surveyed in J. Danuser, *Die staatlichen Hoheitsrechte des Kantons Graubünden gegenüber dem Bistum Chur* (Zürich, 1897), while pertinent historical documents can be found in Muoth, ed., *Codex*, vol. 6.

These developments were not in themselves untypical of Europe in the thirteenth and fourteenth centuries. The Mainz-Worms City League of 1254 (*rheinische Bund*), the League of Swabian Cities of 1331 (*schwäbische Städtebund*), and such alliances of the nobility as the *Löwenbund* and the *St. Georgesbund*, although of varying origin, had much the same purpose as the House of the League of God: the maintenance of regional autonomy in the face of ambitious neighbors. But where these were transient associations in the building of centralized, territorial principalities, the League of the House of God was a permanent structure that disappeared only in the nineteenth century.

The circumstances under which the second of the three Raetian leagues, the Upper or Gray League (*Oberbund* or *Grauer Bund*), emerged are still less assimilable to the experience of the defensive alliances of southern Germany.[11] The League of the House of God had encompassed an area already unified by centuries of church jurisdiction and by its original status as a Carolingian Hundred; it was, moreover, geographically exposed to its enemies, accessible from Austria over the modest St. Luzienstieg saddle or through the Inn River valley in the Engadine. The region that united as the Gray League occupied, on the other hand, the long, isolated, steppelike Upper Rhine valley—a long twisting valley sealed off from inner Switzerland and the south by high mountain passes, from the north by impassable mountain walls, and from the east by the broken valley itself that descended from alpine springs in a succession of sudden plunges over densely wooded drops and abrupt little falls. Still narrower valleys radiated out of the Rhine, following the meanderings of tiny tributaries running from

[11] For the history of the Gray League see Peter Badrutt, *Die Entstehung des Oberen Bundes* (Chur, 1916); F. Purtscher, "Der Obere oder Graue Bund," *Bündner Monatsblatt*, April, May, June 1924; and I. Müller, "Die Entstehung des Grauen Bundes," *Bündner Monatsblatt*, May 1941.

37

remote glaciers and the "eternal snows." Nor was this geographical diffuseness compensated by the unifying imprint of some central political jurisdiction. The abbot of Disentis had for a time played a role in the Upper Rhine valleys similar to the one played by the bishop of Chur in the Churer Hundred. Having acquired extensive gifts of land from Bishop Tello in the eighth century and Otto I in the tenth, and having secured jurisdictional autonomy from local vassals through a grant of imperial immunity (*Reichsunmittelbarkeit*) in 1048 and through a declaration of the abbacy's independence from the bishopric by Pope Honorius in 1125, the abbot seemed on the verge of hegemony in the Upper Rhine valley. But his lesser ecclesiastic authority and the greater independence of the free lords and free peasants in the *Oberland* combined to defeat him before his hold was secure, and he never succeeded in emulating the successes of the bishop. Eventually, he became an important participant in the creation of a democratic league in which he was never more than an equal partner.

The Gray League was created, then, not to preserve the independence of the Upper Rhine factions against a forcible unification by a domestic overlord or an external power, but to foster a needed unity in a land torn apart by physical diffuseness, internecine factionalism, and competitive disintegration. During the thirteenth century, the free lords of Vaz had acted as peacekeepers in the region, but with the death of Donat von Vaz in 1338, the lineage died out, leaving behind a spreading lawlessness. By the middle of the fourteenth century, the devastation was ubiquitous—a miniature War of the Roses with a hundred participating competitors engaged in mutual rapine. Toward the end of the century, both free lords and free peasants, weary of the unending combat, responded to a call from the appalled abbot of Disentis and met in 1395 to put an end to the feuding. The meeting produced the treaty of peace (*Landfriedensbündnis*) that became the basis for the later Gray

League.[12] As parties to the treaty the abbot of Disentis, the free lords of Rhäzüns (who had been most deeply implicated in the feuds leading to the treaty), the free lords of Sax-Misox, and the free valley people of Lungnez obliged themselves to forswear all use of force and unilateral action in reconciling differences. A court of arbitration (*Schiedsgericht*) would henceforth serve to mediate disagreements. Although free peasants were recognized in the pact, they were in no way favored; indeed, the treaty has sometimes been viewed as an alliance of lords to protect their interests (*Herrenbund*), a view which is probably equally unwarranted. In fact, the treaty was without effect on substantive relations between competing political forces in the valley because it did little more than freeze the status quo, guaranteeing to the contracting parties the rights and prerogatives they enjoyed upon entry.

In 1424 the pact was elaborated, and its membership enlarged. The executive authority of the court of arbitration was extended in a fashion that eventually made the Gray League the most centralized of the three.[13]

If the League of the House of God had been the result of a compound threat from within and without, and the Gray League had been born of purely internal strife, the League of Ten Jurisdictions (*Zehngerichtenbund*) was produced exclusively by an external threat. Comprising a fairly self-contained semicircle of interdependent valleys lying on the border of Austria but well insulated from it by mountains, the region had enjoyed relative tranquillity for a long period. It had been unified under the ubiquitous family of Vaz, whose influence seems to have been very widespread during this era. The expiration of the Vaz line, which in the Gray League had generated only chaos, created no dif-

[12] The text of the treaty can be found in Conradin von Moor, ed., *Codex Diplomaticus*, vol. 4 (Chur, 1865), no. 194.

[13] The text of the Pact of 1424 can be found in Constantin Jecklin, ed., *Codex Diplomaticus*, vol. 5 (Chur, 1865), no. 15.

ficulties here, for the Vaz estates were transferred intact to Frederich von Toggenburg, who was able to acquire jurisdiction over the entire area of the later league by 1390. Under a single, uninterferring Toggenburg lordship, and thus unencumbered by the divisive quarrels of a feuding petty nobility, the free peasant communes of this region were able to nourish considerable local autonomy. Their unique status was further enhanced by the presence at Davos, the most important of the communes, of a large, influential colony of German-speaking immigrants from western Switzerland. These so-called *Walser*, with little experience of Raetian collectivism and mutualism but with a highly articulated sense of individuality, had been given in 1289 the right not only of settlement but also an extraordinary degree of self-rule by the free lords of Vaz, who asked in return only fealty and military support.[14] Their enviable independence and their peculiar notions of self-reliance acted to catalyze the traditional Romansh communes of the area, who had in any case an extended tradition of self-government of their own dating back to the mutualistic common associations of the prefeudal era.

Together, these *Walser* and Romansh communes pre-

[14] The *Walser* were apparently driven from their original settlements in Wallis (hence, the name) by deteriorating economic circumstances. They generally settled in the highest valleys that were of little use to the lords into whose fiefs they fell, and tended to keep to themselves. A rapid rise in population forced them to migrate from their two original settlements at Davos and the upper Rheinwald valley to surrounding regions. Their Germanic culture and alien architecture (wood in place of the usual Romansh stone) accelerated the Germanization of Raetia considerably—simultaneously Romanic collectivism with an unusually pronounced individualism. See Erich Branger, *Rechtsgeschichte der Freien Walser in der Ostschweiz* (Bern, 1905); Hans Kreis, *Die Walser: Ein Stück Siedlungsgeschichte der Zentralalpen,* 2d ed. (Bern, 1966); Karl Meyer, "Über die Anfänge der Walserkolonien in Rätien, *Bündner Monatsblatt,* July-September 1925; and Peter Liver, "Ist Walserrecht Walliser Recht?" *Bündner Monatsblatt,* February 1944.

sented a picture of self-aware autonomy unique throughout Raetia and probably throughout Germanic Europe in the fourteenth century. It was only natural that they established permanent avenues of commerce and communication among themselves, and more natural still that, when the beneficent Toggenburgs followed most of their titled contemporaries into an heirless void in 1436, they looked to a mutual security alliance to ward off the vultures circling the Toggenburg carcass. The covenant they signed pledged mutual aid, forswore separate alliances, and affirmed traditional rights and freedoms.[15] The treaty created no new rights, nor did it terminate fealty to "rightful" feudal overlords (the legitimate Toggenburg successor, whoever he might be); it was not, in other words, a declaration of independence or a call to rebellion, but it did protect the League of the Ten Jurisdictions from internal fractionalization and usurpation, and served as a depressant to Austria's voracious appetites—just now being whetted by the death of their domestic competition in Raetia. Consequently, the League of Ten Jurisdictions though most encumbered with unwanted foreign attentions throughout its life, remained the most unusual of the three leagues.

By 1436, then, Raetia had discovered the solution to survival. The declining feudal nobility, menaced equally by economic stagnation and familial sterility, ceased to threaten independence from within. The building of the leagues had thwarted the bishopric and its external allies from absorbing the country from without. The three infant leagues were not formally united until 1524, but they perceived early on the utility of collaboration. The easing of trade restrictions, the arbitration of interleague disputes, and the planning of a common defense were all matters that could be treated only in the context of alliance and cooperation. As early as 1440, the Gray League and the League of the House of God were linked by treaty, and

[15] The text can be found in Jecklin, *Codex*, vol. 3, no. 20.

41

there is evidence of pacts among their component districts still earlier.[16] In 1450 the League of the House of God forged a similar alliance with the League of Ten Jurisdictions. In 1471 the League of Ten Jurisdictions, increasingly anxious about Austria's belligerence, completed the circle through an alliance with the Gray League. Thus, by 1471, all three leagues were directly allied to one another, although not by a single treaty. There is little evidence for the legendary Treaty of Vazerol (its illusory place in Raetian history has been secured by a monument in Chur, the cantonal capital of modern Graubünden) to which the Raetians like to trace their unity, but it does appear likely that representatives of the three leagues were meeting together to discuss matters of common concern as early as 1461.

The three leagues also recognized the interests that they held in common with the young Swiss Confederation, and they were able to establish direct ties with several of the confederation's constituent members (*Orte*). In 1400 the Gray League sought an alliance with Glarus, lying directly to the north; the treaty was strengthened in 1407 in conjunction with the signing of a separate treaty with Uri, just across the Oberalp Pass from the Upper Rhine valley. In 1419 Chur and other members of the League of the House of God allied with the powerful Swiss town of Zürich, creating an advantageous relationship that was renewed and extended in 1470. Finally, in response to the zeal for reconquest of the new Hapsburg Emperor Maximilian I, the League of the House of God and the Gray League combined in an alliance with the seven members of the Swiss

---

[16] There is considerable controversy about whether the three leagues can be regarded as united prior to the pact of 1524. See P. Gillardon, "Ein neu aufgefundener Bundesbrief von 1524 und die Frage nach der ersten Bundesvereinigung gemeiner 3 Bünde," *Bündner Monatsblatt*, August-September 1932, with rejoinders and correspondence by Peter Liver and others.

Confederation as a collectivity, setting the scene for the Swabian War (which we will review below). The abstention of the League of Ten Jurisdictions from the treaty was no more than a prudent reaction to the realities of that league's precarious status under Austria; for in 1474 the Hapsburgs had purchased the feudal rights once exercised by the Toggenburgs over the Ten Jurisdictions, and they had more to fear from Austria than they had to gain from an alliance against her.

It is hard for us to know whether these alliances and pacts were products of foresight—necessary preparation for involvement in inevitable wars—or a factor in precipitating unnecessary involvement in wars that might have been avoided. Like it or not, however, Raetia found itself deeply involved in European affairs by the end of the fifteenth century; its participation was not only to hasten final union among all three leagues but also to mark its history with turbulence and insecurity throughout the three-hundred-year history of the Republic of the Three Leagues.

### RAETIA AND EUROPE

By the end of the fifteenth century, the Hapsburgs had established a dominion that was to make Charles V, at the beginning of the sixteenth century "beyond comparison the most powerful ruler of his day." Although the formal rights of the ecclesiastical and temporal electors of Germany had been maintained, the Hapsburg kings had in practice acquired permanent control of the imperial title from 1438. Maximilian I, with the words *bella gerunt alii; tu, felix Austria, nubes* engraved on his heart, married into the Burgundian and Spanish ruling houses. While Maximilian awaited the dowry of this unromantic union, which came to his descendants as a splendid inheritance encompassing all of Spain and Burgundy as well as Spain's Sicilian and Sardinian kingdoms and its South American colonies, he

43

diverted his attention to the reconquest of Helvetia and Raetia. The communal townships and peasant democracies of the Swiss Confederation were a constant reminder of the dissolution of the empire, and an irritation to the League of Swabian Cities. The burgeoning leagues of Raetia, meanwhile, stood obdurately in the way of Austrian ambitions in the eastern Alps.

The situation allowed neither negotiation nor compromise. Austrian probes in early 1499 into the Raetian valleys accessible by the Inn River valley from the Austrian Tyrol escalated almost immediately into full-scale war. The lines of battle in what became known as the Swabian War extended from Basel to the Lake of Constance down to the southeastern tip of Raetia; they were manned by an army of Swiss and Raetians fighting in their own regional units. The valor of Raetia's troops, fighting against heavy odds one of Europe's most powerful war machines, constitutes a colorful highlight in Raetian history. Badly outnumbered, a small detachment of Raetians managed in the justly celebrated battle at the river Calven to slay 5,000 Austrian soldiers while losing only 300 of their own. One of Graubünden's best known heroes, Benedict Fontana, won immortality at the Calven when he revivified a Raetian assault that had been stalled by a formidable line of Austrian pikes; hurling himself upon a half dozen lances, thereby breaching the impenetrable line, Fontana is said to have cried with a dying breath: "Fresh now! Forward Comrades! Heed not my wounds, I am but one man. Today men of Graubünden, or nevermore!"

The war itself was a less pretty affair, consisting on the Raetian front of little more than a "wild chaos of raids and depredations in which innumerable castles and villages went up in flames, and whole valleys were plundered— during all of which only three larger battles were waged."[17]

---

[17] Friedrich Pieth, "Der Schwabenkrieg," in Jecklin, *Bündnergeschichte*, p. 143.

Nevertheless, three battles were enough. Maximilian, increasingly preoccupied with the Turkish threat and the enmity of Venice and France, which had already resulted in the loss of the pivotal city of Milan, withdrew his thwarted army. On September 22, 1499 he signed the Treaty of Basel. Neither Swiss nor Raetian independence won formal recognition, but the treaty did signal an end to overt Austrian attempts at coercive reincorporation of the two mountain confederations into the empire. Hapsburg rights in Raetia were not abrogated, but the leagues had maintained their modest sovereignty. From this point on, Europe acknowledged the existence of an independent Raetia, while Raetia itself recognized its own role in European affairs. While Helvetia was gradually withdrawing into a defensive neutrality, Raetia was plunging into active involvement, acquiring for itself a minuscule empire.

Since the overwhelming successes in the Burgundian wars a century earlier, the reputation of Swiss and Raetian mercenaries had been inordinately high. Some Milanese pharmacies of the period are reputed to have sold flesh strips from freshly slain Raetians to a superstitious public that apparently believed some part of the Raetians' boldness might be imparted in this fashion.[18] For the Swiss, however, participation in the Italian campaigns that had become central to the Austrian-French confrontation brought their engagement to a sorry end. With their defeat at Marignano in 1515, a defeat that prompted the French king Francis I to strike a medallion reading "Francis has vanquished those whom only Caesar was able to defeat," they retired from the field. Their once formidable pike-armed phalanxes could withstand neither field cannon nor the overwhelming numbers of the new national armies; they could be deployed effectively only in the mountains in self-defense. The day of the mercenary was over.

[18] Similarly, a soldier displaying the severed head of a Swiss or Raetian mercenary received a hero's reception in Italy.

Raetia, on the other hand, never really was presented with neutrality as an option. Austria was too near, too threatening, the leagues themselves too interested in extending their income and security. In the course of the long papal-Venetian campaign to oust the French from Lombardy, Raetian mercenary units—"Protectors of freedom and of the Church," as they had been dubbed by Pope Julius II—had crossed and recrossed the fertile Adda river valley lying directly south of the Raetian mountains. Encompassing an area equal to Raetia, the Tellina valley (*Veltlin* in German sources) through which the Adda flowed was populated by Italians owing allegiance to the duke of Milan and having nothing in common with the mountain people to the north. But Raetia had long been eyeing the valley's strategic location and had been pondering the possibilities inherent in its own feudal rights in the valley, which had been granted to the Churraetian bishopric by the Milanese archdiocese. The issue was resolved in 1512, when military units from Raetia occupied the valley as a tactic in the successful campaign to restore the Sforzas to power in Milan. The Roman-Venetian conquest of Milan that Raetia thus abetted proved short-lived, but Raetia's own stay in the Tellina valley became permanent. Claiming to exercise the bishop's tenuous rights of feudal overlordship, Raetia subjected the entire valley to its rule, annexing the adjacent counties of Bormio to the east and of Chiavenna to the west as well.

Raetia thus entered the sixteenth century with a bellicose colony that its internal structure was not suited to handle, and an involvement in external affairs wholly disproportionate to its diminutive size and resources. It did not yet even possess a unitary administrative structure. Raetia's first order of business then had to be federation. But its real business for the next three centuries would continue to be survival—not so much for its own sake but for the sake of the regional autonomy and unique self-sufficiency that had set it apart from the rest of Europe in its formative centuries, and that would continue to mark its futile efforts at tranquillity and real independence with such moving poignancy.

# CHAPTER III

# Raetia to 1800—The Republic of the Three Leagues

GRAUBÜNDEN had spent over 700 years acquiring independence; it would spend nearly 300 more defending it, only to see it lost to Napoleon's armies. As burdensome and terrible as the years of independence often were, they were years of glory for the Raetian people. They constitute a separate chapter not only in this survey of the Raetian past but also in the very history of Europe.

## THE ACT OF FEDERATION

The Swabian War had pointed to the need for closer cooperation among the three Raetian leagues. The unexpectedly complex responsibilities of ruling the Tellina valley transformed the need into a political imperative. The religious schism introduced by the Reformation lent to this imperative a social and structural urgency that made it irresistible.

In the early autumn of 1524, representatives from each of the jurisdictional communes (*Gerichtsgemeinden*) into which the leagues were divided assembled to draft a treaty of confederal union. With them were Hans von Marmels, the lord of Rhäzüns, and the abbot of Disentis, both of whom had played a constructive role in the discussions leading up to the meeting. The leagues were not directly represented, other than by their constituent communes, and the bishop of Chur, once again a hostile foreigner, was notable by his absence. The Act of Union, the treaty that was negotiated at this gathering, quickly came to be seen as the constitution of the Republic of the Three Leagues (*Freistaat der Drei Bünden*), but it was not in reality a creation *ex nihilo*. Much of it was a codification of earlier treaties and precedents: the opening paragraph speaks of "a *renewal* of our understandings and treaties, with clarifications. . . ."[1] Nevertheless, the treaty in its central provisions was thoroughly innovative, a change of state as well as in degree, and a radical improvement on the unwieldy system of bilateral alliances that had prevailed in the previous century. In foreign affairs the leagues were made subordinate to the federation; separate alliances were prohibited; war and peace became matters for the majority of communes to decide; and the Valtellina was given a federally administered colonial structure. In domestic matters, a referendum was instituted that gave to the communes exclusive control of all legislative activity. The only instrument of the central government was a three-man commission (*Häupter*) made up of the heads of each of the leagues that, with the assistance of an elective assembly (*Beytag*), prepared the referendum and executed the will of the communes. In the new structure power was an inverse function of level of organization. The central "federal" government had almost none, the regional communes had a great deal. But a common framework for action had been established, and if it was to prove inadequate to some of the challenges which were to confront the republic, it nevertheless provided the people of Churraetia with several centuries of real though fitful independence, and a measure of autonomous self-government rare in Germanic Europe.

Unfortunately, the Act of Union did not accomplish the defeudalization and secularization of Raetian society. It

[1] The text from which this paragraph is cited can be found in Constantin Jecklin, ed., *Codex Diplomaticus*, vol. 5 (Chur, 1865), no. 38. A lucid paraphrase and elaboration of the founding document is provided by William Plattner, *Die Entstehung der Freistaates der Drei Bünde und sein Verhältnis zur alten Eidgenossenschaft* (Davos, 1895), pp. 255–263.

imposed a new political veneer on an underlying social and economic structure that was little changed. The veneer would probably have cracked had not the communes challenged feudalism in a more fundamental way. The challenge came with two historic declarations—the first issued in the year of the Act of Union, the second two years later—that were the Raetian expression of a more sweeping revolution that was enveloping Europe: the Protestant Reformation.

## THE REFORMATION

While Luther was nailing up his ninety-five theses in Germany, Ulrich Zwingli was leaning out from his pulpit in the Grossmünster in Zürich, urging a less bombastic but equally far-reaching program of religious and social reform for the Swiss. From Zürich the new gospel spread, chiefly through Johannes Comander, a disciple of Zwingli, to Graubünden where the conditions seemed still more ripe for the Reformation. Church power and church corruption dallied together with a brazen insolence, while the political abuses of spiritual authority were as flagrant in Chur as in Rome. The cloisters had become "centers of stupidity and immorality."[2] The bishop of Chur, more often than not, seemed content to play the puppet to Austria, simultaneously exacting from his Raetian subjects every last tithe, every last hour of labor service that he could.

Under these conditions, reform could not afford to await the gradual spread of the new gospel, which did not reach its full influence until the late 1530's in Graubünden. Thus, in 1524 the communes met in Ilanz and promulgated the

[2] E. Camenisch, "Die Reformation in Graubünden," in Fritz Jecklin, ed., *Bündnergeschichte In Elf Vorträgen* (Chur, 1902), p. 183. Camenisch has also written a history of Protestantism in Graubünden, commissioned by the Evangelical Church: *Bündner Reformationsgeschichte* (Chur, 1920).

First Articles of Ilanz, a moderate and cautious document not unlike the conservative Mandate of Faith under which mild reforms were introduced in Catholic Inner Switzerland. It remedied only the most egregious abuses of the church, once again insisting that the bishop confine himself to church affairs, ruling that priests were to be maintained without burdening the communes they served, and assuaging the economic plight of peasants indentured to the bishopric.[3] The prudent restrictions of the First Articles of Ilanz were, however, Band-aids on a compound fracture. Bishop Ziegler was in that comfortable exile that had become the wont of Austrian-supported clerics, and implacably opposed the most restrained reforms. Meanwhile, a Milanese offensive, abetted by treachery, had led to the occupation of part of the Tellina valley (in the short War of Müsso Castle of 1525–1526), happenings attributed by many directly to the disloyalty of the bishop. At the same time, the new creed was gaining wider acceptance, in part because of the reformers' success in a well-publicized Great Disputation with representatives of the church in 1525. Passions were outstripping prudence—a half-organized rabble overran the bishop's inner courtyard during the same year—and the only alternative seemed to be a radical elaboration of the Ilanzer Articles. As a result, a second set of articles was fashioned in 1526 that called for the wholesale secularization of the new Republic of the Three Leagues. The bishop was deprived *in toto* of his vestigial political and legal prerogatives, losing also his powers of secular appointment. The Churraetian church was placed under the permanent surveillance of the republic. Priests, as well as the new Protestant ministers, were henceforth to be elected by their parishioners, a reform that led to the emergence of church communes (*Kirchgemeinden*), which continue to

[3] Both the first and second sets of Ilanzer Articles are reproduced in Jecklin, *Codex*, vol. 5, nos. 37 and 38. Their name derives from the capital of the Gray League, Ilanz, where they were drafted.

play a vital role in modern civic life. Finally, many church tithes and other feudal obligations were reduced or abolished, the remainder being permanently fixed against arbitrary future increases.

The Articles of Ilanz shared a common ethos with the several peasant declarations that came out of the Peasant Revolt in Germany during the 1520's. Yet while the German documents were desperate petitions of a failing rebellion, the Ilanzer Articles were positive law enacted by a sovereign republic capable of giving force to their provisions. Their most stunning achievement turned out to be creation of circumstances where confessional coexistence was possible over several centuries. The communes themselves were left to choose their own persuasion; in some cases a single commune encompassed Catholic and Protestant communities that cohabited a village, and sometimes even a common church, in relative harmony (for example, in Churwalden).

The ambitious tolerance of the Second Ilanzer Articles helped produce mild, humanistic, and even reform-minded successors to Bishop Ziegler, who died in 1451. Their willingness to cooperate in minimizing religious friction, expressed concretely in their submission to the so-called Six Articles subordinating them still further to the authority of the League of the House of God, reinforced the climate of formal religious parity in the country.[4] So patient was the mood that communes converted to the new faith often waited patiently for the death of their priest before securing a converted minister. This general feeling of good will was externally enhanced by the duke of Milan's decision to formally recognize Graubünden's rights in the Tellina valley following the second War of Müsso Castle in 1532.

Graubünden was tranquil, but Rome was not; otherwise Raetia's peace might have endured. But the storm of the Counter-Reformation generated by the papal bull *Licet ab initio* (1542) engulfed Italy in waves of inquisition and persecution, sending disquieting ripples into Raetia. Polit-

---

[4] Texts of the Six Articles are given in *ibid.*, no. 40.

ical developments followed that were even more unsettling. Since the 1530's Milan had been in the hands of the Spanish, thus the Hapsburgs; Graubünden's passes and the Tellina valley, natural arteries for Hapsburg blood from the Austrian heart to the new Italian limbs, became the focus of the most intense Hapsburg interest. Austria's French enemies meanwhile pondered the benefits of abrupt surgical interdiction of these life-sustaining arteries. The small mountain republic of Graubünden thus found itself the theater of a major diplomatic and military struggle between France and Austria for European hegemony. Two political parties emerged, aligning themselves with the contending powers, while traditional families were forced to choose up sides in a game many would have preferred not to play, especially as the contest took on an increasingly ominous confessional tone. The Hapsburg party became almost exclusively Catholic, the French party predominantly Protestant, despite the trauma of St. Bartholomew's Massacre in 1572. Raetia soon was split into two hostile camps divided by family, religion, and politics, and kept apart by a mountain of foreign money. The few honest neutrals who aspired to an alliance with the Swiss were foiled by the incapacity of the confederation—itself torn asunder by religious distrust—to agree on conditions for Raetian entry. The seven Catholic cantons were overtly hostile to Raetian membership, particularly in the aftermath of the short-lived but bitter War of Kappel—an internecine religious struggle which cost Zwingli his life. With Zwingli died his dream of a united Protestant Europe with a united Switzerland at its center; and with that dream went Raetia's only hope for a way out of its debilitating European entanglements.[5]

---

[5] "Although the battle of Kappel (1531) was little more than a skirmish, the death of Zwingli made it a turning point in European history. His great concept of a united Switzerland, a great European power, allied with Venice and the German Protestant princes, died with him. . . . His death was a disaster to Protestant Europe, and it was followed by three centuries of Swiss disunion, the effects of which are still ap-

Attempts at reform from within, which followed the failure to gain security from without, were equally unsuccessful. Despite the periodic prohibitions against accepting foreign monies (as pensions or outright bribes) and reform efforts aimed at curbing the arbitrary use of force by courts turned lynch mob, things got progressively worse.[6] The failure was due in part to the impotence of the central government in the face of widespread disregard for laws and treaties, but its central cause was probably the continuing devotion of the communes to local power in the face of problems that clearly required central resolution. The Great Reform Act of 1603 hence moved to weaken further central controls that needed to be strengthened, leaving tragically unfulfilled hopes for an end to corruption in the administration of subject territories, the reestablishment of religious parity, and the regaining of federal unity.

Graubünden thus entered the seventeenth century torn apart by religious enmity and political factionalism, its institutions ridden with cynicism and corruption. Disunited and disspirited, it found itself without the insight to bring about inner reform and without the sense of common purpose to resist outward aggression. The first half of the century proved to be the most difficult in the history of the republic—a Time of Troubles that quite nearly destroyed it.

---

parent." E. Bonjour, H. S. Offler, and G. R. Potter, *A Short History of Switzerland* (Oxford, 1952), pp. 161–162. Also see M. Valer, "Die Beziehung Graubündens zur alten Eidgenossenschaft," in Jecklin, *Bündnergeschichte.*

6 Efforts at reform included the *Pensionerbrief* adopted in 1500 well before the Act of Union as a prohibition against accepting foreign pensions (see Jecklin, *Codex*, vol. 5, no. 36); the *Kesselbrief* of 1570 that renewed the same prohibition (*ibid.*, no. 46); the *Dreisieglerbrief* of 1574 that outlawed the use of force or political courts in settling intercommunal and interleague disputes (*ibid.*, no. 45); and finally the Great Reform of 1603 the thirty-seven articles of which dealt with the entire gamut of corruption and abuse in Raetia and its subject territories (*ibid.*, no. 49).

54

## THE TIME OF TROUBLES

In a war involving all of Europe, Raetia could hardly be a primary consideration: what happened to it during the Time of Troubles was little more than a footnote to the Thirty Years' War, in the course of which all of central Europe was laid to waste.[7] Yet for the individual Raetian, the footnote was the entire book of life; what happened to him *was* what happened to Europe. Within a dozen years he watched his country ravaged by successive French and military occupations dictated less by local tactics than by grand strategy. Each invasion occasioned new depredations, each initiated a spree of wild bloodletting in which the victims of earlier invaders took their merciless revenge on their onetime tormentors under the protection of the new invaders. No man, no party could feel secure, for the vicissitudes of distant armies could turn victory into disaster, celebration into assassination, or statesman into traitor in the course of a single alpine night. Those condemned at dusk could find themselves executioners at dawn, while their judges from the night before stared at them in terror from the block. The individual was trapped in an endless nightmare, "the whole land writhed and shrieked in the

[7] The Time of Troubles (*Bündnerwirren*) coincides with the birth of Raetian historiography. Contemporary accounts, albeit inaccurate in historical detail, provide a vivid picture of the period as it must have been experienced by the local population. Among the best of this plentiful genre are the following: Bartholomäus Anhorn, *Pündtner Aufruhr im Jahre 1607* in Conradin v. Moor, ed., *Archiv für die Geschichte der Republik Graubünden*, vol. 6 (Chur, 1862); Fortunat von Juvalta, *Raeti commentarii vitae* published as *Denkwürdigkeiten* in Theodor von Mohr, ed., *Archiv für die Geschichte der Republik Graubünden*, vol. 1 (Chur, 1853). Fortunat Sprecher von Bernegg, *Geschichte der bündnerischen Kriege und Unruhen* in Conradin von Moor, *Archiv*, vol. 3 (Chur, 1856); and a rare history of the era written in Ladin, the Raeto-Romansh dialect of the Engadine, Jakob Anton Vulpius *Historia raetica*, in Conradin von Moor, *Archiv*, vol. 7 (Chur, 1866).

throes of a man-created hell, filled with blood, famine, pestilence and death."[8]

The chain of events leading up to these disasters began many years earlier with the signing of an alliance between the Raetian Republic and the Venetian Republic. Venice was Raetia's southern neighbor, a fraternal republic, an excellent trading partner, and an important source of income for a large group of Raetian guildsmen, primarily confectioners, who resided there. The alliance seemed natural enough, and was supported by France. Henry IV had disposed of the Huguenot problem, had won the Swiss Confederation over to what became a permanent alliance, and had secured in 1602 a separate alliance with Raetia itself; he was thus pleased to see the renewed collaboration between Raetia and Venice. But the duchy of Milan—Hapsburg now, as we have seen—was profoundly discomfited at a liaison that left its vital routes to Austria in the hands of countries in the French camp. Fuentes, the Spanish governor of Milan, secured the support of Austria to take retaliatory measures. Provocative fortifications were hastily erected on the very threshold of the Tellina valley, while covert agitation was sponsored to stir up the already ripe resentments of that valley's deeply Catholic, pervasively anti-Raetian and anti-German population.

Emboldened by these external developments, Raetia's Spanish party under the Engadine leadership of the Planta family struck at the French party within Raetia. Chur was seized by armed communes in 1607, and unlucky French party leaders were tried for treason, mostly *in absentia*. The aristocratic French-leaning family of von Salis and evangelical ministers like Blasius Alexander and Georg Jenatsch, who constituted the real leadership of the French party, had made off in escapades that were to be repeated over and over again in the next thirty years. The resurgence of

[8] F. Grenfell Baker, *The Model Republic* (New York, 1892), p. 322.

the Spanish party and with it the Spanish cause made renewal of the Venetian alliance, which came up for reconsideration in 1613, out of the question. Henry IV had been assassinated in 1610, Louis XIII was preoccupied with new Huguenot rebelliousness, and the Austrians were able to press their case unopposed. The alliance was allowed to expire and the Hapsburgs apparently won a victory. Yet just as the initial invocation of the Venetian treaty had catalyzed the Spanish party into successful action, so its involuntary termination revitalized the complacent French party. Anti-Hapsburg factions soon had effected a counter-inquisition in the Protestant jurisdiction of Thusis. With the voluble pastor Jenatsch at its head, a makeshift kangaroo court tried and banished the two leading Plantas, Rudolf and Pompius, confiscated all their property, and handed down sentences on 157 more followers of the Plantas' Spanish party.

The cycle of action and reaction now accelerated. Repelled by the arbitrary performance at Thusis, factions antagonistic to the French party organized their own inquisitional court at Chur, which remained a center of Hapsburg sentiment. The decisions of Thusis were all duly reversed, a new roster of villains supplanting the old. The von Salis party countered with a court of Davos reaffirming the judiciousness of Jenatsch's work at Thusis. And so it went: court matching court, lynch mob matching lynch mob, a rising howl of dissident vengeance and impassioned violence drowning out the whispers of impartiality and justice of the once democratic republic.[9]

Miraculously, despite the widening anarchy, there had

---

[9] Peter C. Planta suggests that Raetia during this period was in "complete anarchy: the sovereignty of the jurisdictional communes, supposedly expressed in the legal majority, had been transferred to a revolutionary assembly; the government, insofar as one can speak of a government, was in the hands of a revolutionary tribunal; and justice had been reduced to a deadly instrument of party vengeance." *Geschichte von Graubünden* (Bern, 1913), p. 213.

been no overt foreign intervention until 1620. But the Spanish party was losing the vindictive internecine struggle and felt itself increasingly in straits from which only Austria could rescue it. The Austrians complied in the summer of 1620 with a timely offensive from the Tyrol into the Münster valley, coordinated, in what was probably more than a fortuitous accident, with a major rebellion in the Tellina valley. While Austrian units were sweeping Raetian resistence from the field, deeply embittered Italian Catholics were slaughtering Raetian colonials, residents, and their families in their subjugated Italian homeland. Six hundred died, including hundreds of women and children incinerated in the evangelical churches where they had sought refuge. The trauma of the combined events shattered what vestiges of unity Raetia possessed: the predominantly Catholic Gray League urged total surrender to Austria, the Tellina valley appeared irretrievably lost, and a foreign army stood poised for the kill over Raetia's supine form.

Once again, however, Georg Jenatsch roused his crumbling party to fierce opposition. In a lightning campaign of terror that included the melodramatic murder of Pompius Planta in his own castle at Rietburg and a rampage in the Austrian-leaning Upper Rhine valley that invites comparison with General Sherman's journey of rapine, Jenatsch confronted Austria with unexpected problems. What Austria had hoped to accomplish by the exploitation of internal divisiveness and by military intimidation it was now compelled to obtain by conquest. Nonetheless, obtain it by conquest it did. The Münster valley and the Engadine, cleared briefly by Jenatsch's bold maneuvers, were easily retaken, and Austria soon controlled the entire republic. Its grasp secure, it forced upon Raetia the humiliating Articles of Milan which construed the Hapsburgs as rightful masters of the Engadine and Münster valleys, and of the League of Ten Jurisdictions. For all practical purposes, the remainder of Raetia became an Austrian military province.

The French-oriented Protestant party fled northward to Zürich; those unable to escape were dealt with summarily by Rudolf Planta's vengeance-seeking Spanish party or by the Austrians directly. Blasius Alexander, Jenatsch's reformed colleague, for example, was imprisoned in Innsbruck, where he died.

Under the umbrella of Austrian occupation, Capuchin monks introduced a second Counter-Reformation, pressing their advantage with particular vigor in the devoutly Protestant Prättigau valley in the all-Protestant League of Ten Jurisdictions. Reformed Raetians could tolerate only so much, however, and the Prättigau persecution ultimately produced a violent if short-lived uprising.[10] In 1622, the local population, without any apparent outside leadership, took up brooms, field implements, and axes and set upon Austrians and Capuchins with a rage fired by piety. The surprised occupation forces fled in terror, while Georg Jenatsch and von Salis capitalized on these local heroics by raising an army throughout the republic. Exploiting surprise rather than numbers, Jenatsch and von Salis with no more than 2,000 men expelled the Hapsburg forces altogether from Raetian territory. It took the Austrians little time to recognize the pathetic frailty of the "army" that had swept them from the field, however, and within two months they returned to Raetia with a force of 10,000 men seeking revenge. The valleys of the Engadine, the Münster, and the Prättigau were plundered with all the violence that shame and projected dishonor could muster. Livestock

[10] A striking contemporary account of the uprising is offered in Johann Guler, *Rechtfertigung des Prättigauer Freiheitskampf*, first written in 1622, published in Conradin von Moor, ed., *Archiv*, vol. 10 (Chur, 1877). His opening remarks, characteristic of the period's fervor, implore: "Let us die in our simplicity: Heaven and Earth will be witnesses to the truth that you slay us by brute force and without right." The full objective account of the insurrection is given by P. Gillardon, *Geschichte des Zehngerichtenbundes* (Davos, 1936).

was randomly slaughtered, villages were put to the torch, and participants in the rebellion were hounded quite literally to death. The humiliation of the Articles of Milan was imposed afresh with a new Treaty of Lindau. The winter of 1623 was one of despair, famine, plague, and death: the only edible staple was boiled grass. The many pious Protestants who cried out for deliverance from the persecution of Catholicism by death had their prayers answered by starvation, disease, and Austrian lances. Further resistance was unthinkable. Salvation could come only from the outside, from the legions of Louis's France.

In fact, France had finally settled its Huguenot problem. With Richelieu as the monarch's chief minister, France seemed ready to take up the Austrian gauntlet once again. Striking convenient alliances with Venice and Savoy, the French were able in 1624 to drive the Austrians not only from Raetia but also from the Tellina valley. Once again the tables were turned—supporters of the Hapsburg cause rushing hastily into exile, friends of France returning to a foreign-supported eminence. Yet as the bog of European politics became ever more slippery with muddy intrigue, it became clear to Raetian statesmen on both sides of the conflict that the simplistic cleavages of the past would no longer serve them or their country. With each passing day, Richelieu's manipulative cynicism became clearer, even to the loyal French party. His interest in Raetia was patently a variable function of his interest in the European power balance. Thus, when Raetia's sovereignty in the Tellina valley no longer suited his purposes, he negotiated the secret Treaty of Monsonio (1626) that turned over effective power there to the pope. When French troops were withdrawn from the valley in 1629, papal forces replaced them. The dimming of France's Raetian star added luster to Austria's. The French party felt betrayed, the Austrian party vindicated. When renewed war broke out between Austria and France in 1629, the Raetians were not disposed

to support France. As a result, Austria occupied Graubünden for still a third time, bringing with it not only renewed
Protestant persecution but also a species of pestilence not
yet experienced in the eastern Alps: bubonic plague. More
than one-quarter of the already decimated population per-
ished of the new disease, an astonishingly large number in
view of Raetia's almost exclusively rural character. The
mortality rate in towns like Chur and Disentis was presumably even higher.

It was not France but Sweden that this time drew the
Austrians away from Raetia. Attacking vigorously in the
north, it compelled Austria to abandon its north Italian
campaigns and rush its forces to the new front. Raetia
watched passively as the Austrians retreated and French
troops returned to Graubünden under the leadership of a
sympathetic former Huguenot leader, the duke of Rohan.[11]
Rohan unfortunately turned out to understand the needs
of Raetia better than he did those of France; he won the
loyalty of the local population through a series of well-
intended promises concerning the restoration of Raetian
rule in the Tellina valley, upon which, however, an irri-
tated Richelieu refused to make good. Initially, Richelieu
simply refused to allow his forces to retake the valley. Then,
when Austria's ominous victory over Sweden in 1635
prompted him to do so, he continued to temporize about
its disposition. In this fashion he squandered the considerable good will that had been created by Rohan's sympathetic presence.

[11] The duc de Rohan is a rather peculiar and enduring hero in
Raetia's historical consciousness—a first-class hotel in modern Chur
carries his name. His role as a friend of Graubünden who was duped
by Richelieu has probably been romanticized to the advantage of his
reputation as a loyal naif. Yet it does seem clear that he viewed his
ouster from Raetia as a personal tragedy, at least according to the
memoirs he set down in Geneva during the year separating his tenure
in Raetia and his death at the Battle of Rheinfelden. *Mémoires sur
la guerre de la Veltline* (hgg. v. Zurlauben, 1758).

By 1637 France was again an unwelcome guest. Georg Jenatsch, still the liveliest and most resourceful figure on the Raetian scene, engineered still another coup in the service of his country's independence. A friend to the French only because he had deemed their aid valuable to the Raetian cause, he did not hesitate to betray them, nor even the Protestant faith, when they appeared to jeopardize Raetian independence.[12] In a dramatic public gesture, Jenatsch abruptly converted to Catholicism, signaling to his followers his disillusionment with France. At the same time, he assumed covert leadership of the Spanish party, promising in secret negotiations to help drive the French from Graubünden if Austria would guarantee the return of the Tellina valley to a fully autonomous Raetia. His daring diplomatic gambit succeeded, and by the end of 1637, supported by an Austrian army poised helpfully on the frontier, he expelled the French. Two years later, after a long mission to Madrid, the Treaty of Eternal Peace was ratified making good on the Austrian promise to restore the Tellina valley to Graubünden. Although the treaty was regarded as restoring the *status quo ante bellum*, it included provisions (the so-called Capitulation of Milan) barring Protestants from residence in the Tellina valley that were to become the source of later tensions.

[12] Georg Jenatsch is possibly the most controversial and romantic figure in all of Raetian history. A reformed minister, a rebel, a soldier, a diplomat, and a statesman, his name became synonymous with the unexpected and the daring. He pursued his vision of a strong, independent Raetia throughout his life with a passion to which everything else, including his religious conviction, was subordinated. Hence, his reputation as a great patriot has always had to contend with his reputation as a great scoundrel. The widely read nineteenth-century novel *Jürg Jenatsch* by Conrad Ferdinand Meyer gives currency to some extravagant distortions about Jenatsch—for example, to the fanciful myth that he was romantically involved with the daughter of Pompius Planta, the Austrian party leader whom in collaboration

Two years later another treaty with Austria formally acknowledged Raetian independence, while recognizing the vestigial feudal rights of the Hapsburgs in the League of Ten Jurisdictions. These rights were in any case to be sold back to the republic within a decade to pay off part of the staggering debt Austria had accumulated in the endless war. Georg Jenatsch, the chief protagonist of this thirty-year Raetian struggle for survival, did not live to witness the peace his violent intransigence and his remarkable diplomacy had finally secured. In 1639, in a final act of that monstrous vengeance, which he himself had so often exploited, he was struck down by assassins. His troubled passing brought an end to Graubünden's Time of Troubles.

The era of the Thirty Years' War had not solved any of Raetia's difficulties: it remained divided within by factions sympathetic to opposing foreign powers, and continued to depend on foreign patronage, especially Austria's, for its precarious independence. Yet it had survived as a sovereign republic—a most remarkable feat in view of the wars and disruptions it had undergone. Raetia now had a century and a half of relative peace to try to work out its internal problems.

## THE EIGHTEENTH CENTURY

The price Raetia had had to pay for its continued independence was a passionless friendship with Austria that persisted until the French Revolution. Alliance with the Swiss Confederation might have permitted a more autonomous foreign policy, but the seven Catholic cantons remained uncompromisingly hostile to Raetian entry; the League of Ten Jurisdictions and the League of the House of God were simply too Protestant. This enmity thwarted

---

with others he murdered. A much more accurate, if unnecessarily dull, portrait is painted by Alexander Pfister in *Georg Jenatsch: sein Leben und seine Zeit* (Basel, 1939).

all efforts at an alliance, even in the period during the War of Spanish Succession when the Swiss were trying to forge a broad alpine *Defensionale* to protect their neutrality. The best Raetia could do was a partial alliance between Zürich and its own two Protestant leagues in 1707. By the middle of the eighteenth century, it ceased to send representatives, even as observers, to the Helvetian Diet and came to be viewed, "against its own will, in the eyes of most of the Confederation, as an alien power."[13]

Austria naturally welcomed Raetia's estrangement from the confederation. Its own stature had been secure since it sold back to the republic its vestigial prerogatives in the League of Ten Jurisdictions following the Peace of Westphalia, and it now found itself with exclusive access to Raetian ears.[14] Its influence was decisively confirmed when Charles II, the last Hapsburg, died in Spain and France claimed the Spanish throne; for in the war that followed, Raetia, after toying with neutrality and the renewal of its lapsed alliance with Venice, was persuaded to support Austria. In the Pass Treaty of 1707, Raetia ceded to Austria rights of unlimited passage of men and material through the mountains. Austria thereby secured a permanent and direct lifeline with its army in Italy—a circumstance that

[13] Friedrich Pieth, *Bündnergeschichte* (Chur, 1945), p. 254. See also Johannes A. von Sprecher, *Geschichte der Republik der Drei Bünde*, 2 vols. (Chur, 1872), which gives a good general picture of Raetia in the eighteenth century. The second volume has recently been reedited by R. Jenny and has appeared with valuable supplementary material as *Kulturgeschichte der Drei Bünde* (Chur, 1951); it is an invaluable source of economic and social data on the century under review here.

[14] Raetia purchased back its rights in the Eight Jurisdictions for 75,000 florins—almost 2 million francs at the 1936 value according to Gillardon, *Geschichte*, p. 200f.

The dependency on Austria that ensued did not, however, impede Raetia's remarkable traffic in mercenaries with other countries unfriendly to Austria. In 1696 there were 8,800 Raetians in French service—well over 10 percent of the Raetian population!

contributed vitally to its subsequent routing of the French and its reconquest of Milan, despite the loss of the Spanish throne to the Bourbon pretender. As compensation for benevolent neutrality, Raetia was given crucial concessions in tariffs and trade and a promise of eventual revision of the Capitulation of Milan of 1639 which had so prejudiced the status of Protestants in the Tellina valley. A second Capitulation in 1726 executed the promise, while a third in 1762, contrived by the ubiquitous von Salis family, improved the lot of Protestants still further, albeit at the cost of permanently losing the good will and friendship of the Venetian Republic.[15] The important thing to the individual Raetian must, however, have seemed the long era of relative tranquillity that the relationship with Austria promoted. Far-off alliances, occasional military transports, and reports of contested successions were to him of much less consequence than local efforts at political reform and economic rationalization. The real landmarks of eighteenth-century Raetian history are thus the reform acts and the emergence of institutions like the Economic Society.

Most of the political reforms had as their objective the further democratization and decentralization of authority within the leagues. The twin powers of dominant towns and dominant families were a rising danger to Graubünden's form of participatory government. The communes

[15] The third Capitulation was a reward of sorts to the von Salis family, who, in defense of its own interests in the Splügen pass port system, had helped Austria to thwart a Chur-Venetian plan to provide a more direct trade route between Italy and the north at the expense of the Splügen system. The consequence of these intrigues was the breaking of relations between Venice and Graubünden in 1766, and the expulsion of a large colony of Raetian tradesmen and guildsmen.

The von Salis family had figured in almost every significant crisis of the seventeenth and eighteenth centuries, for it was the most prominent and prolific family in the land. Of 63 members of the Republic's accessory parliament, 11 were at one point von Salis's; this family also dominated the mercenary service. Cf. Planta, *Geschichte*, p. 336.

of the League of Ten Jurisdictions, for example, brought the leading town, Davos, before a board of arbitration to challenge its peculiar preeminence in the league; its mayor became president of the league as if by natural law, while secondary league offices had come by custom to be occupied exclusively by Davosers. The arbitration board, headed by the statesman Waser from Zürich, handed down only a weak compromise, but the challenge remained a significant symbol of communal discontent.[16] A similar suit was brought by communes of the League of the House of God against Chur and had equally ambivalent results.[17] But the precedent established by their objections facilitated a far more successful and far more vital endeavor when in 1734 an Austrian-leaning bishop preemptorily sold the Münster valley to the court at Vienna. The appalled communes in the League of the House of God raised such a storm of controversy that Austria eventually was moved to sell back the valley to the league at the original cost.

The communes were less successful in containing their own aristocratic families than in curbing the excess powers of the larger towns, for families like the von Salis, the Travers, the Sprechers, the Tscharners, and the Plantas had deep roots in the common Raetian past, often having played

[16] The text of the so-called *Waserische Spruch* can be found in Jecklin, *Codex*, vol. 5, no. 54. The League of Ten Jurisdictions presented manifold complexities to the Arbitration Board. One of the ten, Davos, enjoyed a privileged status both as the largest jurisdiction, and as an original *Walser* settlement; another, Malans, was both an independent jurisdiction within the league, and a subject territory of the republic as a whole (which has purchased Austria's feudal rights in the commune); a third, Maienfeld, had to be treated simultaneously as a free commune, as a subject territory of the Raetian Republic, and as a fief of Austria. No wonder, then, that the best the Arbitration Board could do was recommend that the presidency (*Landamman*) of the league henceforth rotate among the communes, rather than being restricted to Davos.

[17] The text of the Second Act of Arbitration, the *Malanser Spruch*, is given by Jecklin, *Codex*, vol. 5, no. 58.

crucial roles in national defense or movements toward unity. Their position was grounded in convention and consensus —a certain deference to their heritage—but not, as in aristocratically controlled cities like Bern or Luzern or Freiburg, in any hereditary right to office. Consequently, the somewhat disproportionate influence of such families in Graubünden's nominally egalitarian political structure was difficult to restrict: deriving from custom rather than law, there was little law could do to contain it. The only major reform of the period, the Great Reform Act of 1684, addressed itself only to obvious corruptions like the maladministration of the Tellina valley and the acceptance of foreign bribes. There could be no question, however, about the locus of real sovereignty in republican Graubünden: the communes remained *the* voice of the collectivity throughout the republican era.

During this same period, pressures for other more profound kinds of change were being brought to bear on Raetia. A watery but for Raetia amply potent brew of Enlightenment prescriptions gradually seeped from Paris to Basel and Zürich, and thence on to Raetia's more populous towns where they were reconstituted in suitable alpine form for local consumption. A Society for Friends of Agriculture was created, and it immediately initiated publication of a reformist agricultural magazine directed at a lay audience of peasants and cowherds. *Der Sammler*, as it was called, urged reforms on its readers with the fervent spirit of the great *Encyclopedia of Arts and Sciences*, though with only minimal success.[18] Road-construction programs got

---

[18] First published in 1779 as *Der Sammler: Eine gemeinnützige Wochenschrift für Bündten*, it ceased publication in 1784; it reappeared from 1804 to 1811 as *Der Neue Sammler* under the revitalized Economic Society. It was from the outset a paragon of Enlightenment journalism, combining rational and scientific discussions of agriculture and economics with popular exhortations to improvement. But like so many other reformers, the editors of the Sammler seemed to get

under way that were to transform Raetian trade and commerce. The bridging of the once impassable gorge of the Via Mala on the Splügen Pass in 1739 proved a turning point in a transportation revolution that would culminate over a hundred years later.[19]

The spirit of the Enlightenment was also evident in educational reforms patterned on the models of Swiss pioneers like Rousseau and Pestalozzi. As early as 1761, a progressive teachers' seminary was founded in Haldenstein. Legal reforms led to the introduction of a new criminal code at the beginning of the eighteenth century,[20] and the first all-Raetian federal court in 1766.[21]

---

through only to the converted. A reader complained in the last issue of 1779 that the weekly was neither bought nor read by the peasants and dairymen for whom it was intended.

[19] Rudolf Jenny, Graubünden's current archivist, has reviewed the history of Graubünden's passes and commercial roads in *Historisches Exposé—San Bernardino: Graubündens volkswirtschaftliche Bedeutung in historischer Zeit* (Chur, 1963). The significance of geography and transportation are the focus of our study in the next chapter.

[20] In 1716 a new criminal code (*Malifiz-Ordnung*) based on the German *Carolina* was ratified for Raetia; though hardly rational in the sense of Beccaria, Bentham, or the later legal reformers, the code did ameliorate the arbitrary harshness of prevailing feudal precedents. In any case, the code could not bind the semisovereign communes, who controlled through the higher jurisdiction (*Hochgericht*) criminal affairs. Cf. Peter Liver, "Aus der bündnerischen Strafrechtsgeschichte," *Bündner Monatsblatt*, March-April 1941.

[21] The Raetian Federal Court established in 1766 had jurisdiction only over foreign criminals and vagabonds who ranged in hordes through the sparsely populated mountains robbing at will, thus creating a truly federal rather than a local problem. In early editions of *Die Räuber*, Schiller had been moved by these conditions to speak of Graubünden as an "Athens of today's rogues." His remarks occasioned a literary controversy that still smolders.

The new court did little to mitigate the situation or improve Raetia's reputation, for the jealous communes never gave it the authority to operate forcefully. It was disbanded in 1761, then re-created in 1799 for another futile eleven-year trial period. Cf. P. Gillardon, "Das

If the Enlightenment effected a series of far-reaching socioeconomic changes in Graubünden, it also produced a major reaction whose character and consequences can still, as we shall have an opportunity to see in the final chapter of this study, be observed in the present canton of Graubünden. But Raetia's tortuously eventful journey to an ambiguous modernity was interrupted at the end of the eighteenth century by the intrusion of still another European cataclysm—the French Revolution. This time the constitutional structure of the republic, which had barely survived the Time of Troubles, proved wholly inadequate to the challenges of war and crisis. When the revolution was over and Napoleon's armies were comfortably ensconced in much of Europe, the little Republic of the Three Leagues had disappeared from the map of Europe. An unlikely experiment in independence and local self-sufficiency had come to a likely end.

## Loss of Independence and Union With Helvetia

The French Revolution found Raetia as divided as it had been at the outset of the Time of Troubles, a grim and prophetic omen of things to come.[22] The French party —its loyalties wholly with the monarchy—had survived the long century of Austrian predominance in Raetia; under the still ubiquitous family of von Salis it reemerged as a potent force in the revolutionary era. Meanwhile, an Aus-

Kriminaltribunal gemeiner III Bünde in der zweiten Hälfte des 18. Jahrhundert," *Bündner Monatsblatt*, April 1942.

[22] The extensive literature on the fall of the Raetian Republic includes E. Dunant, *La réunion des Grisons à la suisse* (Basel, 1899); G. Hosang, *Die Kämpfe um den Anschluss Graubündens an die Schweiz* (Chur, 1899); Alexander Pfister, *Die Patrioten* (Chur, 1904); Alfred Rufer, *Das Ende des Freistaates der Drei Bünde* (Chur, 1965) and *Der Freistaat der III Bünde und die Frage des Veltlins*, 2 vols. (Basel, 1910); and Robert Steiner, *Der Kanton Rätien zur Zeit der helvetischen Verwaltungskammer* (Zürich, 1936).

trian-oriented coalition including descendants of the notorious Plantas of the seventeenth century had been developing oddly progressive ideas for a "patriotic" reform based on many of the ideas that were to fuel the revolutionaries in Paris. It was no surprise, then, that following the ideological metamorphosis of France after the revolution, the loyalist party of von Salis transferred its allegiance to Austria, while the patriots began to court the favor of the new French Republic. In 1794 an extraordinary representative assembly was convoked, ostensibly to deal with unwelcome by-products of the French Revolution like inflation, trade deficits, and the expulsion of mercenaries from France. In fact, the patriot party quickly seized control of the assembly, turning what was to have been a neutral court of inquiry into an audacious political court styled after the rabid inquisitional bodies of the Time of Troubles. A devastating attack was launched on the Austrian-inclined party of von Salis and particularly on its leader, Ulysses von Salis-Marschlins. Only the refusal of the still sovereign communes to ratify the raucous proceedings of the assembly saved Raetia from still worse divisions.

The discontent and factiousness that infected Graubünden had long since wasted the spirit of the Tellina valley. Its population responded to the revolution with a major insurrection of their own. Raetia's corruption had been their misery for almost 300 years; they would endure no more. Napoleon, not yet quite prepared to sever the valley from Raetia and incorporate it into the newly created Cisalpine republic (as its leaders demanded), offered to Raetia the alternative of accepting both the Tellina valley and the adjacent subject territories of Bormio and Chiavenna into the Republic of the Three Leagues as fully equal members. But Graubünden's response to this generous offer reflected only the worst in its decentralized political structure. Each effort to reach a decision was obstructed by indecision, procrastination, divisiveness, jealousy, and impetuosity. Even within the prorepublican patriots, fears of "Romanization" if the all-Catholic Tellina valley was accorded full membership in the republic acted to mitigate natural enthusiasm. After a prolonged period of grace, Napoleon's impatience overtook Raetia's indecision. Both the Tellina valley and Bormio and Chiavenna were joined to the Cisalpine republic, and a rich potential canton was lost to the nascent Swiss Confederation about to be born. Regrets were short-lived, however, for Raetia itself now appeared in danger of losing its own independence. A leader of the patriot party acknowledged sadly:

> We are in the position of a man to whom a death sentence has been given, but who is allowed to choose the manner and hour of his death. Which of us would not, in such circumstances, reflect and temporize and await salvation by an angel from heaven? But no angel will come, and the dread words must sooner or later be heard in Graubünden: "The hour is come."[23]

Graubünden's alternatives, in fact, had been narrowed to following its own former colonies into the Cisalpine republic, submitting to an Austrian protectorate, or entering the Swiss Confederation under the watchful eye of republican France. It could no longer choose to remain fully independent. The Austrian-oriented von Salis party naturally was attracted to the protectorate option, while the patriots—reasoning that "between the twin evils of either becoming outright vassals of Austria or, under the guise of being free Swiss, becoming French vassals, choice must opt for the latter"—turned toward union with Switzerland.[24]

[23] Jakob U. von Sprecher in a letter to Gaudenz von Planta cited by Pieth, *Bündergeschichte*, p. 313.

[24] Johannes B. von Tscharner, cited in Planta, *Geschichte*, p. 354. The Patriots' campaign had the support of most Enlightenment *philosophes*; typical of the agitated pamphlets contributed by rationalist foreigners to the cause were the well-known German historian

The occupation of Switzerland by the French and the subsequent promulgation of a new unitary Helvetic constitution specifically inviting Raetian participation (in 1798)
should have decided the issue in favor of the patriots, but
the communes were still unready for decisiveness. They
rejected the proposal in a referendum by a margin greater
than four to one, and underscored their ire with a vindictive campaign against the patriots that was contrived to
return power to the von Salis party. What followed was a
lengthy charade in which Raetia managed to postpone its
loss of independence only by surrendering its vestigial dignity. Its contortions, no less agonizing than during the Time
of Troubles, were wholly futile; the country fell hard; in
its collapse its poets could only rue:

> Fall poor pine trunk, fall poor tree;
> For O! We fall as hard as thee. . . .[25]

The charade played itself out as a game of international
seesaw. The ascendancy of the von Salis party following
the rejection of the Helvetic Constitution by the communes
provoked the French into intimidation. An army appeared
on Raetia's northern frontier, glaring up the Rhine valley
toward Chur. The three leagues, unable to raise an army of
their own in their state of disunion, permitted the Austrians
to invite themselves in with an army to counter the French.
Unwilling to tolerate a standoff, the French commander in
Switzerland, General Massena, seized upon the outbreak
of hostilities between France and the Second Coalition to
send 35,000 men sweeping through Graubünden. General

---

Heinrich Zschokke's *Freie Bündner, verlasst die braven Schweizer
nicht!* (*Free Raetians! Abandon not the brave Swiss!*) and his slightly
more restrained *Soll Bünden sich an die Vereinte Schweiz schliessen?*
(*Should Graubünden join United Switzerland?*) both penned in the
closing years of the century.

[25] From "Two Deportation Poems" written in 1799 by patriots in
exile in "2 Deportierten-Lieder," *Bündner Monatsblatt*, September
1859.

Hotze's 6,000 Austrians retired under duress, permitting the patriots to once more assert themselves. A provisional government was established whose main business appeared to be introducing the Helvetic Constitution into Raetia. In April of 1799, patriot leaders signed an Act of Union in Chur making Raetia into a "canton" of the Helvetic Union.

What "see-ed," however, also "saw-ed." Before the new arrangements could be institutionalized, the Austrians managed to retake Graubünden and held it for the next fourteen months. Johannes Ulysses von Salis again seized the reins of government, and the patriots again had to flee; the horse von Salis now rode was hitched to an Austrian team whose movements were guided exclusively by the commands of General Hotze.

Within a year "saw" reverted to "see": Suvarov's coalition army had been frustrated in its dramatic attempt to engage the French in central Switzerland and had retired from the field. Napoleon had become First Consul of the reorganized French Republic and now commanded France as well as its armies. The following spring he defeated an Austrian force at Marengo. One month later Raetia was reoccupied and the Helvetic Constitution was again being forced upon the Raetians. The traditional leagues and communes disappeared almost immediately in the unfamiliar maze of administrative prefectures and districts so dear to the Napoleonic reformers. A seven-man council led by the patriot leader Gaudenz Planta presided over the new cantonal structure. Yet even these radical institutional changes failed to end the charade completely, for the Austrians tenaciously held the Engadine and Münster valleys as well as the Bergell and Oberhalbstein regions, and encouraged the local populations to retain their traditional forms of government. Even in French-held sections, enmity provoked by the unremitting billeting of foreign troops and the economic costs of occupation continued to obstruct the full implementation of the new constitution. When in 1801 a thoroughly revised version of the Helvetic Constitution was submitted to the people of Raetia, it was rejected by an overwhelming margin, 8,825 to 1,799. Although this disavowal had no impact on the outcome, since the Helvetian government resourcefully decided that the new constitution had been accepted despite the opposition of Graubünden and a majority of other cantons, it signaled the beginning of overt opposition to the new order. Shortly after the referendum, Gaudenz Planta was arrested and a mild insurrectionary attempt was made to restore the constitution of the Raetian Republic. French troops were able to quash the rebellion swiftly, but its lesson was not lost on Napoleon. With consternation he had watched the spreading resentment to the extreme centralization of the Helvetic Constitution and to its disdainful supercession of all traditional institutions. The formation of a new party loyal to the concept of union but demanding a new federalism that would acknowledge the traditional rights and independence of the individual cantons moved him to an act of statesmanship that was perhaps the most remarkable of his career. At the end of 1802, he invited sixty-three representatives of the Swiss cantons to Paris and after prolonged consultation with them promulgated a new Swiss Constitution. Its provisions, influenced but not bound by recommendations of the delegates, embodied an ingenious mediation of the traditional cantonal structures and the requirements of the new federalism.[26] The Constitution of Mediation although it confirmed the loss of the Tellina valley for Raetia, was in its recognition of traditional communal structures and cherished forms of self-sufficiency a most welcome revision. The increasing acceptance with which Raetians viewed the Constitution of Mediation and the later instruments of 1815 and 1848 gave a substantive and permanent character to the

[26] The texts of the relevant portions of the Constitution of Mediation are given by Jecklin, *Codex*, vol. 5, no. 64.

formal loss of independence suffered in 1799. The "unbroken spirit and indestructible awareness of freedom of the people" that had carried Graubünden through "so many storms, so many misadventures and so much guilt" could carry it no further.[27] The independent Republic of the Three Leagues was dead.

## GRAUBÜNDEN AS A SWISS CANTON

With the promulgation of the Constitution of Mediation in 1803, Graubünden ceased to have an independent history. Its destiny became inseparable from Switzerland's: its problems became Swiss problems, its misfortunes the shared sorrows of the larger republic, and its freedom the concern of millions of men. Raetia's modern fate in the struggle with modernity will preoccupy us vitally in subsequent chapters, but its formal history ends here.

[27] Planta, *Geschichte*, pp. 375–376.

# PART III: Old Free Raetia and the Emergence of Freedom

Of old sat freedom on the heights,
  The thunders breaking at her feet:
Above her shook the starry lights:
  She heard the torrents meet.

There in her place she did rejoice,
  Self-gather'd in her prophet-mind,
But fragments of her mighty voice
  Came rolling on the wind.

Then stept she down thro' town and field
  To mingle with the human race,
And part by part to men reveal'd
  The fullness of her face.
            —Alfred Lord Tennyson

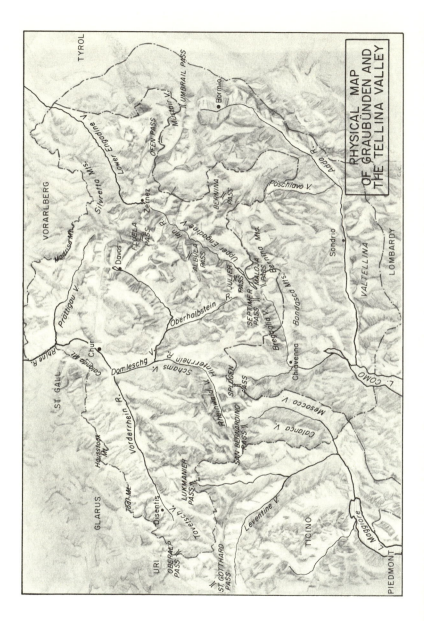

PHYSICAL MAP OF GRAUBÜNDEN AND THE TELLINA VALLEY

# CHAPTER IV

# The Alpine Environment

FROM Aristotle through Montesquieu to contemporary geo-political theorists like the Sprouts, students of politics have insisted on the interdependence of politics and the physical environment. Geography has been treated as a natural generic factor in the study of almost every major political construct in the theorist's lexicon, and freedom is not an exception. Thus, the emergence of freedom in Graubünden, a land in which geographical influences have always been predominant, appears to be particularly amenable to a study of the conditioning effects of the physical environment. To neglect the geographical in exploring the conditions of freedom in *Alt Frei Raetia* is to risk bypassing that country's essential character—to miss what the Swiss themselves view as their country's organic alpine integrity. Richard Weiss underscores the need for "recognizing that the entire alpine culture is an integral, self-enclosed organism whose parts are mutually determined and must be seen and explained in relation to one another."[1]

To accept the necessity of elaborating Raetian notions of freedom in the first instance in the context of geography is not, however, to predispose the argument to any one understanding of the meaning of freedom, nor even to hypothesize a salient causal relationship between geographical and political factors. Nevertheless, it is to raise the ques-

---

[1] Richard Weiss, *Das Alpwesen Graubündens* (Erlenbach/Zürich, 1941), p. 14. F. Grenfell Baker likewise insists "The topographical peculiarities of the Graubünden must never be lost sight of in all questions affecting their history, as these are very largely responsible for the social and political conditions of the people." *The Model Republic* (New York, 1895), p. 299.

tion of how freedom emerged in Graubünden within a geographical perspective, to insist on the theoretical priority of environmental conditions in assaying the origin of political ideas that were later to be molded by more obvious social, economic, and institutional forces. The question can hardly even be posed, however, without depicting the physical environment of Graubünden, not in the language of professional geographers, but in terms of those more obvious characteristics that seem capable of influencing either directly or through the secondary conditions they precipitate the development of Raetian freedom.

## THE PHYSICAL ENVIRONMENT

The geographical map of Switzerland, in general, and that of Graubünden, in particular, make generalizations about topography as difficult as they are risky. The country is full of paradoxes that are sometimes overlooked by map readers in a hurry. One of the most characteristic of the erroneous and confidently misleading generalizations made about Switzerland states that "the political map of Switzerland is largely the result of its physical map."[2] André Siegfried, a more careful student of the country, speaks more accurately: "Nature has permitted Switzerland to exist, but it did not create Switzerland; that was done by man."[3] Switzerland's geography is in fact a paradox. Superficially, it suggests unity, but when examined circumspectly it reveals internal diversity and a fluidity of potential borders.[4]

[2] J. Christopher Herold, *The Swiss Without Halos* (New York, 1948), p. 10.

[3] André Siegfried, *Die Schweiz: Eine Verwirklichung der Demokratie* (Zürich, 1949), p. 29.

[4] Hermann Weilenmann writes that "the mountains, which elsewhere divide peoples from one another, constitute in many parts [of Switzerland] not frontiers closing off the outside, but barriers dividing the territory of the state itself. Switzerland is not a land foreseen in the blueprints of the planet. Not having been created by nature, it has

On a relief map it appears crossed with mountains, yet today over 85 percent of the population lives below 700 meters in country which though hilly is hardly mountainous. The country is rural; yet its more recent history has been dominated by the larger towns and cities that sweep in a great northeastern diagonal from Lake Geneva to Lake Constance.[5] Although the map of Graubünden is somewhat more limited and certainly more homogeneously distinctive than that of the Swiss Confederation as a whole, many of the same paradoxes appear along with some peculiarly regional ones. Paradox and dualism seem as much a part of the geography of Graubünden as they are of the concept of freedom itself.

We can view Graubünden's physical environment from two vantage points: from without, as if we were regarding it from some great distance; and from within, like an eighteenth-century traveler working his way through a geological labyrinth. From the outside, it is Graubünden's geopolitical location in the center of Europe and its overwhelmingly mountainous character that are most easily discerned. From the inside, a remarkably variegated topography and a raw, uncompromising climate are most prominent.

From without, Graubünden is a paradox. Its two chief characteristics, the central accessibility of its location and the isolated remoteness of its mountainous topography, have had a different and often contradictory impact on its politics. Its accessibility is undeniable, for Graubünden is in the center of Europe and at the vortex of European

---

to be the product of the men who inhabit it." *Pax Helvetica: oder die Demokratie der Kleinen Gruppen* (Zürich, 1951), pp. 23–24.

[5] These include Geneva, Lausanne, Neuchâtel, Biel, Freiburg, Bern, Solothurn, Basel, Zürich, and Schaffhausen. It is true that the small mountain cantons, the so-called *Waldstätte*, dominated the early and, in the formative sense, archetypal period of Swiss history, but this predominance lasted only a few centuries.

commercial and military traffic. To the west lies Switzerland (traditional Helvetia), to the northeast Austria and then Bavaria, to the south Italy. Its frontiers are more exposed than those of any other Swiss canton. Of its nearly 700 kilometers of frontier, 466 face foreign countries, one-quarter of the entire 1855-kilometer Swiss frontier.[6] Graubünden serves, moreover, as the watershed of Europe. From its mountains, waters flow to the Adriatic, the Black Sea, and the North Sea. The major headwaters of the Rhine, the Hinterrhein and the Vorderrhein, together drain more than 90 of Graubünden's 150 valleys, while major tributaries of three other European rivers originate in Graubünden's awesome glacial springs: the Adda (the chief river of the Valtellina), feeding into the Po; the Inn (running from the Maloja region out through the Engadine into Austria), watering the Danube; and the Rambach (originating in the Southeastern peaks of Graubünden that presently constitute a Swiss National Park), feeding the Adige (Etsch). Just as the rivers of Europe meet at the mountain springs and alpine glaciers of Graubünden that water them, so the trade routes of Europe meet at the natural crossroads that its strategic centrality has made of Graubünden. Lying squarely on the most direct trade route from north-central Europe to Italy and the vital ports of the Mediterranean, travelers from Paris to Venice, from Vienna to Milan, from Munich to Genoa had but little choice to journey through Graubünden's mountain passes.

From one point of view, then, Graubünden appears to lie at the very heart of Europe, accessible from every direction, vital to trade and traffic, the watershed of a subcontinent. But this is only one view. If the eye wanders from the political map to the relief map, from implications of the

---

[6] A full geographical and geoeconomic account of Graubünden up until 1930 can be found in Gian A. Töndury, *Studie zur Volkswirtschaft Graubündens* (Samedan, 1946) from which many of the statistics in this section have been drawn.

country's location to those of its terrain, a very different and contradictory picture emerges.

In relief, Graubünden appears strikingly mountainous; moreover, its mountains form a natural wall to the outside, the valleys, passes, clefts, and gorges that divide them being almost entirely internal. From the outside, Graubünden appears to be a fortress: ". . . in all of Europe there is hardly a geographically fixed area which is cut off from the outer world . . . in the manner of Wallis and Graubünden."[7] Its isolation is due not simply to the altitude of its mountains, but to the absence of strategic saddles and valleys that might serve as entrances from the outside. On the northern border facing most of Europe (via the Swiss cantons of Uri, Glarus, and St. Gallen), there is a massive mountain wall nearly eighty miles in length which, at all points except one, is virtually impenetrable. Only to the northeast, where the Rhine exits from the mountains at Maienfeld, is there an opening. Yet here too, though the gap is wide, traffic from the north must cross the Lake of Walen and then the Rhine itself, and traffic from the east (Austria and Liechtenstein) must ascend a steep and narrow saddle (the Luziensteig), to enter Graubünden's territory. This is the only relatively level access route into Graubünden in the entire land and the only one of any kind in the north. In the west and in the south, entry can be gained only by scaling high mountain passes, the rudimentary roads of which were and remain passable only in the summer. To the east, only the Inn river valley provides access from Austria, the rest of the eastern frontier being sealed by the high peaks of the Silvretta range and the mountains that today enclose the Swiss National Park. The Inn valley (the Engadine) is itself cut off from the rest of Graubünden by an east-west chain of peaks running across the center of the small country.[8]

[7] Weilenmann, *Pax Helvetica*, p. 78.

[8] The Engadine must depend for contact with the rest of Graubün-

Thus, the paradox: a Graubünden in the center of Europe, and at the crossroads of European trade, yet a Graubünden isolated from Europe by its formidable mountains. A country predestined by its location to play a crucial role in European history and trade, yet a country seemingly fated by its geological character to a history of isolation and particularity. For all of its imposing mountains, however, Graubünden has never been treated as a classical mountain-state. Its most salient features are not its peaks but the passes that cut between them. The geographer Haushofer is thus much closer to the truth when he speaks of Raetia as "the really classical Pass-state in the entire region of the Alps from Dalmatia to Liguria."[9] "All that Graubünden represents," writes Graubünden's most thoughtful historian, "all that it has lived through and suffered—its innermost being as well as the essence of its culture stands written in the history of its passes."[10] Through these passes the granite walls that separate Raetia from Europe are breached; and through them Graubünden has had access to the world. They are the vital bridge between the isolation forced on the land by its mountains and the involvement made inevitable by its geographical centrality. In all of Switzerland there are twenty-two major passes and thirty-one minor ones, and of these no fewer than eleven major

---

den on three high summer passes, only one of which even today can be kept open in the winter: the Julier, the Abula, and the Fluela. The valley has thus often been occupied by foreign armies who have otherwise been excluded from the country. During the Napoleonic period, for example, Austria retained military control over the Engadine well after the rest of Graubünden had been occupied by the French.

[9] Cited by Graubünden's cantonal archivist, Rudolf Jenny, "Graubündens' Passtransit und seine volkswirtschaftliche Bedeutung," *Bündner Monatsblatt*, September-October 1954, p. 326.

[10] Rudolf Jenny, "Wesen und Gehalt der bündnerischen Kultur," *Bündner Monatsblatt*, June 1949, pp. 175–176.

ones and sixteen minor ones are in Graubünden. The paradox of Graubünden seen from without is the paradox of its passes.

Seen from within, conditions are no less paradoxical and ambivalent. Here again, the political map seems to contest the lessons of the relief map. Viewed as an independent state rather than as the Swiss canton it became in 1803, Graubünden is a compact, unified, small nation that might have been expected to excite the admiration of a Pericles or a Rousseau. With an area of only 7,113.5 square kilometers, surrounded, like some huge medieval manor, with a protective mantle of mountains, it would appear to provide ideal conditions for nurturing liberty and fostering participatory democracy. This idyllic image cannot survive an inspection of a detailed relief map, however.

The mountains that from a distance overawe the spectator with their monolithic solidity, resolve, when seen from nearby, into ridges and peaks, hills and valleys, and meadows and forests, broken and divided everywhere by major torrents, lesser streams, and myriad alpine brooks. From afar the mountains appear as an impassable fortress hung from the clouds; from within they are marked by rockslide, water, wind, and snow with countless peculiarities that make each valley a small world unto itself. From afar, we are struck by massive oneness; from within the eye wonders at such unending diversity. Graubünden's 7,000 square kilometers are divided into no fewer than 150 distinct valleys; the mountains that wall off valley from valley are relieved of their severity by more than 8000 alpine meadows, each one enclosed by woodlands, defined by gorges, cut off by precipitous bluffs and rock-strewn river beds. Seven of Graubünden's eleven major passes lie entirely within the country, linking together valleys that might otherwise be foreign countries; only four lead to the outside world.[11] And four major Raetian valleys lie outside the ring of

85

mountains that encircle the country, more accessible to the outside than to the Bündner heartland.[12] The entire Inn river valley (Engadine), although within the ring, stands to the south of the rest of Graubünden separated by a ridge whose lowest pass elevations are over 2,300 meters. The very area of Graubünden, diminutive even by Europe's land-poor standards, is misleading, for flattened out it would approximately triple.

Viewed from within, then, Graubünden remains a paradox—a small manageable country unified by its rocky frontiers, on the one hand, a diversified and divided collection of independent valleys as separated from one another as from the outside world, on the other. Its peculiarities, however, are not limited to the ambivalent configurations of its mountains. The elevation of its inhabited valleys, the poverty of its soil, and the absolute paucity of natural resources are derivative features of the mountain environment that have uniquely affected Graubünden's geopolitical background.

The important valleys of Graubünden, unlike those in many other areas of Switzerland, lie at considerable heights between still higher mountains. Thus, while elsewhere in the Alps the inhabitants enjoy their mountains from distant plains or from protected river valleys no higher than 500 meters, in Graubünden men are compelled to inhabit and toil in the arms of their inhospitable mountains. The

[11] Only the Oberalp, the Lukmanier, the Splügen and the Umbrail passes are actually on the Raetian frontier. The Fluela, Abula, Julier, Maloja, Bernina, Bernardino, and Ofen connect valleys within the country.

[12] Three of these valleys lead directly into Italy: the Münstertal (south of the Ofen Pass), the Puschlav (south of the Bernina), and the Bergell (below the Maloja at the upper or southwestern end of the Engadine). The first two have historically been particularly vulnerable to Austrian influence. A fourth valley, the Messoco, leads south from the San Bernardino Pass down into the Italian-Swiss canton of Ticino.

canton of Valais (Wallis), for example, although generally regarded as mountainous, is dominated by the broad Rhône river valley which lies at a very modest altitude. The capital of the canton of Glarus, another "mountain canton," is at an elevation of 780 meters, and most of the canton's population resides at this amiable elevation despite the fact that the mountains around the Linth river valley rise to 3,000 meters. In contrast, 188 of Graubünden's 221 communes lie above 700 meters, and one of them, Juf, is the highest year-round settlement in Europe (at 2,100-plus meters). The entire upper Engadine valley lies at 1,800 meters and such major towns as Davos, Lenzerheide, and Zernez are over 1,500 meters. In Switzerland at large, only 4.6 percent of the population lived above 1,000 meters in 1930; in Graubünden, 55 percent of the population did so.[13] By 1970, while the rate for Graubünden remained almost 50 percent, it had dropped to less than 3 percent for the nation. The mountains of Raetia are, then, to be approached not simply as possible historical determinants of ancient institutions, but as the major reality of everyday life in Graubünden—in the past and today. Perhaps here more than in their geographical configuration on political and relief maps, they affect the forms that freedom has taken in Graubünden, not as a prime cause but as a continuing presence.

[13] All of these figures are from Töndury, *Studie*, p. 5ff., and are for the year 1930. The urban-rural ratio has obviously shifted markedly in favor of the cities in the last forty years but the population of Switzerland, and especially of Graubünden, still remains remarkably dispersed. Graubünden has always been unusual in this respect. In the supposedly mountainous canton of Valais only 30.6 percent of the population lived above 1,000 meters in 1930, while in the original "mountain canton" of Uri no more than 8.6 percent did so. However, in Switzerland at large according to 1970 statistics less than 3 percent of the population lived above 1,000 meters; see Switzerland, *Statistisches Jahrbuch der Schweiz: 1972* (Bern, 1972).

If Raetia's valleys are unusually high, its soil is unusually barren. Dusted with a poor and infertile top-soil capable of nurturing only the hardiest grasses and shrubs, 30.5 percent of Graubünden's surface is neither arable nor forestable nor in any other manner agriculturally usable.[14] Approximately 30 percent more can be used only in the summer for grazing. Another 22 percent is woodland, leaving only about 25 percent for haying, winter fodder, and "agriculture," if that indeed is the term for an agrarian economy that can devote no more than 1 percent of its land to grains, vineyards, and vegetables. There is certainly adequate moisture, but the climate makes for long winters that may last from September to June. It is seldom very cold—no frigid Canadian air mass skulks to the north—but almost always cool; even in the summer the strange, glistening presence of the "eternal snows" on higher crags and northern rock faces are enduring reminders of nature's vindictiveness in the Alps.

Nor is the paucity of soil in Raetia compensated by an adequacy of natural resources. Legends of gold have abounded, but with the two exceptions noted below real resources, construed in the widest sense, are appallingly scanty.[15] The few low-grade ores to be found are not worth mining, and there are no fuel deposits (coal, oil, natural gas). Moreover, Graubünden's physical environment puts transportation and trade at a severe disadvantage. The country is land-locked, a factor that, as Switzerland's vulnerability to the Axis in World War II demonstrated, can impede or even cripple national independence; moreover, its many rivers are entirely unnavigable. Indeed, their whimsi-

[14] Töndury, *Studie*, p. 4. This must be compared to a Swiss national average of 22.5 percent, a figure that would be considerably lower if Graubünden were not included in the average.

[15] Literature and mythology abound with wishful stories about hidden deposits of precious metals in the otherwise unyielding mountains. See, for example, Arthur Zimmermann's romantic novella *Das Gold von Parpan* (Aarau, 1906).

cal proneness to spring flooding makes them more of a threat than an aid to transportation. Road construction is also fraught with difficulties in the mountains, natural road-beds being virtually nonexistent.

There are several exceptions to this general scarcity of resources, but they have become significant only in the most recent times and thus have not affected the conditioning of Graubünden's political ideas and institutions. The canton does today control fully one-quarter of Switzerland's potential hydroelectric resources, a vital statistic in assessing Graubünden's modern economic position but clearly irrelevant in historical terms. Likewise tourism—of considerable economic importance today—becomes important only as Graubünden's natural beauty is understood as a resource and a commodity. But until the nineteenth century, the tourist trade was no more than a trickle of wealthy young Englishmen spending their obligatory year on the Continent. Indeed, until Rousseau and the Romantics taught European man something about the aesthetics of nature, the mountains were regarded by most as obstacles to the mundane pursuit of agriculture, commerce, and war rather than as catalysts in the transcendental pursuit of beauty. Historically speaking, then, it may be said fairly that Graubünden had *no* natural resources whatsoever.

## Two Paradoxes: The Direct Effects on Freedom

Two related paradoxes have emerged from this sketchy geographical portrait, one based on a view of the country from without, the other upon a view from within. First, we need to look at the direct impact of these ambivalent conditions on the idea and practice of freedom; then, we may note the possible indirect effects of some of the secondary and derivative characteristics explored above.

We have seen that, viewed from without, Graubünden appears predisposed by its geography both to centralism

89

and involvement (its strategic location) and to insularity and isolation (its hostile mountains). As might be expected, the effects of each are both different and in conflict with one another. Raetia's centrality clearly has been an obstacle to national independence and political autonomy. Powerful neighbors (the Venetian Republic, Hapsburg Austria, France) for whom trade and military mobility across Raetia's passes have always been critical functions of national interest have persistently maneuvered to acquire diplomatic, economic, and political control of the small country. And although Raetia, despite these pressures, managed to preserve its political autonomy over a number of centuries, it could not avoid an ongoing and largely unwholesome involvement in European power politics. As we will see in Chapter VI, this involvement brought about the most serious and compromising consequences for the development of free political institutions. Small nations are disadvantaged by their size from the outset; set down among large, predatory neighbors not only their freedom but also their very survival becomes problematic.

Yet the isolation imposed on Graubünden by its mountains has worked against the vulnerability of its location, securing it from the kinds of permanent cultural influences and episodic military occupations that might have made the development of autonomous institutions completely impossible. The contradiction between isolation and centrality, however, did not result in a standoff for Graubünden. The mountains, protective as they might have been, were a fortress with open portals and stairways built into its bulwarks. The very passes that attracted ambitious neighbors rendered Graubünden vulnerable to them. Thus, in practice, the contradiction between the country's geographical centrality and its geological insularity is resolved in favor of the former, and thus in favor of the kinds of interference and intervention by foreign countries that are associated with centrality. This conclusion, extended to

90

Switzerland at large where the situation is very similar, gives little support to the popular assumption that mountain nations like Helvetia or Raetia owe their independence and much of the freedom that independence makes possible to their mountain environment. Indeed, as has been pointed out with regard to the early Swiss Confederation, the very opposite is true: "The Confederation achieved independence," Peter Liver has prudently written, "not because of its location on the Gotthard pass, but in spite of it."[16] Much the same is true of Raetia: it secured independence and developed free, participatory institutions not because of but in spite of its magnetic passes and geographical centrality. Viewed in the larger perspective from the outside, the geography of Graubünden cannot be regarded as a cause or even as a conditioning factor in the development of Raetian freedom; indeed, to the degree that we can resolve the geographical-geological paradox, it operated as an obstacle to autonomy.

Seen from within, Graubünden's geography precipitates a somewhat related paradox. The country's apparent unity and compactness as seen on a political area map conflicts with its evident diffuseness and diversity as seen on a relief map. The image gained from an area map is one of a small, unified, easily governed principality that might easily be traversed on horseback in a single day, in other words of a country providing many of the critical conditions of participatory democracy. Yet the image of easy communications, limited diversification, and potential political homogeneity suggested by an area map cannot survive a simple glance at the realities of a relief map. The real physical geography of Raetia leaves an indisputable impression of manifold diversity and potential political diffuseness. And just as in terms of their effects centrality is dominant and isolation recessive in the external configuration, so diversity is dom-

---

[16] Peter Liver, "Alplandschaft und politische Selbständigkeit," *Bündner Monatsblatt*, January 1942, p. 19.

inant and unity recessive in the internal constellation of characteristics. The effects of diversity on political institutions and on the emergence of freedom are obviously likely to be at considerable variance with those of compactness. Where a unified, political compactness might have favored central government and unitary administration, diversity in fact encouraged divisiveness, political disintegration, and potential weakness in the face of external aggression. The history of Raetia's three leagues and their multiple parts and factions demonstrates over and over again how injurious to independence and to freedom a geographically inspired factiousness can be. At the same time, the inaccessibility of adjacent valleys to one another dilutes the sense of commonality and accentuates political particularism in a fashion that cannot help but obstruct the practical functioning of participatory institutions and the emergence of consensual democracy. Whether consensus is a prerequisite of the general will (natural consensus) or a consequence of it (artificial consensus), it is in fact patently disadvantaged by a disparate geography and the parochialism associated with political heterogeneity.

There is another side to diversity, however. Heterogeneity complicates and obstructs unification and administrative control from within and from without. The lack of central government that weakens Graubünden's common resolve and renders it vulnerable to outside powers is inherently difficult to exploit. To control a country from the outside is usually to control its capital city, its governmental bureaucracy, its central communications nexus, and its national army and police powers. But a country vulnerable precisely because it lacks such centralized power systems is not really vulnerable at all. To control Raetia would mean to control through military occupation every valley and village and village "fraction" in the land. An army occupying Chur no more controls Graubünden than does one in Milan or

Vienna.[17] Diversity can be a strength as well as a weakness.

The effect of heterogeneity on the forms taken by liberty and political participation only confirm this. Although diversity is hardly conducive to a countrywide consensus (and in this sense is contrary to the spirit of direct democracy), it does encourage an exceedingly decentralized confederal form of government that depends upon vigorous political activity in relatively autonomous local government units; these units, by their very nature, provide ideal conditions for maximum political participation by all citizens. Historically, the diminutive size and disproportionately extended autonomy of Raetia's local communes led to active participation on a scale unknown elsewhere in Europe. Thus, although geographical conditions in Graubünden cannot be said to have fostered federal democracy, at the level of central government, they did favor an exceptional degree of regional participation in political affairs and gave to Raetian concepts of freedom a Rousseauean flavor that some theorists today like to call positive liberty.[18]

Regional diversity in Graubünden has also robbed central government of the possibility of consensus while giving it to local government to an exceptional degree. Where the weak central government of the old Republic of the Three Leagues had neither the means to discover a public will nor the authority to execute it, local communes managed not only to establish common goals by consensus but also to pursue them as a collective. The remarkable uniqueness of the institutions developed by these semiautonomous communes will be explored in Chapter VII. Here what

[17] During the French revolutionary period, for example, successive French and Austrian armies occupied disparate regions of Graubünden without ever gaining full control of all of it. See Chapter III.

[18] In Swiss constitutional terminology, the term "federalism" refers to regionalism rather than centralism; to speak of "federal" questions is to speak of issues of cantonal and communal autonomy, not central government control.

seems crucial is the importance of geographical diversity in providing conditions that made any but regional, small-scale forms of democracy impossible. The kind of large-scale central government that elsewhere in Europe led to a defensive preoccupation with freedom as a set of libertarian rights held against a distant, alien bureaucracy was simply ruled out by the topological contours of the land. The notion of freedom in Graubünden thus developed as an integral feature of political participation in small communities of like-minded men. No sane comparativist would want to conclude from this that Graubünden's geography "caused" its notion of freedom to be fashioned in unique ways, but there do seem to be grounds for claiming an indirect, noncausal relationship. On the other hand, it is evident that geography overall has exercised an ambivalent influence, the competing effects of which have worked against one another. Hence, in a more general way, neither of the two paradoxes depicted here can be said to have had decisive effects on the emergence of freedom in Raetia. There are, however, a number of derivative geographical characteristics that have had certain indirect effects on the conditions under which freedom emerged in Raetia, some of which appear to be more salient than the kinds of obvious relationships explored above.

## THE INDIRECT EFFECTS ON FREEDOM

A people who live and work in the mountains (the factor of altitude), on land that yields its scant fruits most reluctantly (the factor of unarable land and harsh climate) and that has no compensatory resources in fuels and ores (the factor of resource paucity) are not necessarily directly affected in their political thinking and organization by such peculiarly adverse conditions. But such an environment can hardly fail to have a major impact on the development of their individual and collective character, their life styles and attitudes, and the fundamental economic premises of their physical existence. These in turn, perhaps more than geography itself, have a profound effect on the meaning and significance of political activity and the notion of freedom associated with it.

The most universal and overwhelming feature of life in an environment characterized by an inhospitable climate and a dearth of agricultural and mineral resources is its simple physical hardness. This is perhaps the most salient single consequence of the several derivative characteristics noted here and is in turn responsible for peculiarities of character and communal life that have had a significant bearing on the development of freedom in Graubünden.

Most importantly, the severity of life in Raetia not only prevented the evolution of an agricultural economy but saved the Raetian people from the bondage of an agrarian culture. Ironically, the soil of Graubünden was too barren to permit it to enslave the people who lived off it. Every recent account of village life in traditional rural Europe has focused on the deadening relationship of bondage between man and soil in the preindustrial and nonindustrial countryside. Edward Banfield's classic study of the moral rigidity and collective despair of a south Italian village, Peter Laslett's nostalgic but grim journey through rural village records in seventeenth-century England, Marx's and Engels's own faithless depiction of the inescapable conservatism of a peasantry chained to its hearths by its plows—each confirms the deep incompatibility of political consciousness and autonomous institutions with an agricultural mode of life.[19] However much like the Greek *polis* or the New

[19] See Edward C. Banfield, *The Moral Basis of a Backward Society* (New York, 1958); Peter Laslett, *The World We Have Lost* (London, 1965); and Frederick Engels, *The Peasant Question in France and Germany*, in Marx and Engels, *Selected Works*, 2 vols. (Moscow, 1951).

England town these farm villages appear to be, however much we look fondly back to the small-town mutuality of spirit that characterized the "world we have lost," we cannot avoid recognizing that agricultural man lived in a stultifying dependency to his land, the yoke of subsistence forcing his head and body forever downward into the soil he tilled. The Raetian peasant was spared these burdens by the very conditions that made his life so austere. Land that will nurture neither grains nor vegetables can support only the most limited populations, precluding the burgeoning of families and townships that elsewhere in Europe brought eventual poverty to seemingly fertile areas. Graubünden thus remained wholly provincial, with a population that today hardly exceeds 160,000 occupying a land which encompasses one-quarter of Switzerland's area. In the typical peasant village, portrayed here by Oscar Handlin, "disaster chained the peasant to his place. The harshness of . . . burdens immobilized those upon whom they fell, made the poor also poor in spirit."[20] In Graubünden, free from a land that refused to support him, the peasant turned harshness into a discipline of individuality, a teacher of autonomy. He held an intuitive conviction that his rural mountain life, his uncomplicated involvement in a pastoral economy that left him considerable leisure time, was inextricably bound up with his independence and his freedom. This conviction finds parallel expression in the more sophisticated observations of such historians as Henry D. Lloyd, who contends "that a mountainous country favors hardihood and independence of character and makes the political and economic domination of an oligarch difficult to establish or maintain is a commonplace of history."[21] When Montesquieu speaks, then, of the way in which mountains

[20] Oscar Handlin, *The Uprooted* (New York, 1951), pp. 21–22.
[21] H. D. Lloyd, *The Swiss Democracy* (London, 1908), p. 2.

favor the reign of liberty, we need to think not so much of the protection they afford against the outside as of the hardiness they impose within.[22] At the most practical level, the physical sturdiness of the mountaineer makes him especially well suited to self-protection and military combat. The reputation of Helvetian and Raetian mercenaries was well earned—a product of an environment that made men hard without depriving them of spirit, that could toughen a man without crippling his body or exhausting his energy (as happened almost always with the peasant farmer).

Just as the hardness of pastoral life in the mountains made the alpine cowherd or huntsman a fine soldier, the harshness of the alpine climate left him ample time to utilize his fighting skills. The six-month winters that so limited his agricultural alternatives freed him as a soldier in a manner unknown to the lowlands farmer.[23] He could join his entire village in a communal fighting unit (the Fähnlein) to defend his region, or, with the capacities, experience, and leisureliness of the professional soldier, embark on more distant and extended campaigns.

In addition to these advantages, the terrain that helped to give the Raetian his much envied military skills put him at an unusual advantage in employing them, for the lightly

[22] Montesquieu writes: "Liberty . . . reigns, therefore, more in mountainous and rugged countries than in those which nature seems to have most favored . . ." and suggests that "the barrenness of the earth renders men industrious, sober, inured to hardship, courageous, and fit for war." *The Spirit of the Laws*, trans. Thomas Nugent (New York, 1949), Book 18, pp. 272–273.

[23] Peter Liver remarks: "Dairy farming in the mountains does not place the kinds of demands on energies of the population that the more diversified agriculture of the fruitful plains does; the mountaineer is thus more readily available for political and economic undertakings than is the plains-peasant." "Die staatliche Entwicklung im alten Graubünden," *Sonderabdruck aus der Zeitschrift für Schweizerische Geschichte*, vol. 13, no. 1, 1933, p. 233.

clad, swiftly moving footsoldier was nearly unbeatable in the mountains. The heavily armored mounted knights of the Middle Ages lost their tactical value in terrain where a man could maneuver more facilely than a horse, while the large national armies of later eras could not be deployed in the country's narrow valleys and steep passes. Not even modern armies with hostile ambitions can do more than lay siege to Graubünden's alpine fortress. As recently as World War II, the national defense plan for the whole of Switzerland envisioned falling back from the plains to the mountains of the interior—the vaunted "redoubt" strategy —where an obdurate defensive war could be effectively waged. It is not even clear that atomic weapons, apart from the greater efficacy of fallout at higher elevations, would be of much tactical use against a nation built on one, massive, countrywide natural air-raid shelter.

Militarily, then, the hardiness of character nurtured by the physical hardship of life in the mountains seems to have favored both personal and collective independence. There is also an attitudinal dimension to this independence syndrome. The typical alpine cowherd spent his summers almost entirely alone with his livestock on some high mountain alp well above even the sparse summer villages. Personal solitude appears to have played a significant role in the formation of individuality and independence of character. "The fairly long periodic stays of the mountain peasant," writes one historian, "in lonely isolation on high mountain meadows and alps, where each had to depend on himself, and where each could be his own master, contributed to a heightening of the peasant's defiant self-awareness."[24]

[24] P. Liver, *Von Feudalismus zur Demokratie in den graubünd-nerischen Hinterrheintälern* (Chur, 1929), p. 37. The mountain peasant's outdoor life was as little like the farmer's hearth-chained existence as the burgher's urban ways. The spirit of the Raetian's sense of forced communion with nature is richly evident in an

This sense of self-sufficiency was perhaps even more enhanced, though far less so today than formerly, by the limited economic autarky enjoyed by the alpine peasant. He grazed his cows, milked them, produced a variety of dairy foods both for consumption and for sale; he cut the hay and stored the fodder for the long winter, and he acted as midwife when they calved in the spring. Like peasants everywhere, he was involved in a modest home economy that could meet almost all of his family's daily needs. Yet the mountainman was unique since he did not become a slave to that economy. He could appreciate the organic harmony of life-cycles and participate fully in every phase of a labor process; yet he never needed to risk paying the farmer's price of bondage to the soil. Neither the fragmenting, self-alienating labor specialization of the industrial epoch nor the life-sapping toil of agricultural society threatened his individuality.

Even so, traditional Raetia was not a country preoccupied with individualism, and Raetian man did not consider his freedom to be an extension of his own person. There was nothing in Graubünden comparable to the English natural rights tradition that understood freedom as an extension of the property each man was thought to have in his own person. This may be because individuality, in an environment vulnerable to manifold natural disasters, did not and

eighteenth-century poem that caustically attacks the city dweller and contrasts urban and rural life:

FROM A COUNTRYMAN TO A RICH BURGHER
On softest beds you sleep, and I on softest clay;
Within grand walls you dwell, in unwalled fields I stay;
Great artists paint your portrait, Nature colors me;
You, sick with satiation, I of every sickness free;
You pay a Swiss to guard you, my faithful dog guards me;
You slake your thirst with darkened wines, the clearest
    springs cool me.

By the probably pseudonymous poet Ewald, in *Der Sammler*, 1780, no. 51.

could not dictate the form social and economic life was to take. Avalanches, rockslides, sudden summer blizzards, floods, and a multitude of less decisive catastrophes left the individual and his livestock in permanent jeopardy. Only collective labor and common decision making afforded protection against nature's hostility, the more so in earlier times before technology became available in the war to subjugate nature. Thus, as the hardness of life molded a man's sense of autonomy, it also compelled him to cooperation and collective action. The sturdy individual could survive the mountains that had toughened him only by compromising his individuality in favor of the group. When Raetia was first settled, the forces of environment must have seemed both overwhelming and ineluctable:

> A separate existence for men in the mountains at the time of the settlement and initial cultivation of the land was unthinkable. The individual would have perished in the struggle with nature. Only as a member of a group such as the clan, or the *Markgenossenschaft* which arose out of it, could the individual and his family survive.[25]

Compare this stark reality with the situation of the agricultural peasant whose conditions have fostered neither individuality nor social collaboration. Nature has left the farmer with too little time and energy to cultivate a separate, self-reflective existence; but it has treated him just a little bit too well to force him into mutualist cooperation with others, especially where social structures have permitted him his own land (however minuscule the parcel). In many agricultural societies, the result has been a self-destructive selfishness, what Banfield has characterized as "amoral familism," wholly inimical to the development of institutions of social

---

[25] Georg Ragaz, *Die Entstehung der politischen Gemeinden im Schamsertal* (Disentis, 1934), pp. 66–67. A full portrait of the Raetian *Markgenossenschaft* follows in Chapter V.

collaboration.[26] Combine this with the apathetic cynicism spawned by the farmer's total powerlessness in facing nature's episodic terrors—a pestilence of insects, an untimely hailstorm, spring floods can still ruin a vital crop even in the present age of technological farming—and the background for the farmer's conservatism, his lack of political consciousness, and his inability to cooperate becomes obvious.

The mountaineer involved in a pastoral way of life, on the other hand, with his peculiar mixture of acquired independence and compulsory mutualism, developed an early and pronounced social consciousness. Awed and threatened by nature, he was nevertheless able to treat with it, to impede its avalanches with stakes, to curb its rivers with clay embankments, to soften its terrors with mythology and superstition. A ruined crop meant disaster and probable starvation for a farming family: the mountaineer was not so vulnerable. In common labor with his neighbors, the less mortal perils of the mountains could be thwarted. Consequently, in spite of his individualism, the Raetian's concept of freedom was far less individualistic than might have been anticipated. For him freedom came to mean "not individual emancipation from his obligations to the whole, but the right to bind himself by his own choice."[27] Without prejudice to Rousseau's intentions, we might well choose to say that the mountains "forced the peasant to be free" in a sense similar to that in Rousseau's *Social Contract*.[28] An economic and cultural study of alpine life thus suggests that

[26] The antisocial principle underlying the ethos of "amoral familism," according to Banfield, is to "maximize the material, short-run advantage of the nuclear family" at the expense of any form of more extended cooperation or mutual help. *The Moral Basis of a Backward Society*, p. 83.

[27] Weilenmann, *Pax Helvetica*, p. 255.

[28] Jean-Jacques Rousseau, *The Social Contract*, ed. G.D.H. Cole (London, 1913), Book I, Chapter 7, p. 15.

101

in the mountains of Graubünden "each man is forced to participate."[29] Compulsion and participation, voluntary obedience to a common will and emancipation from the tyranny of nature and unreason, are here coupled together in concrete institutional forms very much in the fashion envisioned not only by Rousseau but also by Kant and later neo-Idealists. Yet, at least in Graubünden's small history, none of the "protototalitarian" terrors attributed to this political mode by neo-Lockean liberals has been in evidence,[30] for the physical environment of Graubünden seems to have endowed its people simultaneously with a sense of uncompromising autonomy and a feeling of constructive mutuality, both of which have found their way into Raetian notions of political consensus and citizenship. Autonomy never slipped over into an exaggerated politics of pure self-interest (in the style of American pluralism); yet collaboration never became an indefeasible rationale for statism and monolithic conformity (in the style of certain socialist republics). Indeed, because there was no state, no bureaucracy apart from the citizenry, the polarization between alienated individual and encroaching state that precipitates these widespread perversions never took place. It is difficult to become anxious about the perils of totalitarian collectivism when the collectivity in question is a commune of several hundred citizens who govern themselves directly in an ongoing process of deliberation and political action.

It would be dangerous to conclude from these remarks, however, that the indirect effects of the physical environ-

[29] Weiss, *Das Alpwesen*, p. 163. The citations from Weilenmann and Weiss are of more than usual interest because they are concrete observations about pastoral life by historical students of Switzerland who have no theoretic axes to grind.

[30] For the liberal distrust of idealist approaches to freedom see Isaiah Berlin, *Two Concepts of Liberty* (Oxford, 1958); Karl Popper, *The Open Society and Its Enemies* (London, 1945); or J. L. Talmon, *The Origins of Totalitarian Democracy* (New York, 1960).

ment in Raetia were entirely unambivalent. The physical strenuousness of alpine existence may have made men sturdy and independent, and encouraged political mutualism, but it also made them bitter, stolid, cold, superstitious, irrational, and violent; and it often informed their collaboration with a spirit of petty contentiousness quite incompatible with the pursuit of consensus. Life in the mountains hardens the skin and perhaps toughens the will, but it inspires in the mind a terrible and lasting fear that in turn nourishes irrationality, superstition, and violence.[31] It can freeze a man's outsides and leave his insides in turmoil; it can give him a leaden, hard-headed exterior that is but a cover for a seething, restless spirit. Even the architecture of the large, free-peasant houses suggests this tension:

> He who passes through the powerful, imposingly arched portal of an Engadiner house into the vaulted entrance hall, through the static, unmoving cubic mass that constitutes the outer walls into the lively agitation of the inner rooms, must be astonished by the logic with which the Bündner's own essential being is here reflected—the calm of his outer appearance concealing the agitated passions of his inner life.[32]

How like Rousseau's description of the Swiss in Geneva this is: "Under a phlegmatic and cold manner," he writes, "the Genevans hide an ardent and sensitive soul easier to move than to control. . . . The men are only too capable of

[31] The folktales of Graubünden are notoriously raw, as G. Fient has made clear in *Das Prättigau* (Davos, 1897), tending to fearful brutality rather than to pastoral charm. See A. Büchli, *Sagen aus Graubünden* (Aarau, n.d.) for a representative collection.

[32] Jenny, "Wesen und Gehalt," p. 181. This characteristic tension is widely appreciated: Peter Liver thus notes "the apparently phlegmatic Bündner, if possessed of an unexpected will to self-determination, is nonetheless riven with the wildest inner passions." *Die Staatliche Entwicklung*, p. 238.

103

feeling violent passions, the women of inspiring them."[33] What is true for Rousseau's independent lake-city men is even more true of our mountain men, who, in the limpid catalog of one close observer, are possessed by "slyness, taciturnity, closedness, cruelty, rawness . . . and an unbelievable tendency to violence and combativeness."[34] A people possessed of anything resembling cool reason, it has been remarked, would have abandoned the mountains at the very outset.

Manifestations of this turbulent temperament are to be found at every dangerous turning, every unsavory episode, in Graubünden's history: the use of the courts (*Strafgerichte*) as instruments of personal-public vengeance during the Time of Troubles (during the Thirty Years' War); the disastrous party feuds at the time of the collapse of the Republic of the Three Leagues in the aftermath of the French Revolution; the frequent misuse of the communal militia (*Fähnlein*) to settle vendettas, the assassinations and plots that characterized every unheaval; and the pettiness and bitterness of so much of public life right through the nineteenth century. Whether climate can really be held even indirectly responsible for such manifestations will necessarily remain speculative; nevertheless, the apparent tension in the Raetian personality evinced in the common portrait that emerges out of our discussion ought to be entered as a caveat to the more decisive tone of the previous section, for this tension is still one more indicator of the ambivalence that enclouds the effects of the physical environment on Raetia's political history. If the mountains have disposed the Raetian peasant to an independence and collaboration that have served him well in securing his

[33] Jean-Jacques Rousseau, *Letter to M. D'Alembert on the Theater,* trans. Alan Bloom as *Politics and the Arts* (Ithaca, New York, 1968), p. 118.

[34] Johannes A. von Sprecher, *Kulturgeschichte der Drei Bünde,* new edition by Rudolf Jenny (Chur, 1951), pp. 280–281.

country from external enemies and ambitious local tyrants, they have also disposed him to a brutal inner turbulence that has made him the enemy from whom he and his countrymen in self-government have had most to fear.

Geography, then, has had a profound bearing on the emergence of Raetian man as a free citizen in a self-governing republic, but its expression in ambivalent, contradictory moments and in factors that have worked as much against a free spirit and autonomous institutions as for them simply does not confirm the facile generalizations that have so often been made about freedom and mountain life. When M. L. Tripp attributes Switzerland's freedom to its "relative geographical isolation,"[35] when Peter Liver allows that "the environment of the mountains generally favored the establishment and preservation of personal freedom and communal autonomy,"[36] claims are being advanced that Graubünden's experience fails to demonstrate. The grand generalization that mountains make men free—as in Schiller's bucolic refrain, "in the mountains: freedom!" (*auf den Bergen: Freiheit!*)—seems no more persuasive than the competing shibboleth, "cities make men free" (*die Stadt macht frei!*). Just as oligarchically governed cities have grown up alongside of democratic ones, so unfree mountain states have been as numerous as free ones, not only in the premodern societies of the Andes and the Himalayas[37] but also in the Alps themselves. In fact, Graubünden and the original cantons of the Swiss Confederation (Uri, Schwyz, Unterwalden) are exceptions in a region that has known more

[35] M. L. Tripp, *The Swiss and United States Federal Constitutional Systems* (Paris, 1940), p. 14.

[36] Liver, "Alplandschaft," p. 3.

[37] Ecuador is an interesting case, where a feudal social system has survived more effectively in the Andean highlands (where the capital city Quito is located) than in the industrialized lowlands. The degree of urbanization and other "modernization" factors seem to be of much more significance than geography.

subjugation than autonomy, more class rule than equality. The briefest survey of the history of the Jurassien or the Tyrolean Alps makes this clear.

Geography, therefore, cannot be regarded as a decisive element in the emergence of Raetian freedom, however much it has conditioned the attitudes and institutions upon which political structures have been built. If so modest a review of a single, atypical case can have a general conclusion, it must patently be that though freedom may be favored or prejudiced by environmental conditions, it seems ultimately to be more a function of will than of geography, more the creation of man than his habitat.

That is hardly to say that Raetian man contrived full-blown political institutions out of the void. Raetia entered its earliest period of political history (the Middle Ages) with important political and socioeconomic institutions that were to play a vital role in coloring the later emergence of free, democratic structures and ideas.

# CHAPTER V

# Feudalism and Communality

FEUDALISM stands between modern man and both his civilized Greco-Roman roots and his primeval tribal origins—a second womb for a life process that had in fact been going on for millennia. Though we may look to Mediterranean civilization for clues to the abstract character of our culture and thought, we generally go no further than medieval feudalism in seeking the concrete historical antecedents of our political institutions—thus, Joseph R. Strayer's masterful little book *On the Medieval Origins of the Modern State*.[1]

Having been both enlightened and stymied by our examination of the indecisive influence of geography in its ambivalent Raetian expression, we need now to pursue the emergence of freedom in Graubünden with a more traditional look at the socioeconomic setting represented by Raetian feudalism.[2] Graubünden in its feudal period is particularly appropriate to what might be called a pre-political study of freedom, because the original socioeconomic environment in its pristine, prefeudal manifesta-

---

[1] Princeton, N. J., 1970.

[2] The focus on social and economic factors in this chapter should not be allowed to obscure the fundamental immunity of feudal man to sharp, role-related categories drawn from analytic social science. As Fritz Werli astutely notes in his study of medieval constitutionalism, "socioeconomic and legal-political questions were so closely tied together in these pure [medieval] agrarian communities that they cannot be separated out. It would have contradicted the mode of thought of Medieval Man to distinguish with sharp lines different individual facets of his way of life." *Zur Frage der Markgenossenschaften*, vol. 3, *Studien zur mittelalterlichen Verfassungsgeschichte* (Zürich, 1961), p. 29.

tions had not yet been institutionally rigidified or marked by feudal and postfeudal political structures. Raetian feudalism is also difficult to examine, however, because sources are scanty and mostly controversial, while feudal structure, particularly in Switzerland, is unusually complex.[3] The *Swiss Encyclopedia of Biography and History* distinguishes no fewer than twenty-five separate, if overlapping, species of feudal jurisdiction in medieval Germany, Helvetia, and Raetia,[4] each representing one diffuse strand of the yarn of power that only later could be woven into the integral fabric of sovereignty. The diversified structure of social relationships and the variety of customs and mores complicate the picture further. Add to this the confusion created by the uncertain role of the ecclesiastical hierarchy, the overwhelming difficulties of communication in the mountains, and the resulting lack of uniformity in customs and institu-

---

[3] Peter Tuor has bemoaned the "deep darkness that reigns over Raetia's condition in the Middle Ages." *Die Freien von Laax: Ein Beitrag zur Verfassungs- und Standesgeschichte* (Chur, 1903), p. 66. Paul Vinogradoff complains more generally about the "most confusing complex of social groups" with which the German *Grundherr* had to treat. "In Germany," he observes, "the communal element combined with the domanial in all sorts of chance ways which . . . did not develop without difficulty into a firmly established and generally recognized body of rural custom." "Feudalism," *The Cambridge Medieval History*, vol. 3 (Cambridge, 1924), pp. 483–484.

[4] These jurisdictions are as follows: blood *(Blut)*; real *(Echtes)*; free *(Frei)*; peace *(Friedens)*; guest *(Gast)*; mandated *(Gebotenes)*; territorial *(Grundherrliches)*; manorial *(Hof)*; autumn *(Herbst)*; criminal *(Hochgericht)*; annual *(Jahres)*; county *(Land)*; feudal *(Lehnes)*; misdemeanor *(Malifiz)*; spring *(Maien)*; secondary *(Nach)*; civil *(Nieder)*; public *(Offenes)*; punitive *(Peinliches)*; sheriff's *(Schultheiss)*; metropolitan *(Stadt)*; bailiff's *(Vogt)*; 'Fehm' *(Vem)*; and weekly *(Wochen)*. *Historisch-Biographisches Lexikon der Schweiz*, vol. 3 (Neuenburg, 1926), pp. 479–486. These include overlapping and competing jurisdictions, minor administrative variations on a major jurisdictional theme, and even different seasonal sittings of the same court (e.g., spring and autumnal jurisdictions), but they nevertheless do represent legally distinguishable varieties of juridical authority.

tions even within adjacent regions, and the vulnerability to sudden metamorphoses of the precarious socioeconomic arrangements that became institutionalized and the formidable implications of feudal complexity become apparent. Nevertheless, despite the technical problems Raetian feudalism creates, its multifaceted complexity in contrast to the monolithic simplicity of later notions of political sovereignty is precisely what makes it so conducive to an examination of the manifold interaction of society, economic life, the development of political consciousness, and the emergence of a peculiarly Raetian notion of freedom.

The customary divisions between the Low Middle Ages in its Merovingian and Carolingian phase and the High Middle Ages in its classical phase from the tenth to the thirteenth centuries are not particularly appropriate to the complexities of Raetian feudalism, in part because, as we will see, the Frankish constitutions made only a superficial impact on Raetia. Thus, the periodization that corresponds to subsequent sections breaks the history of Raetia into a prefeudal segment in which we can observe the rudimentary forms of indigenous, prefeudal institutions, a feudal segment in which we can measure the impact of externally imposed feudal institutions, and a postfeudal segment in which we can assess the vector resultant of these competing native and foreign forces.

## FREEDOM IN PREFEUDAL RAETIA

Up until and even after the introduction of the Carolingian constitution in Raetia, the primary economic and social relationships of the mountain peasant were a function of a collective and corporate association known as the *Markgenossenschaft*: literally, the corporation of the mark, or, as we will call it, the association of the common.[5] Other

---

[5] The *locus classicus* for a traditional discussion of the alternative meanings of the Germanic notion of *Genossenschaft* remains Otto von

institutions touched particular facets of the peasant's life. For example, distant courts might occasionally claim jurisdiction over him in some legal quarrel. But only the association of the common involved him wholly on a day-to-day basis and in ways critical to his social and economic existence. If anything like a notion of freedom is to be attributed to Graubünden in this earliest part of its history, it will clearly be related to the institution of the common association.

Defined in terms of its purpose, the association of the common constituted an "organization for the use and administration of the Common Mark."[6] The mark encompassed all land and resources held in common. Such associations were of course to be found throughout central Europe, especially in Frankish Germany during the centuries prior to the rise of feudalism, and they can therefore hardly be regarded as peculiar to prefeudal Raetia. However, their role in Helvetia and in Raetia was both more crucial and more enduring than elsewhere in Germany, perhaps because of the collectivist predisposition given the mountaineer by his harsh environment. Indeed, just because in its broad structure the association of the common pervaded much of Europe does not warrant the conclusion that it was ex-

---

Gierke's *Das Deutsche Genossenschaftsrecht*, 4 vols. (Berlin, 1868– ), particularly the introduction to *Rechtsgeschichte der deutschen Genossenschaft*, vol. 1 (Berlin, 1868) of which, unfortunately, only small portions are presently available in English.

Another classical definition of the mark is offered by Henry Maine, who understood it to be "an organized, self-acting group of Teutonic families, exercising a common proprietorship over a definite tract of land, its Mark, cultivating its domain on a common system, and sustaining itself by its produce." *Village Communities in the East and West* (New York, 1876), p. 10. However, Maine is more concerned with the agricultural village than with the pastoral commune.

[6] Peter Liver, "Die Bündner Gemeinde," *Bündner Monatsblatt*, February 1941, p. 38. Cf. G. Pedotti, *Beiträge zur rechtsgeschichtlichen Entwicklung der Gemeinde, der Gemeindeausgaben und der Gemeindevermögen im Kanton Graubünden* (Zürich, 1936), p. 14, and passim.

clusively a Germanic import into Raetia. The mark's Germanic origins based on the tribal conviction that *usage* of the land was a right enjoyed by all (without contradiction to the king's equally just title to *ownership*) may not have seemed salient to the Romanic population of prefeudal Graubünden. To these heirs of a race of colonists who had settled Raetia in the days of the burgeoning Roman Empire, the rights of usage guaranteed by the common association must have been more easily interpreted in terms of the Roman distinction between *dominum utile* and *dominum directum*, the former conveying to them the hereditary use of common land, the latter reserving to the empire (first Roman, then Frankish) abstract proprietary rights associated with ultimate political jurisdiction. Hence, historians seem to agree that, however many characteristics the Raetian common association shared with its Germanic namesake, it originated earlier, perhaps even "in the most ancient times."[7]

Tracing the anthropological genealogy of the Raetian common association, although it does hint at the unique combination of sources out of which Raetian institutions grew and the autonomous course of development they generally followed, tells us little about the *Markgenossenschaft*. To determine whether it may have afforded its members some sense of equality and autonomy that we would want to associate with freedom, we need to know something more about the character of the land and resources that comprised the mark, a good deal more about what it meant to use and administer the common, and a great deal more about the membership responsible for administration and entitled to use of the common, as well as the effects of membership on political and economic life. In brief, we need

[7] H. Moosberger, *Die Bündnerische Allmende* (Chur, 1891), p. 3. Moosberger's somewhat dated study has the advantage of focusing on Raetia. The more general situation in Switzerland is depicted in comparative terms by Werli, *Zur Frage*.

to learn *what* was used, *how* it was used, by *whom* it was used, and *with what general consequences.*

In its initial phase, the common included not only pastureland and woodland, but "alps, springs, streams, quarries, claypits . . . in short the entire region with every and all of its products and fruits."[8] Like those nearly unknown ancestors who had settled in the mountains in prehistorical times, and like those more immediate forebearers who came as colonists on the spreading frontier of the Roman Empire, the inhabitants of Raetia in the fifth and sixth centuries did not hold private property. The right of usage they enjoyed was to them tantamount to collective ownership, though rightful ownership might be held by others in distant places.[9] Initially, common associations elsewhere in Europe held the same broad rights, but the more fertile and civilized regions quickly fell prey to principles of territoriality and private property that came with the cultivation of land and the so-called realization of feudalism. Common forests were razed to furnish arable land, abstract rights of ownership were formalized by lords who settled on and lived off their property (the growth of manors), and soon such communal rights of usage as survived were limited to vestigial woodlands and marshes of insignificant economic value. But in Graubünden, as we have seen already in the context of geography, the poverty of the soil saved the people from agricultural bondage and spared them from the assault on

[8] Moosberger, *Die Bündnerische Allmende*, p. 5. The terms cited in historical documents are charmingly alliterative, but have lost whatever distinctive meaning they might have had: thus *Grund und Grat* presumably means simply ground, while *Holz und Feld, Wun und Weid, Weg und Steg, Wasser und Wasserleiti* may be taken respectively to mean woodland, meadowland, roads, and waterways. Cf. "Wun und Weid," *Bündner Monatsblatt*, December 1901, p. 267.

[9] "For the practical needs of the peasant, it was more important to possess rights of usage than rights of proprietorship. Hence, the peasant tended to regard usage as synonymous with ownership." Richard Weiss, *Das Alpwesen Graubündens* (Zürich, 1941), p. 294.

communalism that fertile ground inevitably occasioned. Thus the Raetian common association underwent a much more gradual decline than elsewhere. Certain valleys retained common rights of usage over extensive alpine pastures and woods well into the nineteenth century.[10] Moreover, where private property did make inroads into traditional collectivist rights, its effect was assuaged by the institution of common-grazing (*Gemeinatzung*), a practice, the peculiarities of which permit us to see *how* the common was held.

As we have already seen, the only feature of ownership pertinent to the daily life of the mountaineer was usage. Actual proprietorship was a fiction of the legal imagination. Consequently, as individual lots gradually came into the hands of private persons and legal title passed from distant lords to resident landowners, the common association continued to exercise its prerogatives of usage. Despite the rising complaints of landholders, these prerogatives were soon institutionalized through the device of common-grazing (*Gemeinatzung*), a practice that permitted all members of the association (and later the political commune) to herd their livestock across all land, whatever its proprietary status, originally within the boundaries of the old mark. Because most of the private property on which this right was exercised lay between the valley barns in which livestock spent their winters, and the higher mountain pastures that remained communal property where they summered,

[10] For example, all eleven communes of the valley of Calanca (*Calancatal*) remained part of a single economic association that was the direct heir to the original *Markgenossenschaft* until 1865. Other examples of the longevity of the common association can be found in the Bergell valley, the Schamsertal, and elsewhere. For a discussion, see A. Meuli, "Die Entstehung der autonomen Gemeinden im Oberengadin," *Jahresbericht der Historisch-Antiquarischen Gesellschaft von Graubünden*, 1901, and F. Purtscher, " 'Zu Ilanz und in der Grub': Ein Beitrag zur Geschichte ihrer Entstehung," *Bündner Monatsblatt*, April, May, September 1922, pp. 100ff.

common-grazing was in fact a dispensation for seasonal grazing (spring and autumn, on the way up and the way down) on the private lands across which livestock had to be moved.[11] By effectively nullifying the prerogatives of private property, common-grazing preserved the preeminence of usage over ownership that had characterized prefeudal economic relations into and beyond the feudal epoch. Despite opposition by eighteenth-century champions of scientific agriculture (imagine the effect of hundreds of cows grazing their way through diffident little vegetable gardens, promising young vineyards, or hayfields being cultivated for winter fodder), common-grazing has even managed to survive down into the nineteenth and twentieth centuries. As a valued anachronism, it has continued to complicate and encumber Graubünden's economy through the present—in ways that will be of importance to the themes raised toward the end of the book. With its vestiges survives a modicum of Raetia's collectivist heritage.

The third question, who was entitled to common association rights and benefits, is easily answered, though its implications are manifold. Every inhabitant of the territory delimited by the common association, usually an easily recognizable geographical region like a valley, bounded by streams, gorges, or cliffs, had full title to all association prerogatives. To dwell within the common was *ipso facto* to be a member of the association that utilized and admin-

---

[11] J. M. Curschellas gives the following legal definition of common-grazing in his historical survey of the institution: "Common-grazing is an associational right of access (for grazing purposes) to all private land within the association's territory not otherwise exempted from that right; it is a right given every community member with grazing animals, to be exercised at specified times in the fall and spring." *Die Gemeinatzung* (Ilanz, 1926), p. 12.

The economic costs of preserving common-grazing into the twentieth century, indeed in several remote valleys into the present day, have been high, and its survival raises fundamental questions about traditional values and modernization; see Chapter IX below.

istered it, irrespective of class, rank, economic status, or worldly connections. Free peasants, descendants of the originally unfree class of Roman colonists (*coloni*), local propertyowners, and land-holding noblemen with vassal status in the Frankish Empire found themselves in a uniquely egalitarian situation. Bound together by their common status in the association and by their common rights of usage over all collective resources, they developed a sense of equality wholly at odds with the hierarchical, status-conscious thrust of medieval feudalism. This distinctive spirit was to dominate the later emergence of democracy in the Raetian Republic, and give to it a character unfamiliar to free peoples elsewhere; freedom in the Raetian Alps would never have that individualistic bent associated with the evolution of free, commercial cities out of medieval, defensive burgs.[12]

If anything, membership in the common association must have enhanced that sense of corporate identity that has been widely attributed to medieval man.[13] Though it might

[12] Compare the development described here with the picture of the emergence of free cities in the late Middle Ages, Henri Pirenne, *Medieval Cities* (Princeton, N. J., 1925).

A certain amount of controversy has surrounded the argument that the democratic roots of the Raetian Republic are to be found in the old common association: compare Curschellas, *Die Gemeinatzung*, and F. Purtscher, "Der Obere oder Graue Bund," *Bündner Monatsblatt*, April-June 1925, who argue strongly for the connection, with Peter Liver, *Von Feudalismus zur Demokratie in den graubündnerischen Hinterrheintälern* (Chur, 1929), who, although sympathetic to the spirit of the argument, warns against exaggerating either its significance or the historical evidence that can be adduced in favor of it.

[13] Jacob Burckhardt suggests that "in the Middle Ages man was conscious of himself only as a member of a race, people, party, family, or corporation—only through some general category." *Civilization of the Renaissance in Italy*, 2 vols., trans. S.G.C. Middlemore (New York, 1958), I, 143. Erich Fromm observes "Medieval society did not deprive the individual of this freedom, because the individual did not

have made him the equal of lords, the Raetian peasant was probably motivated in his participation in the common association primarily by the demands of physical survival, not by a sense of personal identity that he could not have possessed. We have to imagine relatively simple men, bound together by familial ties, pursuing a common economic goal in communities that must have been more like clans than modern contractual corporations. Participation would have had to have been natural and unselfconscious, a prevoluntaristic expression of physical and social needs. To borrow Ferdinand Tönnies' overused and historically inaccurate but nevertheless useful distinction between community and society (*Gemeinschaft und Gesellschaft*), we can best regard the mountain peasant as a member of an extended personal community where obligations appeared natural and mandatory and where individuality as an extension of the atomized, autonomous person was inconceivable.[14] This collaborative social mode, if it was later to color political institutions and to mediate the tensions normally associated with the autonomy of individuals in a direct democracy, was to do so only in a later, more politically self-conscious manifestation. In this early period where men still wore what Burckhardt has called a "veil woven of faith, illusion, and childish prepossession, through which the world and history were seen clad in strange hues,"[15] no modern notion of freedom could have been at home. Necessity, fear, and superstition, the anticipation of an early death and the

---

yet exist; man was still related to the world by primary ties. He did not yet conceive of himself as an individual except through the medium of his social roles." *Escape from Freedom* (New York, 1941), p. 59.

[14] Much of the history of Graubünden, and not a few of its recent dilemmas, can be convincingly elucidated in the context of Tönnies' ideal types: see *Community and Society*, trans. Charles P. Loomis (East Lansing, Mich., 1957). The original German edition was published in 1887, which suggests that Tönnies' categories are more useful as theoretical than as historical or sociological tools.

[15] Burckhardt, *Civilization of the Renaissance*, vol. 1, p. 143.

certain expectation of more proximate acts of violence, the primacy of social roles and the irresistible claims of family must have combined together to repress entirely any incipient inkling of personal power or individual autonomy that equal participation in the common association might have bred.

The development of freedom in the common association then had to await the raising of Raetian man's political consciousness and the fundamental politicization of his institutions and attitudes that would transform economic and social ties into political bonds, that would convert personal obligations into public contracts, and that would supplant the organically integrated, hierarchical social structure of the feudal epoch with the more familiar dichotomies of individual and state of the modern era. Only when men became capable of perceiving themselves as possessing identities separate from society, could they begin to consider their relationship to the polity in the language of freedom. If the Raetian common association held seeds of a later political style, it was barren of those elements required for them to sprout. The decisive catalyst in initiating the structural and attitudinal politicization of the common association had to come from the outside, and it made its appearance with the coming of feudalism to Graubünden.

## FEUDALISM: ORIGINS AND DEVELOPMENT

That Raetia was not politicized in the fundamental sense noted above does not mean that it was without legal-political institutions on the eve of the feudal period. In economic and social matters, "the Emperor's law," as the Asian proverb has it, did indeed "stop at the village gate." But the common association had never been competent in legal questions, civil or criminal; legal jurisdiction had been, and would remain throughout the Middle Ages, in the hands of loftier authorities. Three separate bodies had a part in this

117

jurisdiction in prefeudal Raetia. There was a civil governor (*rector*) who exercised vestigial administrative functions of what had once been the Roman *praeses*; a quasi-representative assembly known as the *curia* that until its abolition in 806 shared ecclesiastical jurisdiction with the politically powerful bishopric; and the bishop himself who held extensive spiritual and secular powers until the introduction of the Carolingian constitution into Raetia. Indeed, in 773 a certain Bishop Constantius also became *rector*. Thus, power was concentrated in his hands.[16] The overlapping, sometimes conflicting, other times synonymous prerogatives of these three offices, and the lesser ecclesiastic and civil courts of the empire, were codified only in the eighth century, initially as the primarily Roman *lex Romana curiensis* and then under the seal of Constantius's successor Remedius, as the Germanic *capitula Remedii*. However, this elaborate, complicated, ever-changing legal superstructure had only a tangential bearing on the lives of individual peasants. The codified laws enunciating prerogatives and promulgating jurisdictional boundaries probably only applied to the Romanic population, and may even have been limited to those directly under the jurisdiction of the church in the *Bischofshof*.[17] In any case, only in matters of taxation and

16 His successor, Remedius, had the exalted title Prince-Bishop of the Empire. However, the extent to which these offices endowed the bishopric with secular criminal and civil jurisdiction remains unclear. Some have argued that the rectorship under the bishop was a purely honorific spiritual office and that the bishop never possessed juridical authority beyond the confines of his own ecclesiastical court (*Pfalzgericht*) that dealt exclusively with offenses of his own clerical train (*Gefolge*); see P. Mutzner, *Beiträge zur Rechtsgeschichte Graubündens im Mittelalter, Separatabruck aus der Zeitschrift für Schweizerisches Recht*, Neue Folge, vol. 2, n.d.

17 Countervailing evidence from the text of the *capitula* itself suggests, on the other hand, that the codifications were intended to apply to the entire population of Upper Raetia, for the document includes a precise description of all of the major administrative offices in the land. Controversy remains.

criminal jurisdiction could these offices have acquired some significance, and these two powers were ultimately controlled by the Frankish kings themselves. As long as the peasant remained politically unself-conscious in mountain communes that were self-governing in the matters that most concerned him, he must have regarded the *rector*, the bishop, and the distant king with splendid indifference.

Nor did the rigid class structures that were creating a social system of maximum inflexibility elsewhere in Frankish Germany have much effect in the common associations. Class distinctions in Raetia, which was directly on the frontier between Germany and Italy, were in any case becoming blurred in the period before the rise of feudalism. The influence of Frankish institutions had increasingly attentuated the sharp lines among the old Roman classes: slaves (*servi*), colonists (*coloni*), and freemen (*ingenui*). The colonist originally free in his person but bound to the land he tilled fell into an increasingly demeaning personal servitude to the proprietor of the land he worked, especially in the lower valleys where the common association was both less firmly rooted and more vulnerable to erosion. Conversely, the personal slave of Roman times had been pretty much emancipated and found himself elevated to a status not far below the level to which the colonist had ignominiously declined. In time, the two melted together into a general class of Raetian unfreemen within which traditional distinctions no longer applied.

Simultaneously, freemen found their condition to be more and more precarious. Those in mountain communes were relatively well-off, but in the lower regions where more fertile conditions and better communications had attracted the attentive interest of titled landholders they were unable to maintain their economic self-sufficiency. Economic necessity, man's original master and the father of all subsequent servitudes, once more led men to relinquish a difficult freedom for a secure bondage. Thus, the distinctions not

119

only within the classes of free and unfree but between the freeman and the bondsman gradually vanished, and Raetia was left vulnerable not only to the hierarchical ambitions of the Carolingians but also to the uncertain attractions of egalitarianism by default. The initial victory went to the Carolingians.

Feudalism began in Raetia, as it did throughout much of Europe, with the attempt of the Carolingian kings to institutionalize through benefice and vassalage the rights held by their predecessors. Landowners and noblemen who had hitherto exercised considerable jurisdictional independence were taken into the service of the empire as vassals; where locals were deemed undependable, they were replaced as agents of the king by appointed officials whose services would be paid for with a land grant. Both the practice among freemen of pledging personal allegiance and service to a lord (vassalage) and that of bestowing upon deserving freemen tenements (benefice) were known earlier in Merovingian times. But the Carolingians fashioned from these two quite distinct instruments a single device for imposing their government on the disintegral and semiautonomous regions that constituted their far-flung empire.[18] The shortage of money in conjunction with the surfeit of land, the obvious advantages of repaying services with self-sustaining fiefs, and the simple avarice of provincial lords all contributed to the success of the Carolingian experiment in relating the personal bond of vassalage that had originally been unconditional with the granting by contract of land rights. Of course, the identification did not become com-

[18] Marc Bloch makes a good deal of the critical distinction between the Germanic *foedum*, which conveyed only a sense of usage by grace, and *allod*, which gradually became identified with a more proprietary interpretation of land in the vassal setting; he concurs with Montesquieu in viewing the life-fiefs of the Carolingian period as essentially prefeudal institutions. *Feudal Society*, trans. L. A. Manyon, 2 vols. (London, 1965), p. 190 and passim. Cf. Karl Lamprecht in *Deutsches Wirtschaftsleben im Mittelalter*, 3 vols. in 4 (Leipzig, 1886).

plete until considerably later. Under the Carolingians benefice conferred only rights of usage (*dominium utile*) and
not rights of ownership (*dominium directum*). Nor were
these rights yet hereditary. As a result, the essential alodial
character of feudalism cannot yet be detected in the Carolingian phase, a fact that has led observers from Montesquieu to Marc Bloch to treat this era as prefeudal.

Nevertheless, these Carolingian innovations had a significant direct impact on Raetia's civil government and a
less profound indirect effect on the common associations.
The first to feel the influence of the Carolingian constitution were the larger landholders in the valleys. The importation of German noblemen to exercise the emperor's rights
of criminal jurisdiction in what under the new constitution
became the earldom of Upper Raetia required the expro-
priation of those who for centuries had been exercising
rights of usage, for their land was now to be parceled out
as fiefs to the imperial interlopers. Within a short time, the
Churraetian bishopric, its monastic dependencies, and many
of the smaller temporal estates found themselves dispossessed.

On the other hand, the common associations, perched on
less accessible alpine meadows, were to experience the
presence of the earl and his county chiefs (the so-called
*Schultheissen* or bailiffs who administered the *Centen* or
hundreds into which the earldom was subdivided) only
obliquely. In fact, it was not the temporary success but the
ultimate failure of the Carolingian constitution in Raetia
that proved fateful for the political consciousness of the
common associations, for the Carolingian presence catalyzed and then nourished the ambitions of local secular and
ecclesiastic powers who eventually proved to be a much
greater threat to the autonomy of the mountain peasant
and who finally compelled him in defense of his collective
independence into political activity. The failure of Charlemagne's successors was rooted in the very success of the new

121

forms of vassalage they had pioneered. By demonstrating that loyalty could be won and kept by granting lifetime rights of usage over imperial domains, they taught their vassals the secret of treason. These vassals, pretending to a *pro forma* loyalty to their imperial benefactor, could quietly create a system of subvassals using the land granted them by the empire to undermine the authority of the king while enhancing their own. The post-Carolingians quickly discovered that the hierarchy created to solidify their control over the empire had become a wall separating them from their subjects; for their subjects were more loyal to the vassals empowered by the king than to the king who had empowered them. Such loyalty paid more.[19] What is worse, the remedy resorted to by the anxious post-Carolingians was more deadly than the malady it was intended to cure. Their strategy was to put an end to the abuse of self-serving vassals by absolving the indigenous landholders they had originally dispossessed from the jurisdiction of wayward subordinates, just as a prudent commander might bypass and render powerless an untrustworthy captain by permitting the captain's lieutenants to report directly to him. The danger—quickly realized in Raetia where the remedy was tried earlier than elsewhere—was that the new beneficiaries of imperial favor could abuse their new prerogatives for their own gain, the more so because the king had removed them from the jurisdiction of their former lords and the king's only means of local control. Nominally,

19 F. L. Ganshof observes: "The policy followed by the Carolingians failed to produce the fruits they expected from it. The great extension of vassalage, its incorporation in the framework of the institutions of government, the distribution of benefices on a large scale, all ended by diminishing the authority of the king instead of increasing it. Even before the end of the reign of Charlemagne, it had become apparent that the bonds which united a vassal to his lord, bonds which were direct and immediately appreciable by the senses, were stronger by far than those which bound the subject to the king." *Feudalism,* 3d English ed. (London, 1964).

122

this jurisdictional by-pass (which went under the name *Reichsunmittelbarkeit*), by granting chosen locals immunity from the king's vassals, bound them directly to the king and thus enhanced his prestige and power. In fact, it emancipated them from the only kingly authorities capable of compelling their fealty and thus unwittingly destroyed the power of the king and his higher vassals at a single stroke. In Raetia, ecclesiastic and temporal powers favored by the king with these self-defeating grants of immunity went to work almost at once to fortify themselves against the empire. Pursuing ambitious policies of territorial and jurisdictional aggrandizement, they not only succeeded in reestablishing their relative autonomy but also managed to bring feudalism to Graubünden in a pervasive way that for the first time implicated and thus jeopardized the mountain peasant in his common association sanctuary.

The estates that benefited most from the disastrous remedies of the post-Carolingians, and the subsequent decline in the authority of the earl and his county chiefs, included not only the revitalized domains of the Churraetian bishopric, and the Benedictine abbacy of Disentis but also a number of secular noble houses with ancient roots in Raetia.[20]

[20] The variety of secular and spiritual houses in Raetia led to a good deal of conflict. The Churraetian bishopric (*Hochstift Chur*) constituted two separate corporations each of which held discreet feudal and alodial claims: the bishop and his train (*Bischofshof*), and the cathedral chapter (*Domkapitel*) headed by a deacon (*Domprobst*). Disentis and Pfävers, two independent cloisters with immunity from the king's local vassals and thus under his own direct protection (the status of *Reichsunmittelbarkeit*), along with several additional cloisters still dependent on local lords, made up the balance of Raetia's spiritual domains during the period. See Johannes C. Muoth, "Churraetia in der Feudalzeit," in Fritz Jecklin, et al., *Bündnergeschichte in Elf Vorträge* (Chur, 1902).

On the other hand, the church had to contend with several powerful secular estates, the most powerful of which was the house of the free lords of Vaz. Although the line died out in 1338, it played a significant role in checking the spreading power of the bishop from

However, their gains over several centuries cannot be measured exclusively in terms of property rights acquired; although the ecclesiastical estates were much enlarged by gifts of land from Otto I (in 958) and his heirs, the holding of hereditary fiefs that in effect transformed rights of usage into alodial property was no longer exceptional by the eleventh century. The struggle thus no longer centered on land per se, but moved to the increasingly decisive issue of jurisdiction. It was the quest for jurisdictional sovereignty that finally involved and politicized those common association mountain men who for so long had been insulated from feudalism by their mountain habitat and their collective institutions.

The struggle for jurisdiction was a long one that went on alongside the developments we have just described. In the early period of Carolingian centralism, the king through his representatives exercised all rights of higher criminal jurisdiction throughout the Empire and based his claims on the personal bond that was characteristic of all early feudal relations. However, the acquisition of large, independent estates by local powers who in the post-Carolingian period had become economically and militarily autonomous called into serious question jurisdiction based on personal allegiance. Fiefholders came naturally to insist upon their rights of jurisdiction over all persons settled within their domains, irrespective of personal status or obligations. The struggle for jurisdiction hence became a campaign to win recognition for the principle of territoriality (*Landeshoheit*) against the vestigial claims to personal fealty of the empire. In the sphere of "lower jurisdiction" that encompassed civil law and certain petty criminal cases, recognition was easily

---

its alodial holdings in Hinterprättigau, Davos, Alvenau-Brienz, Obervaz, Lenz, and Rheinwald and from its mountain fortress at Belfort (remains of which can still be explored today). For a full discussion, see P. Badrutt, *Die Entstehung des Oberen Grauen Bundes* (Chur, 1916), especially Chapter 4.

won, for in this domain the king's powers had always been delegated to—indeed, in the post-Carolingian period, had been conferred on—regional courts that represented local interests. The winning of "higher jurisdiction" that encompassed criminal law and especially capital offenses was a far more difficult proposition. Jurisdiction of blood (*Blutbann*) governing questions of life or death was the essence of medieval sovereignty. As the symbol of the king's ultimate authority over a political system that was otherwise totally lacking in the trappings of later monarchical centralism, it was indispensable to his imperial claims. As a result, full regional autonomy of higher jurisdiction had to await the full disintegration of the Carolingian Empire and the ensuing transformation of vassalage from a personal into a property relationship. The territorial principle could only be vindicated *ex post facto*, when fiefs had become hereditary and feudal holdings became entirely alodial in character.

The extended struggle between regional powers and the empire touched on the common associations well before the conflict was finally resolved in favor of regionalism, for the small tenants and free peasants were at the very nub of the dispute: over their lives the struggle for jurisdiction was being waged.

## The Impact on the Common Association

The changes that were to transform the lives and collective institutions of the mountain peasant in Graubünden were not initiated in response to the temporary instruments of government engineered by the Carolingians; these, as we have seen, touched them little. They were rather a reaction to local manifestations of the far more permanent and intrusive feudal patterns established during the conflict that followed the gradual decline of the empire. The growth of indigenous feudal estates with aspirations to jurisdictional

125

hegemony within Raetia threatened the autonomy of the common associations in ways that the tentative administrative innovations of the empire never had. The threat touched the individual peasant in at least four related ways: (1) it placed the public character of his common land in permanent jeopardy; (2) it subjected him to increasingly debilitating assessments that endangered his economic self-sufficiency; (3) it redefined and rigidified class structure in ways destructive to his functional egalitarianism in the common association; and (4) it undermined the relative autonomy of his once insular institutions. Collectivism, autarky, equality, and autonomy, the defining characteristics of the traditional common association, were under attack. The response of the mountaineer was largely determined by the nature of the threat.

Raetian feudal estates, newly empowered by grants of immunity from the emperor, were in an advantageous position to increase their landed holdings by enforcement of extant but neglected prerogatives formerly superseded by the king's vassals, by contract, by purchase, or by simple intimidation and usurpation. Whereas the presence of the empire in Graubünden had always been an institutional formality, the revival of the bishopric's power and the rise of such secular powers as the free lords of Vaz who had ancient roots and ancient rights in their own native land were physical realities that could not be ignored. The imperial claim to rights of ownership was an insignificant abstraction to those who retained rights of usage. The same claim in the mouths of ambitious local lords could potentially destroy the very basis of the common association. First arable land and vineyards, then even pasture and woodland fell more and more into private hands that would tolerate no traditional demands for usage. With the owners ensconced on their land, use was at their sufferance, on their terms, and with whatever encumbrances and tithes they chose to impose. Under these hostile circumstances,

126

the maintenance of collectivities that depended on usage rights became an ever more aggravated problem, and its resolution in favor of the common association could by no means be taken for granted.

Even where pastureland and other common land continued to be held and used exclusively by the common association, it was subjected to a variety of assessments, the legal justification of which once again lay in the abstract right of ownership suddenly being exercised by the Raetian nobility. The burden was initially small, including church tithes, labor services, payments in kind as well as a score of petty but irritating exactions like the hen demanded of all residents at Easter (*Fastnachtshuhn*); but it had a cumulatively pernicious impact on the capacity of the mountain peasant to remain economically self-sufficient. After all, his free status had from the earliest times depended on his autarky.

In fact, the growth of Raetian feudalism in its indigenous form had by the eleventh century metamorphosized class structure. The old divisions between freeman and slave had been susperseded by arrangements that made almost all men except princes and their vassals unfree dependents of one sort or another, enhancing the importance of distinctions within the general class of the unfree. For example, the difference between the imperial *ministeriales*, who although nominally unfree were highly regarded administrators in the imperial service, and the indentured serf (*Leibeigene*), who was also unfree but could be sold off by his proprietor like livestock, was much greater than that between the unfree *ministeriales* and the free petty vassal. Similarly, the free but landless peasant was not only inferior in power and status to the unfree *ministeriales* but also at a distinct disadvantage even in comparison to the bondsman (*Hörige*) who tilled the soil of a well-endowed lord. This irony led more than a few freemen to surrender their freedom in return for the economic security of the manor. The transition from free tenancy to mild bondage was nearly

127

imperceptible—little being lost in view of the social and economic impotence of freemen, and a great deal being gained in the way of security. This might not have been true had the form of personal bondage popular in Germany (*Leibeigenschaft*) prevailed in Upper Raetia, but Raetian feudalism tended toward the less demeaning form of bondage to the land (*Hörigkeit*), which proscribed the sale of men separate from the land they worked, thus guaranteeing the security and integrity of their lives and families.[21] What was lost in the transition, then, was not so much freedom, the significance which in feudal Raetia we have already had some doubts about, as equality.

Those freemen who were able to resist the temptations of feudal security discovered that their institutional autonomy was no more secure than their economic autonomy. The avid promotion of the principle of territoriality by Raetian estateholders was an even more potent threat than taxation or labor service, because the struggle for real power had come more and more to be associated with jurisdictional claims grounded on territorial suzerainty (*Landeshoheit*). To supplant the empire in Raetia was not simply to replace it as proprietor but to usurp its jurisdictional sovereignty by compelling a shift in the basis of obligation from personal fealty to territorial allegiance. By the thirteenth century the bishop of Churraetia, who once had to defer to

[21] There is no agreement on the precise extent of indentured serfdom (*Leibeigenschaft*) in Raetia. Fifty years ago, Peter C. Planta contended that it was more widespread than generally thought in Raetia, though "nowheres near as frequent as in Helvetia or Germany." "Die Entstehung der Leibeigenschaft auf dem Gebiet des heutigen Kantons Graubündens," *Bündner Monatsblatt*, February-September 1925, p. 53. A decade later, Georg Ragaz offers a much more conservative estimate, minimizing *Leibeigenschaft's* Raetian significance, in *Die Entstehung der politischen Gemeinden im Schamsertal* (Disentis, 1934), pp. 11–12. Peter Liver, the leading contemporary authority, argued for the more extensive pattern from his very earliest work, *Von Feudalismus*, p. 51.

an imperially appointed bailiff (*Reichsvogt*), had obtained all jurisdictional power, criminal as well as civil, lay as well as ecclesiastic.[22] The growth of the principle of territorial jurisdiction jeopardized the freeman in Raetia by cutting him off from the source of his autonomy—the king and the king's court. One of the most salient prerogatives of the freeman under the empire was the right to judgment before an imperial court presided over by the king's appointed officials and constituted by lay judges often chosen from the freeman's own constituency. Place of habitation—on a local nobleman's alod, for example—could not affect the status of the freeman as long as jurisdiction depended on the relationship of fealty between freeman and king. Territorial jurisdiction abrogated this critical relationship, giving to the land-holding lord an exclusive, even arbitrary power over all residents on his land that the king's agents would never have dreamed of exercising. Once again, the neighborhood bully proved to be a far greater peril than the distant tyrant. As feudalism continued to liquidate itself through that process of "realization" that replaced personal with territorial allegiance, the freeman found himself in an ever more precarious position.

The response of the free peasant to these four kinds of interdependent threats was dominated by two important changes in his collective institutions: (1) the breakup of the traditional valleywide common associations (the so-called *Talmarkgenossenschaften*) into smaller units; and (2)

---

[22] "All of these estates, spiritual as well as worldly, were striving to extend their jurisdiction not merely over the serfs indentured to their land, but over all freemen residing in their territory." *Historisch-Biographisches Lexikon der Schweiz*, vol. 3 (Neuenburg, 1926), p. 701.

In fact, the bailiff's office—responsible for representing the king in criminal litigation—had long since ceased to be occupied directly by foreign vassals appointed by the king. The free lords of Vaz held it throughout the eleventh and twelfth centuries, and it was from them that the bishopric bought the office in 1299.

129

the gradual politicization of the association's economic institutions in the face of the jurisdictional aggressiveness of the bishopric and other Raetian estateholders. The breakup of the larger common associations of prefeudal times was both an inadvertent by-product of the extension of private property and an intended consequence of the attempt to improve and expedite the association's administration and utilization of common land in order to make it less vulnerable to usurpation or seizure by those holding proprietary title. The smaller, more tightly knit unit that supplanted the old valley association was the neighborhood association (*Nachbarschaft*), an entity reflecting the more restricted natural boundaries of a local region occupied by a population concentrated in a small cluster of houses. The neighborhood was in fact nothing less than the rudimentary village community (*Dorfgemeinde*), where men interacted daily on a "face-to-face" basis that would be crucial to the preservation of their autonomy.[23] Its restricted size and intuitively consensual approach to common crises lent to it a special strength in meeting external challenges. Although politicization began with the more encompassing jurisdictional communes, it was the village community that was to become the building block of Raetia's later political superstructure and the principal focus of Raetian democracy right up until the present day.

The commune, however, was not initially a viable enough

[23] Peter Laslett develops the notion of a "face to face society" as being characteristic of a "world we have lost"; its features include intimate knowledge of each citizen by the other (knowing in the sense of being born together), the resolution of crises by "people meeting and talking," and a web of interactions based on intuitive psychology. Because this theory claims a good deal less, it is in some ways more useful in thinking about small, traditional agrarian societies than is the classical model of community propounded by Ferdinand Tönnies in *Community and Society*. See Peter Laslett, "The Face to Face Society," in P. Laslett, ed., *Philosophy, Politics and Society*, First Series (Oxford, 1956), and *The World We Have Lost*.

institution to act politically against the territorial pretensions and jurisdictional encroachments of the Raetian
nobility. It was rather the more extended jurisdictional
communes *(Gerichtsgemeinden)*—originally a contrivance
of the feudal nobility to ensure their jurisdiction over
groups of adjacent village communities—that were implicated in the initial politicization of the Raetian peasant. It
was at this level that freemen of the several neighborhoods
making up a jurisdictional commune began to press for
representation in the local courts that claimed jurisdiction
over them, and sought to make their voices heard in the
appointment of district leaders *(Ammänner)*. And it was at
this level, at some point during the long, drawn-out contest between neighborhood autonomy and feudal hegemony,
that the individual freeman must have reached a stage of
political consciousness where he could explicitly relate his
quest for personal autonomy and collective independence
with the securing of such particular political conditions as
the absence of arbitrary external constraints, active political
participation in his neighborhood, a dynamic consensus
both within and between the communes, and a voice in the
institutions that affected his life. Such conditions, of course,
were not to be produced by rebellion. They required a
long, laborious, evolutionary process that began with the
simple effort to prevent the territorial lord from appoint-
ing nonresident aliens to local offices, then grew into a
campaign to limit his choice to nominees proposed by the
community, and thence into the struggle to restrict the office itself to one of advice and counsel.[24] Even when the

[24] It is impossible to generalize accurately about the nature of this
process. As Peter Liver has observed, "each valley, each small region
of each valley, had its own peculiar course to follow in achieving
autonomy and independence: each began with different circumstances,
each underwent different experiences, each employed different means
in achieving their common goal." "Die Bündner Gemeinde," *Bündner
Monatsblatt*, January 1941, p. 3.
Individual portraits of the development in particular regions can

last vestige of feudal interference had disappeared, leaving civil jurisdiction entirely in the hands of the neighborhood jurisdictions, the contest had only just begun. The symbol and substance of real medieval power lay not in civil but in criminal (or "higher") jurisdiction. Before the neighborhoods could regard themselves as autonomous or the freeman conceive himself as self-governing, the power of the gallows had to be wrested from the territorial lords: "free autonomous jurisdiction, and above all in criminal cases, was the overriding objective of the common man in Raetia's late medieval valleys. . . ."[25]

Not until the sixteenth century, however, when the two Articles of Ilanz abolished all vestiges of feudal dependency and when the constitution of the new Republic of the Three Leagues guaranteed to the individual jurisdictional communes full control of civil and criminal affairs, were the political aspirations of the Raetian peasant fully realized. Unfortunately, by this time other more grave pressures from outside the land were putting into jeopardy the autonomy of the entire republic.

be found in the following: P. Badrutt, *Die Entstehung des Oberen Grauen Bundes* (Chur, 1916); G. C. Cloetta, *Bergün-Bravuogn*, 2d ed., (Thusis, 1964); G. Hofer-Wild, *Herrschaft und Hoheitsrechte der Sax in Misox* (Poschiavo, 1949); R. Hoppeler, "Beiträge zur Rechtsgeschichte der Talschaft Safien im Mittelalter," *Jahresbericht der Historisch-Antiquarischen Gesellschaft von Graubünden*, 1907; Peter Liver, "Alplandschaft und politische Selbstständigkeit," *Bündner Monatsblatt*, January 1942; Peter Liver, "Rechtsgeschichte der Landschaft Rheinwald," *66. Jahresbericht der Historisch-Antiquarischen Gesellschaft von Graubünden*, 1936; Georg Lütscher, *Geschichte der Gemeinde und Freiherrschaft Haldenstein* (Chur, 1962); E. Marthaler, "Untersuchungen zur Verfassungs- und Rechtsgeschichte der Grafschaft Vintschgau im Mittelalter," *Jahresbericht der Historisch-Antiquarischen Gesellschaft von Graubünden*, Part I 1940, Part II 1942; Peter C. Planta, Verfassungsgeschichte der Stadt Chur im Mittelalter," *8. Jahresbericht der Historisch-Antiquarischen Gesellschaft von Graubünden*, 1878; Peter Tuor, *Die Freien von Laax: Ein Beitrag zur Verfassungs- und Standesgeschichte* (Chur, 1903).

[25] Liver, *Von Feudalismus*, p. 62.

FEUDALISM AND FREEDOM

Just about one hundred years ago, as Engels was completing his study of Lewis Morgan's *Ancient Society* and Ferdinand Tönnies was cleaving the history of man into two polar segments called community and society, Henry Maine set forth a general theory for the development of institutions that has been influential into the present day:

> . . . from the moment when a tribal community settled down finally upon a definite space of land, the land begins to be the basis of society in place of kinship. The change is extremely gradual . . . but it has been going on through the whole course of history. We can trace the development of the idea both in large . . . states . . . and also in the smaller . . . village communities and manors among whom landed property took its rise.[26]

The history of Raetia in the medieval period can, as we have seen, easily be made to conform to the lines of this classical portrait. But if Raetia could avoid neither the structural transformations of feudalism nor the emergence of principles of property and territoriality that attended its decline (under a smokescreen called "the realization of feudalism"), it nevertheless manifested enough peculiarities in its passage from antiquity to modern independence to mark its political institutions and notions about freedom and democracy with a unique character, for territoriality never really entrenched itself in Raetia with the implacability it achieved elsewhere. Free men and free communities maintained themselves equally against the constitutions of the Carolingians and the more potent jurisdictional assaults of the local landlords who followed. In the fourteenth and fifteenth centuries, when autonomous village communities began to move together towards sovereign in-

[26] *Lectures on the Early History of Institutions* (London, 1875), pp. 72–73.

dependence for all of Upper Raetia, their spirit was more the product of attitudes and traditions that had *survived* intact through the Middle Ages than of innovations forged during the feudal epoch. "The origin of the Swiss nation," writes J. Christopher Herold in a passage especially appropriate to Graubünden, "is to be found not in the towns, where feudalism had been overcome, but in the alpine valleys where it had never taken root."[27]

The ancient roots of Raetia's political institutions are everywhere evident. That mountain peasants bore arms throughout the Middle Ages, when their brothers in the plain were at the mercy of fiefholders controlling armed professionals, was a consequence of traditional, perhaps even tribal practices that had survived into the Middle Ages rather than of attitudes reflecting a willed rebelliousness against feudal subjugation. Similarly, the economic prerogatives enjoyed by the Raetian peasant at the close of the Middle Ages were less newly acquired benefits of the defeat of feudalism than they were long-held common association usages preserved despite feudalism's apparent successes. That the institutions with which the mountain peasant emerged from the feudal epoch and which he used in securing the autonomy of his communities were survivals of an earlier period rather than reactive responses to feudalism had a profound impact on their defining ethos.

Louis Hartz has convincingly argued that the experiences a country does *not* endure, the elements in a background that are *missing* in its institutional history, may be no less vital to its character than the patent experiences it has undergone, than the factors that do constitute its past.[28]

[27] J. Christopher Herold, *The Swiss Without Halos* (New York, 1948), p. 22.

[28] See Louis Hartz, *The Liberal Tradition in America* (New York, 1955) and *The Founding of New Societies* (New York, 1964). Hartz's approach represents a major contribution to comparative methodology.

In Graubünden, the ethos of the village community and its democratic appendages was collectivistic to a degree that could hardly have been comprehended elsewhere in Europe—exactly because Graubünden, at least in a relative sense, had escaped the provocative oppressiveness of pervasive feudalism. The towns and commercial cities of Renaissance Italy and the Netherlands were struggling to *create* independent polities *within* a hegemonic society, to secure the emerging notion of personality in the midst of the hierarchies of preindividualist corporatism, where rank and status had for so long defined the man. Individuation, atomization, and alienation were characteristic processes through which men combatted and ultimately overcame feudalism. The subsequent history of European political institutions has taken the form of a permanent contest between liberated, atomized man and the vestigial imperial state, given a new lease on life by nationalism, bureaucracy, and technological progress. No history of the West (neither the constitutional histories of Gierke, McIlwain, and Strayer nor the political theories of Hobbes, Locke, and Hegel) has missed the centrality of this dualism to the Western political tradition. Representative government, natural rights, the theory of social contract and consent, freedom as the absence of external impediments on movement, power as a necessary evil, private rights as the final objective of public law—each of these characteristic foundations of our political thought and institutions finds its seeds in the birth of modern European man out of the feudal womb.

But in Raetia, no such birth ever occurred. The common association was an old man who lived through feudalism, rejuvenated to be sure by the war against feudal institutions to maintain itself, but not in any sense the child of those wars. Raetian man thus entered the modern era in command of a sovereign state untroubled by those self-conscious anxieties about political identity that preoccupied the post-Renaissance populations of awesome central mon-

135

archies. Never having been a prisoner of a hierarchical status structure, he could not now affect a liberated individuality. As a participant in local, self-governing institutions that had never been anything other than the direct agency of his collaborative community will, he could only view government as an extension of the interests he held in common with his fellow citizens. The dichotomic separation of the unit person and the hostile body politic was the product of an experience he simply had never had.

In forgoing the struggle for emancipation from feudalism, it is true that the free mountain peasant forfeited many of the benefits of mature individualism—albeit the presence among the traditional Romanic population of Germanic immigrants from western Switzerland did have a certain individuating effect on the tone of Raetian collectivism in a later period; for these immigrants, the so-called *Walser*, brought with them when they came at the end of the thirteenth century strongly, almost eccentrically individualistic attitudes and institutions.[29] But if he forfeited benefits, he

[29] The *Walser* first came to Raetia in 1277, settling in the Rheinwald valley on the northern side of the Splügen Pass. Another colony was founded at Davos in 1289. From these two districts their numbers and influence rapidly spread. Although the treaties facilitating their settlement specified that they were "completely free, having to treat with no one," their impact on Raetian institutions became more and more pronounced. *Walser* usages generally corresponded with the practices of the traditional common association, but their living habits (in isolated, individual cottages still distinguishable today by their wooden architecture), their pastoral economy (individually owned livestock, absence of communal grazing), and their political attitudes were highly individualistic. The presence of the *Walser* in Raetia constitutes a permanent caveat to generalizations drawn from the experience of the Romanic population and thus to the ones propounded here. See Erich Branger, *Rechtsgeschichte der freien Walser in der Ostschweiz* (Bern, 1905); Hans Kreis, *Die Walser: Ein Stück Siedlungsgeschichte der Zentralalpen*, 2d ed. (Bern, 1966); and Karl Meyer, "Über die Anfänge der Walserkolonien in Rätien," *Bündner Monatsblatt*, July-September 1925.

136

also avoided the dilemmas that have made freedom an enemy of the public interest and cast democracy as a potential Leviathan in so many Western political systems. If, despite the *Walser*, he never developed a vigorous tradition of rights, he also evaded up until recently the social pathologies of alienation. He had to forgo the efficiency of central government, but was also spared its voraciousness. Where others looked for ways to limit governments that often seemed no less threatening than the disorder they had been designed to overcome, he saw in his own government nothing more nefarious than an opportunity to enhance his collective autonomy and augment through participation his power over his own destiny. And where, in the larger states, democracy finally came to be seen as an ultimate popular check on governmental powers that were deemed both untrustworthy and irresistible, came to be seen in other words as a way to overcome politics, it remained in Graubünden a vehicle of the public will, a way into politics. The Raetian concept of freedom exhibited a certain immaturity to be sure, but as a result, freedom never came to be thought of as a commodity that might only be enjoyed in the loneliness of the private arena, that condemned men to a solitary sanctuary where only the alienated were considered free, where the most irrational behavior, so long as it was unimpeded by physical constraints or public coercion, had to be regarded as free, and where the most rational and moral behavior, if it conformed to the dictates of law and the public will, had to be deemed bondage.

If our subsequent analysis of Raetian freedom and democracy prove these generalizations to be founded, it will be in part then because Graubünden survived as a face-to-face society throughout the long struggle with feudalism, because it eluded the bondage of a corporatism that would one day release the rest of Europe to a lonely, anxious, competitive emancipation. In Hartz's terms, because Graubünden never knew the full weight of feudal bondage, it would never know the bittersweet, ultimately alienating spirit of individuality that can only be felt by the liberated.

This is not to say that Graubünden was a great primeval duck off whose unruffled feathers history flowed like water. If fundamental values retained their prefeudal flavor, attitudes and public behavior nonetheless underwent important changes. Unlike Hartz's America created in a vacuum and wholly insulated from Europe's feudal past, Graubünden confronted the feudal state from its earliest Carolingian beginnings. If feudalism never succeeded in putting down roots in the higher alpine regions where the common association was well entrenched, the struggle to prevent it from implanting itself, especially in its later and more virulent local manifestations, politicized the Raetian consciousness, and gave to its natural communities the vigorous self-awareness of a willed self-preservation. Freedom, though it remained tinged with collectivity and a sense of collaborative participation, could no longer survive as an unthought consequence of traditional social conventions and prepolitical institutions. To preserve it in the face of feudalism required not only a self-conscious act of will but also a consciousness of the meaning of autonomy that inevitably led to what social scientists today would probably call political mobilization.

Yet for all of this, confronting feudalism was very different from experiencing it, fighting against it very different from struggling to rise out of it. By heightening the mountain peasant's political self-awareness and catalyzing the politicization of his institutions, feudalism in fact created the conditions that permitted his traditional communitarian values to live on, to outlive feudalism itself by half a millennium.

The structure of institutions into which these values found their way constituted the political framework of the Republic of the Three Leagues, Raetia wearing the mantle of sovereign independence. However, before we can examine that structure in following up the point of view advanced here, we need to look at the very special problems that independence created for individual autonomy and participatory democracy, for the way in which Graubünden met, or did not meet, these problems was a major conditioning factor in the emergence of a mature notion of freedom in the Alps.

# CHAPTER VI

# Surviving Independence

AN important chapter in Switzerland's book of traditional wisdom is devoted to the presumed interdependence of freedom and sovereign independence. Independence is thought to be indispensable to freedom: hence, "territorial inviolability also means moral and spiritual independence."[1] Yet at the same time freedom is regarded as prerequisite to independence: thus, "the first line of our national defense is our domestic politics."[2] Appealing as this line of reasoning may seem in a land that has enjoyed both free institutions and independence for centuries, there is nothing self-evident about it. Padraig Pearse is said to have proclaimed: "I would rather be a prisoner in a free Ireland than a free man under alien rule," suggesting that independence may be a better friend of nationalism than of individual autonomy. In a more philosophical vein, Isaiah Berlin has contended that "the transference . . . of sovereignty from one set of hands to another does not increase liberty, but merely shifts the burden of slavery."[3]

In any case, the relationship cannot be simple, for the meaning of sovereign independence is itself a question that neither history nor theory has satisfactorily answered, especially in Raetia. When is an extravagantly decentralized confederal political system, incapable of national legislation or national defense, a sovereign state? And if it is not, how is it possible to speak of its independence? What, on the other

[1] Ernst Uhlmann, "Defense of the Nation and of Freedom," *Yearbook of the New Helvetic Society: 1963* (Bern, 1963), p. 91. The identification is even posited in Uhlmann's title.

[2] Gonzague de Reynold, *Selbstbesinnung der Schweiz* (Zürich, 1939), p. 3.

[3] Isaiah Berlin, *Two Concepts of Liberty* (Oxford, 1958), p. 48.

hand, constitutes decisive interference from the outside? Friends have often proved themselves a greater threat to independence than enemies, for the blandishments and briberies proffered by allies are far less resistible than the military ambitions of declared foes.

Raetia, as we have seen, emerged from the Middle Ages with a set of political institutions nurtured by ancient usages, conditioned by the mountains and transformed by the confrontation with feudalism. In the setting of national independence following the establishment of the Republic of the Three Leagues, these institutions reached maturity, along with the notions about freedom and participation that they had generated. By the end of the sixteenth century, Raetia found itself facing the kinds of questions that we have raised here, not as abstract philosophical queries but as a matter of survival. Its institutions were exposed to foreign subversion and potential physical extermination. Its freedoms were jeopardized by the imperial aspirations of its neighbors and by its own awkward attempt at colonization. The belief that neighborhood autonomy rested on political independence was put to a critical test that lasted almost three centuries.

## AN INDEPENDENT RAETIA: ORIGINS AND SIGNIFICANCE

We already have some grasp of how little the notion of sovereignty—as it emerged from the tangle of medieval jurisdiction—had in common with the later centralist tradition encapsulated by Bodin and Hobbes who identified it with indivisible legislative power, particularly in Graubünden where feudalism had never successfully implanted itself. Because dependence had meant subjugation to jurisdictions originating outside the neighborhood, compulsory labor service, payment of debilitating taxes, tariffs, and tithes—because, in short, dependence had been a function of loose and multiple ties, the bondage of which could only be indirectly felt, independence could only mean

141

jurisdictional and economic autonomy for the collective from the entire set of relationships associated with feudalism. The preservation of traditional communal practices, the securing of jurisdictional autonomy—these alone constituted the Raetian notion of independence. Territorial inviolability vis-à-vis the outside world, decisive legislative competence located in a recognized authority, central administration capable of executing the sovereign's will, all of those biases so appropriate to the monarchomachist experience of England and France fail to touch the situation of independent Raetia. Raetia's was not so much a country-wide struggle for *de jure* recognition by foreign powers as an internal battle fought by individual neighborhoods for autarky and jurisdictional autonomy from every interference, most of all from the integrative aspirations of local princes with visions of a splendid alpine kingship secured in its independence by a natural mountain fortress. Whereas for Bodin sovereignty could exist only as a function of central power, for the peasant of Graubünden it could flourish only in the absence of central power. The centralization that elsewhere was regarded as the prerequisite of independence was in Raetia the very force against which the struggle for local independence was waged.

An inscription to the village constitution of Avers, reflecting on the independence the community had achieved by 1622, strikingly depicts the manifold character of the Raetian notion of sovereignty:

We have by God's grace a lovely freedom;
We have the power to invest and to divest;
We have our own seal and staff, our own stocks and
    gallows;
We are indebted, praise God, neither to prince nor
    to Lord,
We owe nothing to anybody but God the Almighty.[4]

[4] Text cited in Georg Sprecher, *Die Bündner Gemeinde* (Chur, 1942), p. 3.

The power to appoint their own officials ("invest and divest"), full jurisdictional autonomy in criminal affairs ("stocks and gallows"), and independence from landed and other noble powers—these were the marks of the sovereign neighborhood.

The fragmentary and untypical character of the Raetian notion of sovereignty is further reflected in the piecemeal fashion in which it came to be acquired by the units which eventually comprised the Republic of the Three Leagues. Today, independence often means the promulgation of a new constitution and the substitution of a new flag for the Union Jack or the Tricolor; it can be accomplished in the time it takes to cry "Uhuru!" In Graubünden it was won only over centuries through a process by which village communities acting alone or in coalition were able to acquire by war, by litigation, by usurpation, by purchase, and by compromise. Each of these limited prerogatives in combination constituted medieval sovereignty. Thus, to take a single example, nearly one hundred years before Raetia was formally constituted as an independent republic, the free peasants of the ancient earldom of Laax bought from the declining Werdenberg family for three hundred gold ducats the few vestigial prerogatives still exercised by them. They acquired by this purchase the symbols and substance of what for them amounted to sovereign political autonomy.[5] However, this entailed neither economic autarky nor

[5] The original contract of sale was very broad; it reads, in part: "To the honorable, pious people, the freemen of the Forest of Flims, who are called the Freemen of Laax, and to their heirs and successors [go] our Earldom of and dominion over Laax in the Churraetian Bishopric—along with all jurisdictional prerogatives, stocks and gallows, water, fishing and hunting rights appurtenant thereto, as well as whatever bondsmen are attached to the land. . . ." Peter Tuor, *Die Freien von Laax: Ein Beitrag zur Verfassungs- und Standesgeschichte* (Chur, 1903), p. 87. The subsequent treaty between Laax and Bishop Johannes is given in Constantin Jecklin, ed., *Codex Diplomaticus*, vol. 5, p. 26. The current Emperor Sigismund ratified both the treaty

military independence. Within six years of emancipation, the free commune felt itself compelled by external threats to place itself under the protection of the bishop of Chur. Yet to say that protectorate status robbed the commune of control over its external security would hardly be accurate, for its military impotence had prevented it from ever acquiring sovereignty in the first place. It seemed more prudent to risk subordination in matters of common security to the same feudal powers from which autonomy had recently been won than to risk a completely indefensible independence.

Eventually, the growing body of autonomous communes found a more permanent solution to the problem of mutual security: the forging of multilateral military alliances. The threat to autonomy was clearly reduced when the parties to the alliance were uniformly democratic and shared the same long-range interest in regional autonomy. The growth of regional leagues in the fifteenth century can be interpreted primarily as a movement aimed at the preservation of those newly acquired communal prerogatives associated in the free peasant political consciousness with sovereignty.

Independence came to Raetia, then, as a paradox scattered over time and place, in bits and pieces, two steps forward and one step backward: the abolition of feudal overlordship followed by military alliance with the ex-lord; the achievement of jurisdictional autonomy guaranteed by confederal mutual protection, the effective operation of which required the surrender of certain jurisdictional prerogatives; and the extension of independence through collective mutualism. Independence through collaboration remained for the new democratic neighborhoods of Raetia the effective formula it had been for individuals within the early common associations.

In 1524 this process of confederal aggregation for survival

and the original agreement of sale in the very same year (1434), thus providing a guarantee of relative autonomy for the freemen of Laax within the protective framework of the bishopric.

culminated in a formal pact creating a federal republic out of the three leagues, which had served as independent protective associations throughout the fifteenth century. The constituent bodies were not the leagues themselves—what the Raetians understood as sovereignty had never been vested in them—but the "individual communes of the Three Leagues."[6] For the very first time, the new Republic of the Three Leagues represented a territorial entity capable of clearly identifying and defending specified frontiers, and may thus be regarded as independent in the more conventional sense. Nevertheless, it was not the conventional integrity of the territory of the new republic that most concerned the free communes, but rather their own safety and independence in the face of subversion from internal aggressors still trying to resurrect ancient feudal estates.

Consequently, the two so-called Articles of Ilanz of 1524 and 1526 were of much greater significance than the formal declaration of independence. The chief danger to internal autonomy continued to be the aspirations of the bishop of Chur, whose capacity to wreak havoc was being systematically augmented by Hapsburg Austria. The first set of articles met the danger head-on and divested the bishop of all but his clerical functions construed in the narrowest possible sense. The second abrogated his remaining jurisdictional prerogatives and placed firm limits on other vestigial feudal obligations that might prove injurious to communal autonomy.[7] To the free peasant, this quashing of an ecclesiastical overlordship that for centuries had waged war on his communal independence was a far more telling victory

[6] The phrase was used in the original text in Jecklin, ed., *Codex*, vol. 5, p. 83. The historical circumstances of the pact are given above, in Part I.

[7] Texts in Jecklin, ed., *Codex*, vol. 5, p. 78ff. and p. 89ff. The two sets of articles are elaborated in detail by William Plattner, *Die Entstehung des Freistaates der Drei Bünde und sein Verhältnis zur alten Eidgenossenschaft* (Davos, 1895), p. 248f.

than the contriving of a confederal political structure exhibiting the conventional properties of sovereignty.

Not that the victory was complete: the Articles of Ilanz were only an "extension of tendencies which for more than a century had dominated the constitutional development of Graubünden," and hence need to be thought of as an episode in an on-going process of political development.[8] The bishopric had been deprived of its secular powers, but not of its natural power. It continued to enjoy ecclesiastical immunity from the republic's secular jurisdiction, it retained extensive holdings in land throughout the League of the House of God (e.g., in the Schanfigg valley, where it held estates and the prerogatives that attended proprietorship well into the seventeenth century), and it nourished a growing intimacy with foreign powers for whom the Catholic church had become an instrument in a policy of territorial aggrandizement. The Articles of Ilanz were thus followed by further compulsory treaties aimed at the complete political dispossession of the church. In 1541 the cathedral chapter (*Domkapitel*) of the bishopric, a body within the church but competitive with the bishop's court, persuaded the communes of the secular League of the House of God (*Gotteshausbund*) to join it in curtailing still further the activities of the bishop. The incumbent was compelled to sign what became known as the Six Articles, which restricted the episcopal seat to natives of Graubünden and placed the bishop's activities under the general purview of both the cathedral chapter and the league.[9] These measures still did not provide adequate protection against the dangers of clerical subversion by the bishop on behalf of un-

---

[8] Peter Liver, *Von Feudalismus zur Demokratie in Graubündnerischen Hinterrheintälern* (Chur, 1929), p. 106.

[9] The text is given in Jecklin, ed., *Codex*, vol. 5, p. 99. A full account of the relationship between the bishopric and the republic is given in J. Danuser, *Die staatlichen Hoheitsrechte des Kantons Graubünden gegenüber dem Bistum Chur* (Zurich, 1897).

friendly outside powers. During the Time of Troubles (in the period of the Thirty Years' War), treaties were forced on Raetia by Spain and Austria rescinding the Six Articles, once again opening the way to appointment of a foreigner in the Hapsburgs' service to the bishopric. As recently as the eighteenth century, Austria continued to exercise a decisive influence (through its Imperial Electoral Commission) over the Churraetian appointment; indeed, its success led it to treat the bishopric as an imperial enclave immune to every secular jurisdiction of the Raetian Republic.

If the Articles of Ilanz failed to interdict completely foreign manipulation of the bishopric, they also were unable to terminate the rights of foreigners to enjoyment of prerogatives over Raetian territories that they owned by legitimate prior contracts. For example, Austria, despite its hostile posture in the Swabian War and again in the Time of Troubles, exercised certain legitimate prerogatives (including the collection of some taxes) in the League of the Ten Jurisdictions (*Zehngerichtenbund*) for a century after this League had been integrated into the "independent" Republic of the Three Leagues. Not until 1652 after Austria made a flagrant attempt to annex the entire League in the name of its traditional rights did the Ten Jurisdictions manage to purchase their complete independence—and then only through an unusual confluence of events that made Zürich and Bern willing to pay the outrageous ransom demanded by Austria.[10]

---

[10] In 1622, during the Time of Troubles, the League of Ten Jurisdictions had been compelled to accept the Treaty of Lindau that "ripped from it eight of its ten jurisdictions. Though no one spoke of the terminal dismemberment of the League, what else could it mean when four-fifths of its territory was removed from the Republic's jurisdiction and turned over to Austria? Not only were the old freedoms and rights abrogated, the original constitution of the League was seized and deposited in Innsbruck." P. Gillardon, *Geschichte des Zehngerichtenbunds* (Davos, 1936), p. 169. Regaining full independence for the League of Ten Jurisdictions thus became vital to the survival

Independence, then, had a diverse and fragmentary meaning for Raetia. It meant neither integral sovereignty at the central level of the confederal government nor personal independence for the individual neighborhood resident. It required only the autonomy of neighborhood communities to determine their own collective destinies. As in the old Helvetic Confederation, where "the freedom for which the cantons had fought was their communal independence, not the freedom of the individual in the state or from the state,"[11] the freedom sought by the Raetian free peasant was simply the continuation of that participatory mutualism he had known since the seventh century. The autonomy of the local group was paramount. The status of the federal system or the individual personality was secondary.

In one of those characteristic historical ironies, however, it was not foreign interference that most endangered democratic communalism and neighborhood independence, but rather Raetian interference in the outside world. Autonomy can better resist foreign conquerors than successful conquest. Its future in the Republic of the Three Leagues was increasingly jeopardized by the republic's acquisition of subject territories and its subsequent involvement in the affairs of the major European powers.

## THE COSTS OF INTERNATIONAL INVOLVEMENT: THE TELLINA VALLEY EMPIRETTE

We have already suggested the degree to which Raetia's geographical centrality and the attractiveness of its moun-

---

of the republic as a whole. A full account of the relationship of the eight implicated jurisdictions with Austria is given in Ernst Kind, *Über Das Verhältnis der 8 Gerichte zu Österreich* (Weide i. Thür., 1925).

[11] E. Bonjour, H. S. Offler, and G. R. Potter, *A Short History of Switzerland* (Oxford, 1955), p. 103.

tain passes would involve it in European affairs. Not even Helvetia was as crucial to the commercial and military life of the great European powers as was Raetia. Although the Gotthard pass was the most convenient route from the Rhineland to Italy, the French could reach Lombardy and the Mediterranean by more direct routes, while the Germans and Austrians could utilize a number of passes to the east. Graubünden's frontiers, on the other hand, spread south from the Rhine to the borders of the Venetian Republic, and as the north Italian plain became the primary theater of the French-Austrian confrontation that was to dominate European politics from the fifteenth century to the Napoleonic era, Raetia's passes thus became more and more critical.

Initially, there were important advantages in Graubünden's political involvements, particularly for those individual neighborhoods and communes fortunate enough to lie directly on major traffic arteries. Even prior to confederal union, a group of ten so-called ports of entry (*Porten*) had been established on the two major trade routes through Raetia into Italy, providing packing, loading, and transportation services to tradesmen and commercial travelers. Despite the half-dozen or more interruptions in a single journey from the Lake of Constance on the German border to Chiavenna on the Italian border that were caused by the change of jurisdiction from one port to the next (for unloading, valuation, reloading, change of guides and mules, and so forth), most merchants gladly paid the tolls in return for scheduled delivery, and security from bandits and other alpine hazards.[12]

---

[12] The two major commercial arteries were the *Unterstrasse* leading into the *Walser*-settled Rheinwald and thence over the Splügen pass to Chiavenna, and the *Oberstrasse* leading from Chur up and over the heath of Lenz into the Oberhalbstein and thence up over the Septimer or Julier/Maloja pass systems into the Bergell valley. There

149

The communes involved in this lucrative trade reaped not only pecuniary rewards but also the less concrete benefits of contact with an outside world that was eventually to impinge on their domestic tranquillity. They were becoming well acquainted with putative friends who might one day be declared enemies. Like the peasants of Uri at the base of the Gotthard pass, the portsmen of Raetia were also "remarkably well equipped to learn of the political changes in the outside world, to ponder their significance, and to take advantage of them in their actions. Since . . . there congregated on their mountain roads and in their inns and resthouses more travellers, and from a wider range of different countries, than could be found in most cities in the plains . . . , they heard of all the wars and uprisings, of the marriages and inheritances of princes, of the shifts in trade and prosperity among the towns, of the arguments of the theologians and sects, and of the changing fortunes of the struggle between emperor and pope."[13]

---

were six ports on the Underroad including Boden, Thusis, Schams, Rheinwald and Misox. Campodolcino in the St. Jakobstal was initially a Raetian port, but passed immediately into Austrian hands. The Overroad included four ports at Lenz, Tinzen, Stalla, and Bergell.

While the disproportionate number of ports did spread the emoluments around, it also disadvantaged the competitive posture of the Raetian port system. The Splügen pass journey on the Overroad took only twenty hours, against twenty-three for the Gotthard pass. But the constant need to reload and the general disorder occasioned by the decentralization of the system made the Gotthard more attractive to many tradesmen. Despite its difficulties, the system survived well into the nineteenth century. For a full account, see Rudolf Jenny, "Graubündens Passtransit und seine volkswirtschaftliche Bedeutung," *Bündner Monatsblatt*, September-October 1954; Johannes A. von Sprecher, "Über die bündnerischen Portenrechte," *Bündner Monatsblatt*, October-December 1898; H. Pfister, *Das Transportwesen der internationalen Handelswege von Graubünden im Mittelalter und in der Neuzeit* (Chur, 1913); and R. A. Ganzoni, *Rechtsgeschichte der Fuhrleute* (Chur, 1897).

[13] Karl Deutsch and Hermann Weilenmann, unpublished manuscript "United for Diversity," Chapter 8, pp. 13–14. Unfortunately, Weilen-

The information thus garnered could be put to good use when the trade routes that brought Graubünden commercial traffic also drew the unsolicited political attentions of powers aspiring to control both the passes of Raetia and the valleys leading in and out of the pass regions. These attentions eventually propelled Graubünden forward into a quest for security that issued in the acquisition of an unlikely and minuscule empire, a veritable empirette. To defend its passes, Raetia needed to control their southern outlets, the Poschiavo, Müstair, Bergell and St. Jakob valleys leading into Italy. This suggested in turn the need to control the wide Italian river basin into which these valleys issued—the Tellina valley with its capital at Sondrio. Consequently, when in 1512 the opportunity arose to seize the Tellina valley along with the two small counties of Bormio and Chiavenna on its eastern and western borders, the Raetians did not hesitate to imitate their enemies. Unfortunately, they had neither the resources nor the military capabilities to make good on their rashness. Rather than enhancing their defenses, expansion merely increased the area requiring defense and ultimately diminished them. Rather than deterring aggression, the new holdings virtually guaranteed it. Raetia had now constituted itself as a solid wedge from the Gotthard massif to the Venetian plain; it was no longer merely an attractive route of passage, it was unavoidable. As if the Tellina valley were not already trouble enough, Austria, cut off from its Milanese and Spanish allies, was provoked into permanent and active enmity.

Offhand, the acquisition by a small, infertile mountain republic of an adjacent colony as large in area and population and infinitely more fecund than itself might seem to be a stroke of unmitigated good fortune. In reality, it became for Graubünden a "source of permanent decay and

---

mann's death may impede publication of this major study of Switzerland.

unspeakable misery."[14] Colonial rule not only brought structural corruption to the Tellina valley but also increasingly undermined participatory democracy in Raetia. As with Athens and Rome, Graubünden moved into the cynical arena of colonial politics at the cost of stable, popular government at home, confirming again that colonialism even in its least invidious form enslaves the master as well as the subject. "One thinks himself the master of others," writes Rousseau, "and still remains a greater slave than they."[15] The corruption that began in Valtellina was a contagion that recognized no borders: the afflicters soon became indistinguishable from the afflicted.

Initially, exploitation took simple forms, appropriate, it might be said, to the peasant mentality. The executive and judicial offices which comprised the colonial administration were officially put up for sale to the highest bidder who, in reward for his generosity, was permitted to carry out his duties in any manner he chose. Most nominees naturally regarded the redressing of the pecuniary deficit incurred in procuring their jobs as their chief responsibility; no stone was left unturned in their devoted pursuit of this goal. The local population was heavily taxed, judicial pardons and decisions in civil cases were sold on the open market, and funds intended for the mother country were embezzled at will. Corruption was limited only by the confines of the officeholders' imagination. A governor in the town of Tirano had his cohorts "lose" their swords, so that local residents unlucky enough to find them could be fined for possessing unlicensed weapons or for the nonreturn of lost property. Other officials had women seduced and then blackmailed. One judge, displaying as much audacity as ingenuity, passed

---

[14] Friedrich Pieth, "Der Freistaat der Drei Bünde und seine Aufnahme in die Eidgenossenschaft," *Bündner Monatsblatt*, August 1941, p. 239.

[15] *Social Contract*, ed. G. D. H. Cole (London, 1913), Book I, Chapter 1.

an arbitrary sentence of death on anyone who appeared before him, for whatever reason. It is a tribute to the catalyzing effect of fear on human generosity that this particular official amassed in fifteen months a fortune surpassing that of his most imaginative colleagues.[16]

That the symbol of sovereignty (the gallows) so recently acquired by the communes of Graubünden had degenerated into an instrument of brute extortion in the provinces was an irony that did not pass unnoticed by the Raetian freeman. But what was to be done? The disease that began in the colonies soon infected the home communes. The sale of colonial offices provoked a spirit of greed, intrigue, and factionalization that did not permit the individual either to ponder the costs of colonialism or to give himself over to guilt. While the people of the Tellina valley resorted to futile bloodbaths to rid themselves of the "Raetian oppressors" (how peculiar the phrase seems!)[17] the village communard in Graubünden was contriving ways to subjugate domestic institutions to a growing avarice that colonial conquest had titillated rather than satiated. In time, it became possible to buy not simply distant colonial offices but

[16] Graubünden's relationship with the Tellina valley has been rued by almost everyone who has written about it: the eighteenth-century German historian H. L. Lehmann, for example, gave this exhortatory counsel: "O dearest Bündner People! If you only decided no longer to sell your offices, but to confer them on worthy men, your subjects in the Tellina valley would be the happiest people on earth—they would build altars to your name, and fame would spread your worthy reputation over the whole earth." *Die Republik Graubünden* (Magdeburg, 1797), p. 239. The circumstances of Raetia's untowards suzerainty over the valley are given in some detail by Johannes A. von Sprecher, "Zustand der Bevölkerung des Veltlins zur Zeit der bündnerischen Herrschaft," *Bündner Monatsblatt*, January-March 1860; and Alfred Rufer, *Der Freistaat der III Bünde und die Frage des Veltlins*, 2 vols. (Basel, 1916).

[17] The best-known of these blood-baths occurred in 1620 under circumstances described above in Chapter III. See also Friedrich Pieth, *Bündnergeschichte* (Chur, 1945), pp. 202–204.

home village mayoralties and seats in Raetia's confederal assembly—to buy them in public forums, often years before the negotiated term of office was to commence. There was still further irony in Graubünden's predicament, for the pervasiveness of corruption in the Tellina valley was in no small part due to the direct democratic mutualism of Raetia's own institutions. If, as H. D. Lloyd has asserted, "empire abroad is wedded to aristocracy at home,"[18] and if empire necessarily corrupts democracy, it is also true that democracy at home subverts empire abroad, that democratic institutions tend toward the corruption of empire. A more aristocratic government appreciating the importance of prudent expertise in colonial administration, a more centralist, despotic government understanding Montesquieu's formula for the relationship between the extent of an empire and the power of the ruling regime might have been less vulnerable to corruption and maladministration.[19] In Raetia's innocent democracy where the people and the government were hardly to be distinguished and where public offices were literally constituted by, of, and for the people, the corruption and abuse of power seemed almost unavoidable.[20] Participatory government had obviated the need for checks on public power. In a pure democracy, where power was in the integral, unseparated hands of autonomous collectivities, there could in fact be no check on the public will. Thus, when publicly purchased offices, the powers of which were exercised over a distance, were subjected to systematic abuse, corrective mechanisms simply were not available. A people unaccustomed to distrusting

[18] *The Swiss Democracy* (London, 1902), p. 16.

[19] *The Spirit of the Laws*, trans. Thomas Nugent (New York, 1949), Book VIII, Chapter 19.

[20] Johannes A. von Sprecher has remarked that "Republics are seldom wise masters: the more democratic the constitution, the greater the danger of misrule . . ." *Kulturgeschichte der Drei Bünde*, ed. Rudolf Jenny (Chur, 1951), p. 496.

government and to placing ongoing limits on the scope of its activities, because they have always identified themselves with government and thus have not developed that alienated cynicism so characteristic of the Anglo-American political outlook, are not likely to be very sensitive to the need for objectivity, impartiality, and restraints in government. Yet without these, there was no way for the Raetian freeman to curb the abuses which he recognized were destroying his capacity for self-government.[21] The country's empirette, then, acted to enhance the weaknesses that were built into its traditional collectivist institutions. And although colonialism was not solely responsible for the corrosion of Raetian democracy, it did catalyze a disintegrative process that might not otherwise have taken place.

For the contemporary individual, this debate was academic. He was caught on the horns of an unsavory dilemma that required him either to forgo an empire and risk destruction of his independence from without or to accept colonial responsibilities and expose his democratic autonomy to still graver dangers from within. In choosing the latter course, he was not unaware of the perils he invited: he simply did not know how to evade them. Salvation was not to be had at any price. His real error lay not in the choice he made but in the presuppositions with which he made it, for he had assumed that his external security depended on his control of the Tellina valley and that this dependence justified taking very grave risks. In truth, what he risked he risked in vain. His assumptions were illfounded in theory and refuted by the subsequent history

[21] Periodic attempts at reform were made, but they displayed more good intentions than good consequences—in the main because mechanisms by which they could be enforced in the individual communes were wholly absent. They included such treatises as the *Kesselbrief* of 1570, and the *Dreisieglerbrief* of 1574, along with the futile Reform Acts of 1603, 1684, 1694, and 1794. The failure of the last act robbed the new Swiss Confederation, which was to emerge within a decade, of an early Italian canton.

of his institutions. The Tellina valley brought him neither security nor tranquillity. It not only catalyzed the corruption of his communal democracy but also jeopardized the very independence he had hoped it would secure. In the end this empirette brought him trouble on a scale that completely overshadowed his precolonial difficulties: ultimately it involved him in a sequence of international events that cost him not shades or the semblance of his country's fragile independence, but its very substance.

## Costs of International Involvement: Entangling Alliances

In conducting a foreign policy appropriate to the preservation of collective independence and the maintenance of internal liberty, there were in theory a number of options open to the Republic of the Three Leagues including: complete neutrality (on the model of the Swiss Confederation); permanent alliance with a suitable neighboring power; full integration into the Swiss Confederation (more at the cost of its external sovereignty than of its internal independence); or a flexible pragmatism that would permit a policy of shifting alliances based on a realistic appraisal of its shifting interests. Unhappily, in practice the very forces that catapulted Graubünden into international affairs acted to restrict its freedom of choice. Ideally, the republic might have opted for neutrality in the hope of obtaining the kind of security it had afforded Switzerland.[22] But Raetia's implication in Italian affairs by virtue of its status in the Tellina valley, and the absence of a potent guarantor for neutrality (playing the role France played vis-à-vis Switzerland) placed

[22] On the other hand, Switzerland's famed neutrality leaned heavily on the patronage and support of France. Its laxness is evident in this observation by Edgar Bonjour: "In the eyes of the Swiss, the neutral posture was quite consonant with the passage of foreign troops, the selling of mercenary services to warring states, and the supplying of provisions to alien armies. . . ." *Werden und Wesen der schweizerischen Demokratie* (Basel, 1939), p. 34.

too many obstacles in the way of this policy. The achievement of neutrality by indirection, through incorporation into the Swiss Confederation, seemed more feasible, but it too was precluded; confessional differences within the confederation and the perpetual indecisiveness that characterized relations between the two regions combined to defeat an integration that would eventually be imposed on the country by Napoleon.[23] A permanent alliance modeled on Switzerland's concord with France never was possible for Graubünden, because the only logical partner in such an alliance—Hapsburg Austria—was intent not on partnership but total mastery. Finally, to play the game of realpolitik as a small country required an advantage such as insularity or sea power that the Raetian Republic simply did not possess.

The country found itself in the impossible position of being compelled to play a major role in international affairs without having the power to effect and enforce rational decisions about its own foreign policy. The outcome was a succession of uncertain policies made more for than by Graubünden. Each of the four options noted was resorted to at one time or another, but almost always out of necessity or desperation, rarely as a consequence of prudent deliberation or skillful maneuver. Raetia simply did not have the opportunity to be opportunistic.

The diplomatic history of Graubünden from the fifteenth to the eighteenth century thus reads like the Book of Job. Following its common victory with Switzerland over Austria in the Swabian War of 1499, Raetia moved toward a policy of permanent confederation with its Helvetian allies,

[23] It is difficult to understand how so many non-swiss commentators persist in regarding Raetia as an integral part, or even a permanent ally, of the Helvetian Confederation. No less authoritative sources than W. R. Shepherd's *Historical Atlas*, 5th ed. (New York, 1926) and *Meyer's Historischer Handatlas* (Leipzig, 1911) have fallen into this error. For a correct account of relations between Helvetia and Raetia see Plattner, *Die Entstehung* and Pieth, "Der Freistaat."

only to be thwarted by the Reformation which split Switzerland into warring camps, the confessional differences of which would not be permanently resolved until the Civil War of 1847 and which left the seven Catholic cantons implacably opposed to the admission of predominantly Protestant Graubünden into the confederation. On the heels of this disappointment, like the vulnerable rejected lover in a broken romance, Graubünden quickly found itself the dependent creature of an alliance with Austria. The entente, fashioned by and for Hapsburg interests, afforded the republic none of the protection associated with permanent alliance, but subjected it to all of the individual indignities and collective lesions of an unequal marriage. Its Austrian protector nearly involved it in the costly War of Spanish Succession, and by exposing it to humiliation by Napoleon's armies contributed directly to its final loss of independence.

Eventually Graubünden came to recognize that Austria, in the fashion of today's superpowers, perceived in the alliance only a license for military intervention; in seeking succor elsewhere, the little republic experimented with a secretive pragmatism, encouraging overtures from one of its adversaries, while accepting the covert blandishments of another. But the free peasants of Raetia were novices in a world of cynical experts, and though a certain measure of success was achieved by the remarkable pastor Georg Jenatsch during the Thirty Years' War, most of Raetia's excursions into balance-of-power diplomacy tipped the scales still further in favor of the republic's enemies.

None of these policies effectively secured Graubünden from external intervention by manipulative neighbors into its internal affairs. If explicit coercion was employed against the republic only periodically, troop passage was often compelled, trade privileges were extorted, elections were tampered with, and factional divisiveness was fomented. These subtler forms of intrusion may have ultimately been more compromising to the individual freeman's sense of autonomy than the more explicit threat to national independence represented by military occupation. As we have already noted, the arena of freedom for the individual in Graubünden was the village community. At the level of the neighborhood, intervention by nonovert aggression was more keenly felt than invasion; moreover, by its very nature it jeopardized directly the commune's traditional participatory institutions. The constitution (the Act of Federation) had in any case placed foreign policy directly in the hands of the semisovereign communes rather than in the weak federal executive, which meant that foreign manipulation had to be centered on the autonomous localities. Indeed, the diffusion of power was an open invitation to foreign lobbyists to involve themselves in matters that ought to have been none of their concern. Each individual commune became the object of lavish attention, being subjected equally to the oral blandishments of silver-tongued "ambassadors" who traded in extravagant promises, and the pecuniary endearments of silver-coffered agents who specialized, on a no less extravagant scale, in the invidious art of bribery. When sentiment favorable to a given policy could not be bought outright, foreign powers did not hesitate to establish and support political factions that might act as communal advocates for their cause. This injected into local politics an element of divisiveness and party spirit which exacerbated precisely those centrifugal tensions the decentralized political system had been developed to overcome. Having survived feudalism and war, the politics of commonality was now endangered at its source. As party divisions aligned themselves with more basic religious cleavages, the rare spirit of parity that had informed relations between the two confessions was subjected to ever greater strains. The result for the individual commoner must have been the subordination of his common interests as a mountain freeman seeking a mutual basis on which to build an individual life to the risk-laden temptations of a more worldly success: gold instead of cheese, power in place of tranquillity, prestige in lieu of self-sufficiency. On his mind was not the question of how to maintain the integrity of the neighborhood but how to manipulate the Austrian agent who was manipulating him into giving him a sum sufficient to buy that lucrative sinecure in the Tellina valley; not whether to represent his commune in the Federal Assembly, but whether to sell his services and the Assembly to Spain or to Austria. The honest but subversive encroachments of feudalism had provoked only his stolid resistance: the glint of gold unmanned him. "The last and final instrument of politics was war," Peter Liver has observed about the Time of Troubles in Graubünden, "but the next to last was money."[24] If war is politics carried on by other means, in Raetia bribery was war carried on by other means. Certainly it subverted the autonomy of the communes and the self-sufficiency of the freeman more completely than war ever did. The damage done to the republic by the successive armies of occupation during the Thirty Years' War was negligible compared to the twenty years of mayhem and rapine occasioned by the fratricidal struggles of indigenous political factions obdurately, blindly serving the interests of their country's adversaries.

Raetia's tempestuous and finally unsuccessful pursuit of national indepedence precipitates the critical question of whether sovereignty can have very much meaning in a world of radical inequality among states. Bénes of Czechoslovakia is said to have commented following the Munich Treaty, in what must have been the understatement of the century, "I found out that the big states and nations do not at this time consider the small nations as equals." A simple enough lesson, but one which the smaller nations never quite acquire the cynicism to learn. By 1916 Carl Spitteler, the poet laureate of Switzerland, was able to say to his fellow

---

[24] Peter Liver, "Die staatliche Entwicklung im alten Graubünden," *Zeitschrift für Schweizerische Geschichte*, vol. 13, no. 1, 1933, p. 239.

Swiss: "Every state steals just as much as it can, period. With digestive pauses and momentary lapses men call 'peace.' "[25] Raetian freemen did not seem ever to acquiesce in this realism. Some will deny that they ever possessed anything like real independence. Yet men forged political careers pursuing it and sacrificed their lives defending it.

The dilemma that complicated their task was not so much the power of their enemies as the limitations of their democracy. The parochialism, the limited population and territory, the devotion to locality upon which direct democracy and freedom of participation depended were highly unfavorable to the development of a strong system of national defense. Conversely, the attempt to develop street fighting skills appropriate to the brawling theater of European politics could only undermine participatory democracy (witness the consequences of Graubünden's acquisition of the Tellina valley). Jacob Burckhardt has suggested that the autonomous institutions and democratic spirit of the small nation constitute a species of countervailing power: "The small state exists so that somewhere in the world there can be a point where the greatest possible number of nationals are citizens in the full sense. . . . The small state has absolutely nothing except its real, concrete freedom with which it can fully counterbalance the powerful advantages—the power itself—of the large state."[26] But freedom cannot oppose power, for it exists in the institutional setting only in power's absence. At the level of states, only power can resist power. Yet, as we have noted, the growth of power subverts the maintenance of democracy. Switzerland, the object of Burckhardt's deceptive flattery here, survived as an independent nation neither because of its internal freedom nor even because of its vaunted neutrality. It survived because of its inordinately potent mili-

[25] Carl Spitteler, "Unser Schweizer Standpunkt," *Neue Zürcher Zeitung*, December 16–17, 1914.
[26] Cited by Bonjour, *Werden und Wesen*, p. 32.

161

tary capabilities, Europe's tolerant sense of expediency that regarded nonalliance as an acceptable price to pay for non-enmity, and above all because behind Switzerland stood France. Far from defending its independence with its freedom, Switzerland effectively sold its independence to France to buy its freedom at home. Graubünden spent nearly three hundred painful years attempting to maintain both, and in the end secured neither. Only when it sacrificed entirely the vestiges of its sovereign independence to enter under duress the new Swiss Federation did it finally win for its weary democracy a respite from the ambitions of aggressive neighbors. Whether the rest was worth the ransom of surrender was the question that tormented the freemen of Raetia as they faced the inexorable destiny imposed upon them by Napoleon.

## THE LOSS OF INDEPENDENCE AND THE IMPACT OF DEPENDENCY

The prospect of losing their independence filled the Raetians with consternation and alarm. The compromises that they were forced to endure over the centuries had nevertheless left them unprepared to surrender the sovereign forms of their independence. Yet at the critical moment, the legacy of party fractiousness that had for so long impaired the country's democratic vitality proved too powerful to allow an eleventh hour rescue attempt to succeed. Similarly, the heritage of Graubünden's corrosive maladministration in the Tellina valley extirpated there what little influence the Raetians might have brought to bear in preserving their Italian colonies from the republican pretensions of Napoleon's revolutionary armies. Napoleon appropriated only the symbols of independence; the substance had been slipping away for centuries, as the First Consul was quick to grasp: "Graubünden was once a power in Europe," he observed, "but its independence was forever troubled by the influence of the outside world and by party factions working from within." Raetia's aspirations of autonomy would be better served, he concluded, by federation than by independence. "In the union with Switzerland, Graubünden will discover security for its freedom and a guarantee for its domestic tranquillity and right order."[27]

Napoleon, with characteristic succinctness, had posed what for the people of Graubünden was a burning controversy: would the surrender of independence, by enhancing security, also augment autonomy? Or would it, by compromising collective self-government, injure freedom irreparably? Reflecting Graubünden's extraordinary predilection for divisiveness, two contumacious parties quickly arraigned themselves around the issue. The ill named patriot party fought adamantly for union with Switzerland, and was preoccupied mainly with security as a prerequisite of autonomy and willing to turn over an illusory sovereignty to obtain it. For Raetia the fact that the most probable alternatives to union were an Austrian protectorate or the ignominy of following its own former Italian subjects into the newly forged Cisalpine republic gave the patriot cause an added momentum. The party's philosophical strength derived, however, from Enlightenment attitudes contemptuous, even fearful, of direct democracy, but supportive of individual rights. Conditioned by the libertarian benevolence of selected Enlightenment monarchs, these attitudes carried with them the conviction that pacific foreign relations and extensive state tolerance were at the root of freedom, while self-government and collective autonomy did little or nothing (or worse) for it. Enlightenment figures

---

[27] Napoleon is here quoted approvingly by Jakob Ulrich von Sprecher in his inaugural address as president of the first grand council of the canton of Graubünden in 1803. The text's authenticity obviously cannot be verified, although the same version of the speech is given in the edited manuscript that appears as "Eröffnungsrede," *Bündner Monatsblatt*, May 1903, p. 113.

like the German historian Heinrich Zschokke thus committed themselves devotedly to the patriot cause, imploring the Raetians "not to forsake the brave Swiss," and rebuking them with the avuncular remonstration "Graubünden cannot long exist for and by itself!"[28]

The opponents of union were a more varied lot and included interested advocates of the Austrian cause who came to be known as the Austrian party. Those not in the shadow of Austria pursued more interesting and telling arguments. Their thinking appeared to draw its sustaining vigor from the ancient collective traditions of the common association, to be steeped in communalist beliefs about the interdependence of self-sufficiency, active political participation, and personal freedom. Novel Enlightenment shibboleths promulgating the marriage of unitary statism and individual freedom were not to be trusted. It almost seemed, though no Bündner ever made this claim, that opposition to union with Switzerland was one more episode in the long struggle to preserve a unique collectivism against the encroachments of European political development. The liberal contention that a strong, centralized state could alone secure freedom was too much like the earlier feudal claim that a hierarchically structured corporate state could alone secure social concord. Both represented rationalizations for the imposition of alien power on uniquely self-governing neighborhoods, both claimed to serve the people they would assimilate, neither could comprehend the real character of the face-to-face community. No opponent of union pretended that the republic's formal status as a sovereign state had not been frequently and profoundly compromised; it remained a vital expression of the Raetian people's will to self-government, not necessarily at the level of the republic where loyalty was weak, but at the level of the neighbor-

---

[28] Heinrich Zschokke, *Notwendiger und letzer Zuruf an biedere nachdenkende Vaterlandsfreude* (Chur, 1798), title page, p. 4. See also Zschokke, *Selbstschau* (n.p., 1842), pp. 112–113ff.

164

hood. Indeed, it is possible to think that the compromises foisted so often on the republic at the expense of the federal executive's credibility actually enhanced the potency of the individual communes. Self-sufficiency not only started in the village but also ended there. And village interests were not necessarily injured by the indignities suffered by the republic as a whole.

Even corruption, corrosive as it had been at the local level, was a tribute to the autonomy of the neighborhood: no one could prevent the autonomous village from liquidating the institutions that defined it. Withal, there were multiple aggressors at the Raetian doorstep; infiltrators and traitors sometimes found their way into the parlor; but the inner sanctum retained an inviolable potency, so long as the neighborhood remained the key to the citizen's political activity and the country's sovereign aspirations.

The patriot party's most prudent recourse, in countering these traditionalist attitudes, was to the Raetian Republic's own dismal history. Whatever the merits of an abstract potency, Graubünden's *physical* inner sanctum had again and again been overrun from without or betrayed from within. When the republic was occupied, a great many of its "autonomous" communes were occupied, rations were expropriated, troops were quartered, orders were given—all in a manner that must have offended the individual freeman directly and expressly. The vaunted autonomy of the neighborhood seemed more often the exception than the rule. When independence was not being mocked by Austrian gold, it was being subverted by colonial ambition; when it was not being perverted to the uses of hostile foreigners, it was being perverted to the intrigues of scheming domestic parties. Nor was there the slightest evidence that sovereign independence, if it was anything more than a convenient fiction, had affected these unpleasant realities at all.

At this point, however, it would appear that the patriots

165

were arguing not so much for national freedom as for national security. Their anxieties betrayed an unwillingness to endure any longer the hardships of liberty, and their attitudes, rhetoric notwithstanding, did little more than rationalize a patent yearning for emancipation from the frustrations and vicissitudes of self-government. The president of the new Grand Council (*Grosser Rat*) of the yearling canton of Graubünden conceded in 1803 without a trace of sentiment that the Bündner "Fatherland no longer stands in the ranks of the independent states. But neither will foreign gold and foreign influence ever again arm brother against brother; and in a land that nature created for the domestic well-being of its inhabitants, never again will party factions persecute and destroy one another."[29] Independence, he seems to say, is gone; and the future of liberty is uncertain. But domestic tranquillity and relief from the insatiable ambitions of covetous neighbors and avaricious fellow citizens have been secured, and for these blessings the price has not been too high.

## THE AFTERMATH

Determining the price of federation was to take a century and a half; indeed, the calculations are not yet complete. The patriots won their battle for security through union. Whether in doing so they also lost their freedom remains an unanswered question. During the period of the Helvetic Constitution (s) (1799-1803), no intelligent evaluation was possible. The number and variety of governments generated by the confusion of the times, and the changing fortunes of the revolutionary and Napoleonic wars that brought with them intermittent reoccupation by Austria defy interpretation. The political structure of the old republic was abruptly dismantled to make way for the imitative unitary constitution thrust on all of Switzerland by the revolutionary armies.

[29] Sprecher, "Eröffnungsrede," p. 112.

But the period was too brief, the constitutional innovations too obviously political instruments of General Massena's occupying army, for Graubünden to experience any fundamental changes.[30]

The period of the Mediation Constitution (1803–1814), if less tempestuous and radical, precipitated more permanent changes. The new constitution, more temperate and realistic than its predecessors, provided for the return of Switzerland to its decentralized, confederal traditions, and thus found wider acceptance even in its innovative aspects.[31] The major portion of the new instrument was pointedly devoted to nineteen separate constitutions for the individual cantons, incorporating numerous features from previous cantonal practice. The prerogatives of the federal government were enumerated only afterward. What this meant for Graubünden was the reestablishment of some local autonomy for both the communes and the regional jurisdictional communes (*Gerichtsgemeinden*) and higher jurisdictions (*Hochgerichte*), though not for the defunct leagues

[30] Robert Steiner gives a full account of the period in *Der Kanton Raetien zur Zeit der helvetischen Verwaltungskammer* (Zürich, 1936); the more general condition of Switzerland is given in Gottfried Guggenbühl, *Geschichte der Schweizerischen Eidgenossenschaft*, 2 vols. (Zürich, 1948).

Many Swiss view the Helvetic Republic as a transient contrivance imposed upon them briefly by alien powers; and it is true that Article 1 of the Helvetic Constitution did try to thrust an impossible centralism on the confederation: "The Helvetic Republic consists in an indivisible state. There shall no longer be borders between cantons and subject lands, nor even between canton and canton." Paul Kläuli, ed., *Quellenhefte zur Schweizergeschichte*, vol. 1 (Aarau, 1952), p. 49. Nevertheless, many crucial features of later constitutions first found their way into Swiss practice in the Helvetic period—not least of which were the eradication of privilege, rank and subject state status, and the guaranteeing of individual rights (a tradition, as we have seen, without roots in the Raetian mountains).

[31] Kläuli gives an abrogated version of the Mediation Constitution but omits critical cantonal documents in *Quellenhefte*, p. 57f.

167

of the old republic. Renewed autonomy permitted continued participation in self-government on the pattern of independence, and led many to believe, as had been predicted
by the more sanguine patriots, that the loss of independence was only tangentially relevant to the operation of direct democracy. To be sure, prerogatives pertaining to the
making and executing of foreign policy along with a limited
number of related executive functions were removed from
the purview of cantonal and local policy makers. But the
prerogatives that remained were reinforced and rendered
more salient by the security from outside interference that
the delegation of sovereignty to the Swiss federation now
guaranteed. The neighborhood's power was curbed, but so
were the abuses to which its vulnerability as a quasi-sovereign body had led; its freedom of action was circumscribed,
but its security of movement in the realm left to it was
enhanced. The conditions of the classical liberal social contract seemed met: give up some of your liberty so that what
remains can be assured; the freedom of the jungle serves
men less well than the tranquillity of the Leviathan.

The early history of Graubünden as a canton appears
to confirm these liberal formulas. The device of federalism
had taken much of the sting out of the loss of independence,
while the heightening of security had mollified fears about
the survival of autonomy within the new political structure.
But in the long run the question remained open. Where
the authorities acquiesced in the historical reality of union,
the individual communes continued to test the premises
on which is was founded. The neighborhood remained the
vital link between the individual and his government, and
neighborhood autonomy continued to preoccupy the men
of the Raetian mountains. Their autarky had survived
feudalism and it had survived the flaws of the ever-disin-
tegrating Raetian Republic. It survived the artificial centralism of the Helvetic Republic, and it endured the revolutionary ferment that created that republic. But by the

168

middle of the nineteenth century, this autarky faced adversaries more threatening than it had ever known, for it faced the collecting forces of an increasingly centripetal federalism and of an irresistibly pervasive modernization. Its fate in these two ongoing struggles is our concern in the final two chapters of this inquiry. Before we can intelligently evaluate the evidence of the latest period, however, we need to fix our attention on the meaning of autarky and self-government in the republican period of Raetia's history when these terms acquired their powerful normative significance.

# CHAPTER VII

# Direct Democracy in the Communes

THERE is an old, slightly boastful, altogether telling story that the people of Graubünden like to recall about an encounter between a Raetian muleteer and a foreign prince on the narrow steeps of the Bernina pass: "Give way!" the nobleman is supposed to have thundered, impatient to be by the lumbering mule train. But the obdurate Bündner, standing squarely in the path, merely retorts, "I am a Raetian freeman." The noble lord repeats his command, punctuating it by haughtily making known his princely rank. With this the muleteer springs up and hurls the lord from his horse into the snow, observing curtly: "And I too am a prince."[1]

The Raetian freeman was very much a prince during the period of the Raetian Republic. Within the neighborhood he was self-governing, self-sufficient, and free. His citizenship made him every man's equal, and his autonomy guaranteed he would be no man's subject. The institutions that nourished these sentiments have been a presence before us throughout this exploration of prefeudal, feudal, and independent Raetia. We need now to establish their real character and to discover how they differ from the mainstream of European political development—how the Raetian freeman, using a vocabulary of freedom and democracy we comprehend so well, came to speak so alien and intriguing a political language. It has been too easy to assim-

---

[1] Cf. Johannes A. von Sprecher, *Kulturgeschichte der Drei Bünde*, new edition by Rudolf Jenny (Chur, 1951), pp. 279–280. A common Renaissance aphorism in Graubünden was "Jeder Rätier, ein geborener Ritter" or "every Raetian a born knight."

ilate the Swiss political experience by perverting it to the preconceptions of our own Anglo-American political categories. We can already assume that such categories are inadmissible in the Raetian context of the common association and the neighborhood. What we need to know, then, is what it meant to a muleteer in seventeenth-century Graubünden to conceive of himself as a prince, to be a free man. What in his democracy permitted him to maintain an integral collective identity where elsewhere democracy was being forged as an instrument to reconcile group interests and party cleavages? From what dilemmas did the manifold corruptions of his political life spring? Are there in his notion of freedom as collaborative self-reliance and community autonomy facets of an attitude that promises an alternative to the tired representative systems, the increasingly unworkable mass democracies, that have been regarded as *the democratic way*? Only in the framework of answers to these questions will we be able to understand what the mountaineer fought to defend in his ancient common association against the incursions of feudalism, what he strove to protect in establishing an independent state and acquiring subject territories, and what he feared losing in the merging of his country with Switzerland.

Of course, an institutional analysis cannot do more than suggest the forms in which Raetian man's political attitudes were expressed. But we may hope to find in our institutional discussion of direct democracy in the neighborhood and in the republic as a whole clues to attitudes, to a political climate of opinion, that point to more fundamental issues.

DIRECT DEMOCRACY IN THE NEIGHBORHOODS:
AUTONOMY AND CONSENSUS

It would be difficult to find a more radical example of the thorough application of the principles of confederal de-

171

centralization than republican Graubünden. Despite the Federal Pact of 1524 which, at least on paper, had subordinated both the leagues and their constituent jurisdictional communes to the federal executive, the decentralization process actually accelerated during the life of the republic.[2] Peter Liver thus notes:

> From the feudal period to the present, political organization in the area of the modern canton of Graubünden has been characterized by fractionalization into small local associations. Indeed, the more recent units are smaller than the earlier: the feudal principality smaller than the Carolingian *hundred,* the jurisdictional commune much smaller than the fief, and the modern political commune still smaller than the jurisdictional commune.[3]

In the period of the republic, there were at least five levels of political organization that could claim to possess some features of sovereignty: (1) the neighborhood (*Nachbarschaft*), which as we have seen was the citizen's immediate political arena, and which was later to become the modern political commune (*Gemeinde*); (2) the jurisdictional commune (*Gerichtsgemeinde*) that had emerged from the Middle Ages as the crucial political entity and that became in

---

[2] "The decentralization process went so far during the three hundred year existence of the Raetian Republic, that the very existence of the integral state was called into question." G. Olgiati, *Die bündnerische Gemeindeautonomie* (Zürich, 1948), p. 40. The extraordinary diversity of administrative and governing bodies in Raetia is displayed in the village, communal, and league statutes given by R. Wagner and I. R. von Salis in their indispensable *Rechtsquellen des Cantons Graubündens* (Basel, 1887).

Other works describing the political structure of the Republic include Julius Putzi, *Die Entwicklung des Bürgerrechts in Graubünden* (Affoltern im Albis, 1951); A. Gengel, *Die Selbstverwaltungskörper des Kantons Graubünden* (Chur, 1902); and Peter Liver, "Die Bündner Gemeinde," *Bündner Monatsblatt,* February 1941.

[3] Liver, "Die Bündner Gemeinde," p. 35.

the period of the republic the paramount locus of both sovereignty and democracy;[4] (3) the higher jurisdiction (*Hochgericht*) which, though of considerable significance in feudal times, had become little more than an administrative subdivision by the time of the republic;[5] (4) the league (*Bund*), representing the loose alliances that had originally convened to constitute the Republic of the Three Leagues; and (5) the federal executive (*Häupter*), constituted by the administrative heads of the three leagues—the *Landammann* of the League of Ten Jurisdictions, the *Landrichter* of the Gray League, and the president of the League of the House of God—and complemented in its work by a representative assembly (*Beitag*).

The picture is one of administrative diffuseness and jurisdictional chaos. In a land of under 150,000 people there were no fewer than 305 discrete jurisdictional regions with competitive, overlapping, frequently incompatible claims to jurisdictional autonomy, administrative self-sufficiency, and even to political sovereignty: 3 leagues, 26 higher jurisdictions, 49 jurisdictional communes, and 227 autonomous neighborhoods. Yet for all of this diversity, there was a certain order in the republic's political structure. The burden of the democratic process and many of the attributes of

---

[4] Friedrich Pieth reflects the general attitude when he writes: "The jurisdictional communes were the most important political units in the land. They were the real "states." They exercised autonomous political prerogatives; they legislated both civil and criminal laws; they were self-sufficient, much as the thirteen cantons (*Orte*) of the Swiss Confederation were with respect to one another." "Das altbündnerische Referendum," *Bündner Monatsblatt*, May 1958, p. 138.

[5] The higher jurisdictions (*Hochgerichte*) had once exercised crucial jurisdiction in criminal and civil affairs, but by the seventeenth century these functions had devolved upon the jurisdictional communes, leaving the higher jurisdiction as a vestigial administrative unit with few salient functions. Cf. Johannes C. Muoth, "Aus alten Besatzung-s-protokollen der Gerichtsgemeinde Ilanz-Grub," *Bündner Monatsblatt*, July-September 1897 for an account of developments in one illustrative higher jurisdiction.

sovereignty in fact fell on the 49 jurisdictional communes and the neighborhoods of which they were composed. In many ways they were like minuscule states—semisovereign in their own affairs, posturing in their dealings with one another as autonomous principalities.[6] Not that they were: their relations to one another conformed to the prescriptions of the Federal Pact, not international law, and there were even circumstances anticipated by the pact that would permit the use of federal sanctions against recalcitrant jurisdictions. But sovereignty was in any case an ambivalent notion in Raetia, and, as we have already noted, there is little reason to try to impose the unitary conceptions of Hobbes or Bodin on the essentially fragmented Raetian experience. In terms of Graubünden's republican experience with democracy, there can be no denying the primacy of the jurisdictions and their neighborhoods.

The face-to-face interaction of the people of Raetia took place exclusively at the local level: here they learned to govern themselves; here they sought political styles conducive to consensus. State treaties and foreign alliances have never been the everyday affairs of men: the Raetians were no different than other men. Their politics began at home with mundane problems of taxation, administration, and cooperation. Their assemblies were not merely their occasional formal gatherings to deliberate and vote, but their casual encounters in the market, at church, or across a tavern table. Their political world was a neighborhood,

6 An eighteenth-century observer was moved to the extravagant claim that "each village of Raetia, each parish and each neighborhood, already constituted a tiny republic. . . ." H. L. Lehmann, *Die Republik Graubünden* (Magdeburg, 1797), p. 109. The neighborhoods and jurisdictional communes, however, were not permitted to develop independent relations with foreign states and this prohibition, as Peter Liver notes, prevents us from treating them as "sovereign" within the framework of international law. Peter Liver, "Rechtsgeschichte der Landschaft Rheinfeld," *66. Jahresbericht der Historisch-Antiquarischen Gesellschaft von Graubünden*, 1936, pp. 116–117n.

and their fellow citizens quite literally neighbors. There were few matters of common concern that they could not dispatch within the neighborhood: they fixed communal tax rates and levied other occasional assessments; they administered the use and oversaw the rare disposition of common land; they took full responsibility for their roads and mountain paths (*Weg und Steg*); they devised appropriate formulas for distributing communal income (from the sale of wood or common land); and they continually reevaluated the criteria by which men were admitted into citizenship (criteria which varied remarkably from commune to commune but which generally set a minimum age of sixteen and specified residence requirements). They also nominated and eventually elected men to local and regional offices, including, after the Reform of 1603, the remunerative colonial posts in the Tellina valley. There were a number of important local offices to fill, including district leader (*Landammann*); bailiff (*Weibel*); secretary (*Schreiber*); and treasurer (*Kassier*) of the jurisdiction; jurymen (*Geschworene*) of the regional court; and representatives to the federal assembly (*Beitag*) as well as to the federal colonial commission (*Syndikat*) nominally in charge of the administration of subject territories (though the realities, as we have noted in the previous chapter, were less neat); and in some districts, marshals (*Bannerherren*) responsible for military organization of the neighborhoods.[7]

Despite these offices, however, the democracy of the neighborhood was anything but an electoral democracy where an elaborate representative system served to separate the citizen from his government and where self-government consisted in the annual privilege of electing one's masters. Almost all of the posts noted here were administrative or service-oriented in character. The initiation, deliberation, and ratification of policy remained wholly with the citi-

[7] A full description of these offices is given by Pieth, "Das altbündnerische Referendum," p. 39f.

zenry. Keeping the books or witnessing documents were menial functions that could be farmed out, but real power was not delegated to officials. The relative unimportance of elected office in a direct democracy was underscored in the Raetian neighborhood by the propensity in some regions to allocate offices by lot. In the absence of total cynicism, it can even be contended that the selling of offices was tolerated in part because the election of officers, in the eyes of the Raetians, did not carry the real burden of democracy. To this day, the Swiss seem less interested in the power of offices and the personality of officeholders than the citizens of other less direct democracies. The collegial federal executive with its anonymous rotating presidency continues to embody this predilection of direct democracy for treating the citizenry as the real government and the elected governors as powerless attendants.

Equally revealing of the individual Raetian's involvement in neighborhood self-government was his obligation to participate in the concrete implementation of the policies he deliberated and ratified. Citizenship brought with it the obligation to *do* and to *act* as well as to *will* and to *vote*. Active participation in the communal assembly was only the beginning of the collective work on which the life of the neighborhood depended. For example, the decision to build a new road could not be made in a splendid flurry of democratic spirit and then forgotten, left to some engineer corps to complete. To will the road into being, as it were, entailed building it. Those who willed it built it, and their labor was regarded as an expression of commonality for which no compensation was required. This extraordinary practice, known as common work (*Gemeinarbeit*), had roots in ancient usages of the mark association as well as in feudal notions of labor service; but as a device that permitted men to serve themselves by extending democratic participation to the execution and implementation of policy, and stretching political obligation to encompass active work, common work was unique. Its vitality is evident in the renewed attention being shown it by recent Swiss reformers looking for ways to rejuvenate failing mountain communes, which have lost the spirit of autarky and self-government so essential to their survival.

In the neighborhoods of the Raetian Republic, however, common work was primarily an expression of the anti-representative ethos of direct communal democracy. It was as if the neighborhood citizen had taken Rousseau's injunction that the will, being inalienable, cannot be represented, and adjusted it to the peculiar forms of his own political life. The belief in common work seemed to argue: if politics is both willing and doing, deciding and acting, then the doing and acting are no more alienable than the willing and deciding. Politics is a process that begins with creative deliberation and concludes with work, no part of which, in a real democracy, can be any better delegated or represented than any other part. In the neighborhood, one commentator says, "each knows the other. Each participates directly in all that is to be decided. He even oversees the carrying out of decisions taken. He advises and shares in the decisions affecting administration."[8] The holistic and ongoing character of the individual's political participation in the Raetian commune give real substance to the claim that politics is an activity and that, in Hannah Arendt's terms, "to be free and to act are the same."[9] Certainly the individual appeared to experience none of that atomization that attends freedom in representative systems, none of the

[8] Liver, "Die bündner Gemeinde," p. 17.

[9] Hannah Arendt, *Between Past and Future* (New York, 1961), p. 153. Bernard Crick makes the same species of claim when he writes "there is a reciprocity between freedom and politics, properly understood, not an animosity." "Freedom as Politics," in P. Laslett and W. G. Runciman, *Philosophy, Politics and Society*, Third Series (Oxford, 1969), p. 194. I have examined the context of the claim at some length in *Superman and Common Men: Freedom, Anarchy and the Revolution* (New York, 1971), pp. 51–72.

alienation which so often emerges as the obverse side of individuality in liberal regimes. The sense of self given by his citizenship defined him as an autonomous man *within* the structure of his polity, not outside of it. There is almost a Kantian tone to his conviction that "the particular will of the individual bound to the collective had in the main to be subordinated to the common will of the commune,"[10] especially when the consciously voluntaristic color of this subordination is borne in mind. How far is this formula from Rousseau's construction of freedom as "obedience to a law which we prescribe to ourselves?"[11]

Nor did the individual need fear the imposition of a perverse totalism in the name of compulsory communality—a danger liberal critics of Rousseau constantly reiterate. As a creative participant in the formation of the communal will, the individual needed no guarantees for the containment of communal power; as the instrument of policy implementation, he needed no sacred rights with which to defend himself against the encroachments of an ambitious bureaucracy. In the most fundamental sense, the citizen *was* the communal authority: its will was his will, its needs were his needs, its instrumentalities were his very limbs, and its power was his sweat and his blood. To speak from a liberal constitutional perspective about the dependence of freedom on the separation of powers and the constitutional containment of power is, in the context of the self-governing, face-to-face polity, to speak an alien tongue.

Not that everyday realities necessarily achieved the ideal enthusiastically depicted here. Faces that could look upon one another knowingly could also look with envy or greed or vengeance or spite. A government from which there was nothing to fear because the government was the community

---

10 A. Cahannes, *Bürgergemeinde und politische Gemeinde in Graubünden* (Disentis, 1930), p. 8.

11 *The Social Contract*, ed. G.D.H. Cole (London, 1913), Book I, Chapter 8.

could be its own most frightening enemy, as the experience in the Tellina valley demonstrated. For who was to protect the community from itself? Common work enabled a constructive citizenry to lay down roads, erect buildings, redirect rivers, and hold back avalanches, but it also facilitated community violence and collective vengeance. The organized, armed village (the so-called *Fähnlein*)—vital to a spirited, democratic defense—could also function as an institutionalized lynch mob ready to wreak an unreasoned justice on any who crossed it. In some places, even the forms of democracy appeared to be lacking. In Klosters, for example, the *Landammann* was elected from a set of nominees chosen on the basis of age rather than by open assemblies, a circumstance that has led one observer to claim that, at least in Klosters, "elections were by no means free and the jurisdictional assembly—at which citizens heard so many fine words about freedom—was largely a decoration."[12] Still, the rule seems to have been meaningful direct democracy, for the maladies from which neighborhood self-government during the republic suffered were for the most part intrinsic to direct democracy—necessary, unavoidable pathologies generated by the face-to-face community in the course of its pursuit of self-sufficiency.

Self-government in the neighborhoods was only one dimension of Graubünden's early experience with democracy. The citizens of Raetia were as devoted to democracy in the determination of countrywide policies as they were in the service of local self-government. In the unique idiosyncrasies of the referendum, a device generally thought to have originated in Graubünden, the antirepresentative tenden-

[12] G. Fient, *Das Prättigau* (Davos, 1897), p. 78. Fient, however, was referring to the occasional assembly of the higher jurisdiction, which was in any case a more dubious institution than the village or neighborhood assembly. Moreover, Klosters was in the League of Ten Jurisdictions and thus unusually susceptible to Austrian influence, which would have favored an aristocratic tempering of direct democracy.

cies of village democracy were both confirmed and preserved at the level of the jurisdictional commune and of the republic as an entity.

## REFERENDUM DEMOCRACY IN THE REPUBLIC: AUTONOMY AND DISSENSUS

The founding pact of the Republic of the Three Leagues gave the sovereign right of legislating public policy for the country as a whole neither to a representative central government (Hobbes' "sovereign representative"), nor directly to the citizenry as an integral body (the "people" as sovereign). It was rather the collective will of the jurisdictional communes, as expressed through the federal referendum, that was to constitute the sovereign *vox populii*. All other federal institutions merely serviced the referendum.

In form, the referendum was addressed to the "honorable councillors and communes," to the communes and the communal officers responsible for the actual polling. Balloting took place within the individual jurisdictions or even at the discretion of the jurisdictions within their constituent neighborhoods, but the final tally was by jurisdictions, not by popular vote. The presumption seems to have been that the neighborhoods were responsible for achieving consensus within particular jurisdictions and that the referendum need concern itself only with the forging of consensus among jurisdictions. The will of the republic was thus construed as the collective will of integral jurisdictions, not the corporate will of an organic people or the majority decision of an atomized electorate. The individual citizen spoke *through* his neighborhood. His sovereignty locally enabled him to defer to the commune in which he was sovereign in matters of state.

The jurisdictional communes were by no means carefully drawn electoral districts of equal size and population. Their boundaries were rooted in geography and in history, the product of centuries of collective experience, and any comparability was purely the result of accident. A system of electoral votes was intended to compensate the more outlandish discrepancies in representation, but the system was more designed to uncover a genuine collective will than to guarantee the procedural principle of one man one vote.[13] Indeed, nothing in the constitution obliged the jurisdictional communes to utilize a popular ballot in determining their position on referenda. Some relied on direct assemblies of the entire jurisdiction (*Landsgemeinden*), but others referred decisions back to the neighborhoods where each village was free to conduct its own referendum in its own fashion. In the capital city of Chur, the five feudal guilds around which the town had been politically organized since 1464 were entrusted with ascertaining the views of their members on referenda questions. The position of the city was simply the position endorsed by a majority of the guilds.[14] As in the American presidential electoral system, the filtering of individual votes through several levels of organization could in effect disenfranchise a popular majority if it was too unevenly distributed to win a majority of guilds or neighborhoods or jurisdictions. Tiny majorities in a bare plurality of communes might outpoll large major-

[13] This electoral system took 65 electoral votes (*Comitialstimmen*) and gave 22 to the 17 jurisdictional communes of the League of the House of God, 27 to the 21 communes of the Gray League, and 15 to the 10 communes of the League of Ten Jurisdictions. The extra electoral votes were simply added to the ballot of the strongest communes and resulted in a weighting of votes not merely by League but by commune as well. Cf. Pieth, "Das altbündnerische Referendum," pp. 137–138ff., and R. A. Ganzoni, *Beiträge zur Kenntnis des bündnerischen Referendums* (Zürich, 1890).

[14] Chur, however, was not typical; the only real town in Raetia, the seat of the bishopric, the nominal capital not only of the League of the House of God but of the republic as well, it reflected special circumstances and special problems. Cf. Peter C. von Planta, "Verfassungsgeschichte der Stadt Chur im Mittelalter," *8. Jahresbericht der Historisch-Antiquarischen Gesellschaft Graubünden* (1878).

ities in slightly fewer communes. Yet these numerical considerations, so important in representative systems with a utilitarian understanding of majoritarianism as the convergent will of the "greatest number," hardly seem to have been an issue in republican Graubünden. The point of the referendum was not to count heads or to enumerate interests but to discover commonality, or in its absence to create it.

Thus, within the individual jurisdictions the referendum operated to elicit and structure consensus rather than, in the manner of pluralist pressure systems, to promote and crystallize divisions along which parties and coalitions might form. Dichotomies and cleavages, the essence of democracy as interest-reconciliation, were firmly circumvented. When in open conflict, the deliberation of issues and the expression of attitudes were usually given priority over the efficient resolution of specific policy questions, particularly when it appeared that efficiency was to be had only at the cost of consensus. Raetian democracy was not concerned with interests. It sought to clarify neither majorities nor minorities; the sense of community and the natural consensus that issue from community were its real objectives. With this achieved, the majority-minority question resolved itself.[15]

Consensus within the commune, of course, did not dispose of intercommunal dissensus. The palliation of cleavages across disparate neighborhoods in a manner that would facilitate the operation of the referendum was a serious problem. One ameliorative strategy (that remains popular with the Swiss even today) works on the principle that the more limited the scope of the issue area, the less likely the

[15] "The resolution of the majority-minority question came through the realization of pure democracy and its granting of maximum self-government to the very smallest units of the body politic—the communes." Peter Liver, "Die staatliche Entwicklung im alten Graubünden," *Sonderabdruck aus der Zeitschrift für Schweizerische Geschichte*, vol. 13, no. 1, 1933, p. 212.

emergence of cleavage. Issues with an incendiary potential are better left unraised. In this spirit, the original federal pact of the Republic of the Three Leagues had from the outset circumscribed the activities of the federal government and restricted the purview of the referendum. The constituting bodies "reserved all rights and prerogatives" with which they entered the confederation, leaving to the central executive (the three-man commission known as the *Häupter*) only residual powers of the most restricted kind.[16] Subsequent reforms hemmed in the executive still further. One late draft reform that was never instituted suggests the tenor of this anticentralism perfectly: "In order to suitably contain the power of the Executive, it will not be permitted to decide upon or set its seal to anything whatsoever. . . . All matters of weight will be left to the will of the jurisdictional communes. . . ."[17] In actual fact, the executive eventually lost even those modest discretionary prerogatives with which it had begun. The communes demanded and won, via the referendum, control not simply of such normal activities as the establishment of diplomatic relations, the sending and recall of ambassadors (all of whom, in the absence of permanent Raetian embassies abroad, were extraordinary appointments), the initiation as well as the ratification of state treaties, and the making of war and peace; but they also wrested from the executive administrative discretion over such minor tactical questions as the form and wording of diplomatic epistles and the logistical details of troop conscription, supply, and deployment. These almost insulting expropriations of executive prerogative did not, of course, in themselves act to assuage dissensus since their end result was to enlarge the purview of the referendum in foreign affairs.

[16] Constantin Jecklin, ed., *Codex Diplomaticus*, vol. 5 (Chur, 1883), p. 87.

[17] The full text of the proposed Reform is given in Ganzoni, *Beiträge*, p. 28.

But in domestic matters the communes acting collectively through the referendum had few more powers than the executive. The pact of 1524 had reserved all powers relating to the judiciary and to economic affairs to individual jurisdictions, and little was left for the collective communal will to determine. Federal expenditures were minor, and income was still less. Even highway tolls and customs duties, normal federal revenue sources in a federation, rested largely in the hands of individual communes. Toward the end of the republican period a court was established at the federal level to deal with foreigners and "vagabonds" (probably gypsies among others), but this was mainly a convenience. Criminal and civil jurisdiction at every level remained otherwise with the higher jurisdictions and the communes. Although there is no allusion to an amendment power in the 1524 documents, the referendum was used in the late eighteenth century to manipulate the executive through a series of federal reorganization acts; the three-man executive commission was abolished in 1797 and then, following an abortive constitutional assembly, reestablished the following year. But during more placid, orderly periods, the referendum was in domestic affairs kept within uncontroversial limits where intercommunal cleavages were least likely to surface.

In addition to foreign and domestic affairs, the referendum could be utilized in developing policies for two other issue areas: colonial affairs, which included the administration of the dual-status town of Maienfeld that was half subject and half free; and transport and commerce, including those few taxes and tolls not in the hands of the jurisdictions. These matters were primarily administrative and thus mundanely unprovocative.

The effort to reduce the executive to utter servitude was taxing to the communes and to the referendum in several ways. By treating the organs of the executive (the three-man commission and the consultative assembly) as prepara-

184

tory commissions for the referendum the communes robbed themselves of prudent legislative aid and denied themselves the comfort of executive enforcement of common decisions. The three-man commission could enforce absolutely nothing (police and military power resided entirely with the armed commune or *Fähnlein*), while the consultative *Beitag*, despite its quasi-legislative constitutional status, was reduced to acts of self-effacing recommendation. As modest as the scope of the federal referendum was, what was not within its pale was beyond common action altogether. Conversely, and more painfully, whatever did require common action required action in its least salient minutia as well as in its principled essence. Willing to leave nothing to the executive, the communes were frequently plunged into a morass of trivia in which the sublime became indistinguishable from the ridiculous. Limited in its scope, the referendum nevertheless "extended itself . . . to the important and the unimportant, to questions of profound consequence as well as to the merest trifles."[18] In one case, an inquiry concerning the wisdom of repairing certain barrels and vats in Maienfeld circulated together with the proposed text of a vital state treaty with Hapsburg Austria. In another case, rather more peculiar but hardly atypical, the vision of a crazed peasant who prophesied the impending doom of the republic was written up and circulated as a referendum soliciting appropriate responses. The outcome is not known —the vision prescribed "penance and improvement"—but the capital city of Chur subsequently banned the use of tobacco and the republic appears to have survived.[19]

This idiosyncratic devotion to detail was in part a con-

---

[18] Pieth, "Das altbündnerischen Referendum," p. 144.

[19] Our peasant seer avowed that a voice from the clouds had confided to him "if men do not much improve themselves, and ample penance undertake, God shall root them up and destroy them with a glacial frost." Pieth, *ibid.*, p. 151, tells the story. Compare this with the picture we drew of Raetian man's superstitious temperament in Chapter IV, above.

sequence of the communal distaste for central, executive policy making, and probably also a reflection of the Germanic legalism which, over a number of centuries, has led both the Germans and the Swiss to subject to rigid legislation and even constitutional amendment trivial matters treated elsewhere in the more flexible context of administration, precedent, or common practice.[20] But it was also a manifestation of the conviction that the communes were sovereign and that the popular will had a right to express itself on anything and everything of common interest (albeit on nothing that intruded upon the autonomy of the individual communes). Yet there is nothing in this attachment to self-government that precludes dissensus. The scope of the referendum was in many ways severely limited by the sovereign prerogatives of the individual communes, but its detail, its vulnerability to excruciating minutiae, were open invitations to cleavage. The magic of immediacy, smallness, kinship, and collective necessity that permeated the village and created ideal conditions for consensus was largely dispelled by the more complex and diversified atmosphere of intercommunal politics. When communes had to take decisions involving issues that went beyond their traditional autarky, they found they could no longer count on persuasion, good will, and public-spirited acquiescence. The self-evidence with which the problem of preserving a common wood against the springtime ravages of nature suggested its own answers could hardly be expected to attend the resolution of such complex issues as the preservation of the independence of the republic. Religious, linguistic, and party cleavages which had been dormant in the tranquil

[20] Herbert J. Spiro gives an interesting account of the costs and benefits of legalism both in theory and in the Swiss context in *Government by Constitution* (New York, 1959), Chapters 5 and 15. It is characteristic of the legalistic attitude of the Swiss that their modern constitutions have been inflated to treat questions (e.g., the alcohol tax rate) that are usually left to statutory legislation.

waters of communal politics came to violent life in the stormy currents of intercommunal and international politics, sharp protruding reefs upon which the fragile shell of consensus easily floundered.

Those who designed the Raetian referendum were, however, by no means unaware of these paradoxes. Nor did they respond to the dangers of cleavage by adapting their political structures to the specifications of a pluralist pressure system where cleavages are accepted and utilized to reach a private interest compromise on the character of the public weal. Successful or not, the Raetian referendum was intended to minimize cleavage, to maximize intercommunal consensus, and to make possible at the level of the republic the sort of consensus vital to the neighborhood. Commonality was the aim, not compromise. A sensitive English study of Switzerland in the 1960's captures perfectly the unefficient, participant-oriented (instead of policy-oriented) quality of the Raetian referendum: "The idea," the survey concludes, "that the proper aim of politics is to provide an environment in which people can develop their own sense of identity, whether as individuals or as groups, is one that goes very deep in the Swiss consciousness. It is a very different assumption from the one that has dominated political thinking in most of the rest of the world since the eighteenth century. . . ."[21]

There are several kinds of additional evidence to support this construction of the referendum as an instrument of consensus. The pact of 1524 in fact had anticipated the possibility of serious intercommunal quarrels and had established procedures for setting up *ad hoc* adjudicative commissions the sole function of which would be to arbitrate disputes. The settlements reached by these commissions (constituted by impartial third parties) were final. Appeal could be made neither to the federal executive nor even

[21] "Switzerland: A Survey," *The Economist*, February 22, 1969, p. xi.

to the referendum.[22] In other words, where dangerous disputes potentially destabilizing to the republic emerged, machinery was available to circumvent the referendum, thus preserving it from the kinds of polarities that might undermine its capacity to elicit consensus.

The most interesting testimony to the consensual temper of the Raetian referendum comes from its actual operation. Most striking were the easy access it offered to private citizens wishing to canvass the wider public on issues they deemed significant, and the flexible form in which it permitted responses to be made.

The referendum in the West has most often been a device by which a government can secure popular support for its programs, and permit a popular veto of its innovations. In Graubünden, the referendum was available to just about "anyone in a position to communicate something or to solicit an expression of will from the sovereign communes."[23] Available, that is to say, not only to the federal executive but also to individual communes, foreign states, representatives of subject territories, and private citizens acting entirely on their own. Although only official referenda conducted by the federal executive were obligatory in their decisional outcome, the quasi-sovereign status of the individual communes and their collective claim to full sovereign legislative power gave to their common decisions on unofficial referenda the authority of acts of state. Abuse of these generous arrangements by foreign powers discontent with the results of mere solicitation did lead to reform efforts that ultimately required federal approval for petitions circulated by private persons and foreigners. The Pact of the Three Seals of 1551 (*Dreisieglerbrieff*) included the

---

[22] Articles 10 through 16 of the federal pact, in Jecklin, *Codex*, vol. 5, p. 85. Because the pact was itself an effort to overcome centuries of intercommunal feuding, it is not surprising that it anticipated future strife.

[23] Ganzoni, *Beiträge*, p. 25.

only partly effective "Prohibition: that nobody shall circulate petitions among the communes without [executive] permission."[24] But the real target of this restriction was the manipulative foreign agent who rode through the communes buying up votes for the petition that followed in his wake; private Raetian citizens were little affected. In spite of the occasional idiosyncrasies provoked by the referendum's flexible openness to the will or the whim of individual citizens, it seemed a small price to pay for a vital, participatory democracy in which the citizenry were encouraged to put as well as to answer legislative questions. In a representative democracy such procedures would be disastrous, would usurp the legitimate enterprise of the representative and endanger the legislative process as an efficient device of policy. But in a direct democracy there is no better way to ensure that individuals will continue to feel at one with their government. A natural process of political sedimentation often lays down unintentional walls between the citizen and his government. The best preventive against such alienation in a democracy is plentiful and ongoing activity—a lively citizenry involved in the initiation as well as in the approval of policies. The refusal of the Raetians to distinguish private petitions from public referenda was a prophylactic of exactly this sort.

Perhaps even more telling still were the numerous options provided for in responding to referenda questions. In countries like the United States, where the referendum has been introduced as a useful check on governmental power—a potential popular veto on the legislative extravagances of straying, irresponsibile representatives—its operation has depended on a yea-nay plebiscite that limits the people to unqualified approval or irremediable veto. In a representative democracy, the people can only be permitted the right either to accept the legislative decisions of their parliamen-

[24] Jecklin, *Codex*, vol. 5, p. 107f.

189

tary representatives, or send those representatives back to chambers for further deliberation. Until their representatives choose to communicate with them on a new proposal, the people must wait passively, placidly, patiently. In republican Graubünden, however, the referendum demanded of the citizenry a full response, always critical, often creative, unavoidably detailed, and hence ponderously painstaking. Of course, there was the option merely to endorse or flatly reject, but the wording of the questions and the method by which votes were classified encouraged far more. Thus, a proposal might be subjected to a searching commentary, revisions or improvements might be suggested, and the sponsors might be admonished to reformulate the question or challenged on its salience altogether. Like a decision of the United States Supreme Court, a commune's decision on a given referendum usually took the form of a lengthy and closely reasoned statement which outlined the general background for the position, elaborated concrete arguments and adduced appropriate precedents, and defended relevant principles.

Where the objective is political participation and the engendering of consensus through constant political activity, the casting of yea-nay votes is downright subversive. In fact, toward the very end of the republic, in a period that some might insist called for more efficient, centralized, unambiguous legislation, the communes passed a reform prohibiting yea-nay referenda![25] Participation, not efficiency,

[25] Article 20 of the Reform of 1794 reads: "Referendum questions should not be put in a fashion that restricts responses to affirmation or negation, nor in all-embracing generalities to which no thinking citizen can commit himself; they should be put in a clear, simple way that, in raising the issue, permits to each man a measured, patriotic expression of his own convictions." Jecklin, *Codex*, vol. 5, p. 165. Compare this with the modern referendum in Switzerland, which is introduced in this unambiguous manner: "Do you, dear fellow-citizens, accept the following proposal or not, yes or no?" (although the locu-

appeared to the Raetian freeman as the key to survival for his democracy, and if policy making was further encumbered by the resulting murkiness, then all the worse for policy making.

If, for example, a proposal to maintain free access over the Julier pass during the winter through the use of oxen (trampling the snow, as was the practice then) was put to the jurisdictional communes, they might in place of simple assent or veto suggest that the question be resolved by the communes directly affected or that keeping it open in December and January was adequate to the demands of commerce or that the Septimer pass was more viable as a winter route than the Julier or that horses were better tramplers than oxen or almost anything else that entered their minds as being relevant. Not very efficient, but a guarantee that participation in the referendum would be an act of legislative creation rather than of legislative confirmation or veto. In 1797, in an actual referendum soliciting procedural authority to negotiate with Napoleon on the future of Graubünden and requesting substantive guidelines for those negotiations, more than one-third of the communes advocated turning for advice and support to the Swiss Confederation, a possibility not entertained at all in the referendum proposal.[26]

---

tion "dear fellow-citizens" is an endearing anachronism that testifies to the degree to which traditional communalism has survived even into modern Swiss politics).

[26] For details see Alfred Rufer, *Der Freistaat der III Bünde und die Frage des Veltlins*, 2 vols. (Basel, 1910), vol. 1, p. 237f. Twenty-five pages of text are required to cover the range of responses given by the communes on this one question.

A reasonably accurate historical picture of referendum results in Graubünden can be gleaned from the following: for the period 1464 to 1803 (with very incomplete returns), Fritz Jecklin, ed., *Materialen zur Standes- und Landesgeschichte gemeiner III Bünde*, 2 vols. (Chur, 1907); for 1803 to 1847, Fritz Jecklin, ed., "Die Volksabstimmungen des Kantons Graubünden von 1803–1847," *Bündner Monatsblatt*, May-

The manner in which an initiative was built into the referendum suggests that direct democracy in Raetia, if it compounded the problems of legislative output, enhanced significantly the quality and diversity of legislative input. Recent critics of representative democracy have argued convincingly that the capacity to influence the nature of the decisions and the scope of the options to be placed before an electorate may be much more vital to real democracy than the right finally to vote yes or no on some particular question that has been narrowed, parochialized, and defined in so confined a way as to render the choice itself insignificant.[27] The Bündner peasant may not have been satisfied with the ambivalent or contrary results of a referendum, but he could be certain that the questions it raised were his questions. His fellow citizens might not agree with him, but he could tell them what he thought the real issues were by either introducing his own proposal or responding to someone else's with counterproposals of his own. Faced with impossible choices or look-alike options or unacceptable alternatives, he could remake fundamentally the decisional context until a possible choice, a distinctive option, or an acceptable alternative was on the table.

Political systems spawn their own jokes: the American representative system's inadequacies are especially well revealed by the story of the little old lady who, on emerging

---

October 1921; for 1848–1917, Jules Robbi, ed., "Die Volksabstimmungen des Kantons Graubünden von 1.Februar 1848 bis und mit 4.März 1917," *Seperatabdruck aus der Engadiner Post* (St. Moritz, 1917); and for 1917 to 1937, "Die Volksabstimmungen des Kantons Graubünden von 11.November 1917–9.Mai 1937." (Unpublished manuscript, Graubündner Kantonsbibliothek in Chur).

[27] The critical paradigm for so-called nondecision theory is given by Peter Bachrach and Morton S. Baratz, "Two Faces of Power," *The American Political Science Review*, vol. 56, December 1962. For a theoretical discussion of its implications for freedom, see Barber, *Superman and Common Men*, pp. 75–77.

from the polling booth, was asked whom she had voted for and replied, "Oh, I didn't vote for *any* of them; it only encourages them." The Raetians would not have been able to comprehend the irony, for in an analogous situation a citizen of the commune would have been able to say, "Oh, I didn't vote for any of *them*; I voted to introduce a different set of options that will give us a meaningful choice."

Nevertheless, it is perfectly true that expanding the decisional scope by multiplying the number of available options can produce an egregious muddle where policy output is supposed to be. In the village assemblies natural consensus had made possible extensive policy agreement despite full and creative political participation by the citizenry; but at the level of the republic positive participation in the legislative input process brought with it indecision, inefficiency, and policy paralysis. To ascertain anything resembling an unambiguous public will from the massive tomes of contentious prose that emerged from each referendum was a thankless and futile task. The communes, in every other way chary of their sovereign rights, prudently relieved themselves of this hopeless job, making it the responsibility of the executive commission (*Häupter*) assisted by an *ad hoc* advisory committee (known as the *Zuschuss*). The commission, whose duties in the "Classification of Votes" were regarded as wholly mechanical, had to try to pigeon-hole long-winded, qualification-studded arguments into one of five categories: accepted, rejected, opinion withheld, conditionally accepted, and modified. These categories, particularly the last two, opened the floodgates to a sea of misunderstanding and abuse. The commission was supposed both to resolve all the ambiguities *and* to produce results satisfactory to each of the participating communes. When it did not, communes simply rejected the commission's interpretation and classification of their stated positions. They sometimes even challenged the construction

193

of a rival commune's vote as well, thus: "our vote was not a modification but a rejection, and commune X's was not a conditional acceptance but a modification, so the proposal ought to have failed," etc. The executive learned in time to play its own games. Frustrated in its efforts to interpret the contradictory evidence provided by the communal ballots and thwarted in the implementation of policy objectives by its own legislative impotence, it occasionally contrived to outmaneuver the watchful communes by using a particularly ambiguous referendum to sanction its own point of view, constructing from unrelated and unclear ballot positions a precarious rationalization for itself. So grave did this abuse become in the period of turmoil at the end of the republic when referenda were being circulated like driven snow and answers thrown out more opaque than alpine mist that the communes felt compelled to coerce the executive into legislative submission. The Great Reform Act of 1794 stipulated in Article 23 that the federal executive "shall make precisely clear to the individual jurisdictional communes how and for what reasons each of their votes have been counted and classified."[28] Yet even where the commission sought a judicious interpretation, it often was unable to extract from the chaos of referendum responses an acceptable consensus. Participation was enhanced but policy often was paralyzed. The communes of the League of Ten Jurisdictions, seeking to rationalize and integrate their common defenses, were unable even to reach an accord on so mundane an issue as a uniform caliber for their weapons![29] Too often, the referendum seemed to become a procedural altar on which the substantive benefits of efficient legislation were sacrificed to the participatory rewards of creative legislating.

[28] Jecklin, *Codex*, vol. 5, p. 166.

[29] Cited by P. Gillardon, *Geschichte des Zehngerichtenbund* (Davos, 1936), pp. 243–244.

## DIRECT DEMOCRACY: ASPIRATIONS AND REALITIES

In its aspirations, Raetia's pure democracy set itself tasks of political participation and community-building quite foreign to representative democracy, and not fully intelligible to us if construed in the context of Anglo-American political ideals. We are still, even at the end of the eighteenth century, dealing with institutions, the moving spirit of which was generated by the common association—institutions grounded in autonomy to be sure, but an autonomy of the collectivity rather than of the individual. The suitable Raetian pronoun always seemed to be we: not *l'etat, c'est moi* but *l'etat, c'est nous.* A sense of the dignity of the individual was keenly felt, and indignation was easily kindled, but almost always on behalf of the collectivity. The story is still told of the Austrian vassal who hurled an imperious order at a district leader in the League of Ten Jurisdictions during the era when it was still under Austrian suzerainty, covering himself with the phrase "obey in the name of the prince's rights and the authority of his bailiff!" The district *Landammann* reputedly replied to the effect that "he shat on the prince's rights and the authority of his bailiff." The prince may well want to have a bailiff as symbol of his jurisdiction, he concluded, but the communes were the real master.[30]

The individual could be incensed, but only in the name of the village. It is thus exceedingly risky to read into the Raetian preoccupation with collective self-sufficiency a concern for personal or private rights. As Herbert Luethy has astutely noted, the Swiss in general have always tended to think "not of liberty, but of liberties in the plural, that is of communal and local not individual and egalitarian rights, not of the rights of man or of all men, but of rights acquired or fought for by a community determined to look

[30] *Ibid.,* p. 120.

after its own affairs. . . . In short, their conception of freedom was the primitive or tribal one."[31] The term tribal
may be a little misleading. We have explored the insuffi-
ciency of political consciousness in the primitive common
association above and have suggested that no construction
of the term freedom may be viable in a preconscious tribal
setting. But the notion that freedom is collectivistic in
Switzerland is well founded in the Raetian experience.

Collectivism has fostered an integration of individual
and government that precludes that "dissolution of the
modern representative state into atomized individuals"
so typical of the alienating experience of contemporary
democracy.[32] The position of the government official in
republican Graubünden was hardly to be envied. His
status verged on the menial, his responsibilities were limited to trivia, and his rights were nonexistent. The people of the League of The House of God chose their nominees for president with some care to ensure that minimum
qualifications were met, but they chose the president himself from the two prime nominees by lot since it did not

[31] Herbert Luethy, "Has Switzerland a Future? The Dilemma of the
Small Nation," *Encounter*, December 1962, pp. 25–26.

This impression is again and again confirmed by writers on Switzerland. Edgar Bonjour writes "The modern concern with the freedom
of the individual simply would not have been understood by the traditional Swiss—so completely did they feel themselves tied to the
community in every facet of their lives. They strove for independence
not for themselves personally, but for the collective body. How different this is from the modern Enlightenment view of democratic freedom, that dissolves and atomizes the body of the state into discrete
individuals." *Werden und Wesen der Schweizerischen Demokratie*
(Basel, 1939), pp. 14–15. G. Soloveytchik likewise argues that "it is one
of the essential peculiarities of Swiss democracy that power rests not
with the individual but with a plurality." *Switzerland in Perspective*
(London, 1954), p. 29.

[32] Bonjour, *Werden und Wesen.*

seem to make very much difference exactly who he was.[33] Whenever it came to a contest between an official and the will of the people, the people were irresistible. An Austrian bailiff who took his job seriously enough to challenge a referendum outcome in the commune of Churwalden within the League of Ten Jurisdictions was warned that if "he could not see his way clear to accepting the decision he could not anticipate leaving the village in one piece."[34] Where the referendum functioned as a creative link between citizen and policy there was simply no need for the recall, no need for hard fought party elections and long debates about the merit of competing nominees for office.[35]

Aspirations are of course one thing, the panchromatic realities of Raetian history another. The experiment with direct democracy was costly to the people of Graubünden not merely by virtue of its failures but as the result of its successes. Efficiency suffered precisely to the degree that full participation was achieved, and consensus faltered exactly because the referendum was creative and unstructured. Corruption, factionalization, arbitrariness, violence, disregard for law, and an obdurate conservatism that opposed all social and economic progress were pathologies to some extent endemic to the pure democratic life form. There is not quite an arrogance but an irresistible quality to popular sovereignty when it is transformed from a symbolic source of authority into the actual fount of political power

[33] Alfred Rufer, "Wie der Bundespräsident im Gotteshausbund gewählt wurde," *Bündner Monatsblatt*, September–October 1954.

[34] Gillardon, *Geschichte*, p. 120.

[35] "The Swiss are little inclined to look upon the state as a master; rather they regard it as an agent." Robert C. Brooks, *Civic Training in Switzerland* (Chicago, 1930), p. 131. Simon de Ploige thus quotes a Swiss citizen of the nineteenth century who insists "it is really no matter to us whether the Chamber is composed of this or that party, for it does not govern us. We ourselves are the sovereigns of the country." *The Referendum in Switzerland* (London, 1898), p. 228.

that can undermine impartiality and justice more thoroughly than any tyrant. We have already witnessed the unsavory use of the armed village (*Fähnlein*) as an instrument of vengeance in the old republic. One telling anecdote recalls the treatment meted out to an unfortunate Austrian party leader in the Engadine valley commune of Schuls; it was 1735 and the French-oriented party had just gained the upper hand in an ongoing quarrel with Johann Marina, the Austrian party's leader. Rather than bring Marina to trial for his putatively treasonous activities before the proper authorities, his followers were stoned, some to death, his house was plundered, and he himself was threatened with a dismemberment that he evaded only by a timely escape to foreign sanctuary. The point of the story is not, however, the vindictive cruelty of the victors but the simplistic, boasting self-righteousness of their justifications. When asked by an outsider why Marina had not been brought before the "properly constituted authorities," one of Schuls's citizens, a simple cowherd, snarled in response, "What 'authorities?' We ourselves are the authorities! Before other 'properly constituted authorities' such scoundrels would remain secure. No, we ourselves insist on being the authorities!"[36] A simultaneous tribute to pure democracy and to its potential perverseness.

In the same poisonous spirit, the very conditions of parochialism, naïveté, and well-founded self-importance that lent to Raetia's democracy its participatory virtue left it especially vulnerable to corruption and factionalization. Ironically enough, the alienated, distrustful citizen of a large representative democracy, whose power is a single, anonymous yes or no to candidates and policies thrown at him by a system over which he otherwise exercises no control, is relatively immune to corruption: impotence knows no evil. The problem in Graubünden of course was aggravated by

[36] Friedrich Pieth, *Bündnergeschichte* (Chur, 1945), p. 267. Note, again, the emphasis on *we*.

198

the avaricious manipulation of foreign powers, although it sometimes appeared as if the bottomless coffers of France were so well matched by the limitless resources of Austria that the Raetian communes, having graciously submitted to the blandishments of both, were obliged to knuckle under to neither. Even domestic corruption had a conventional aspect to it that has led some observers to treat it lightly; in the commune of Ilanz-Grub bribery was institutionalized to a point where it could not possibly affect the outcome of elections. Candidates for lucrative offices were expected to remunerate the entire electorate, those who voted against them as well as their supporters. The result was a kind of poll-tax in reverse that encouraged voting without influencing the outcome.[37] Nevertheless, as we have seen in Raetia's unhappy experience in the Tellina valley, the effect of money on the spirit of communal democracy was unmitigatedly nefarious.

Give government to the ignorant and you are sure to have a democratic tyranny of unreason, some would say; the experience of Graubünden, where political prudence so often seemed compromised by economic and scientific ignorance, was hardly a refutation of this cynicism. In political affairs the individual Raetian was remarkably well informed. He grew up in politics, listening to his father and neighbors distilling political wisdom from the chaos of European affairs. By maturity he was not only thoroughly familiar with the minutiae of various league and jurisdictional civil and criminal statutes but could pass on

---

[37] "The system of bribery," Peter Liver observes, "was finally so general, that payments in gold were no longer viewed as bribery but simply as a necessary condition that had to be fulfilled before one could even get into a particular transaction or electoral discussion." "Die Staatlichen Entwicklung," p. 240. Johannes C. Muoth provides details on such practices in one small commune in the Gray League in "Alten Besatzungsprotokollen der Gerichtsgemeinde Ilanz-Grub," *Bündner Monatsblatt*, July-September 1897, pp. 157–161.

technical questions relating to Raetia's treaty obligations to Venice or the Swiss Confederation. No referendum question was too complicated, no jurisdictional quarrel too entangled for him to comprehend. This profound civic competence was reinforced by the very activity it nourished, for as the citizen's political education permitted him an active and prudent participation, his regular participation augmented his civic wisdom.[38]

Yet for all this sophisticated worldliness, the communal citizen displayed a persistent and astonishing ignorance of almost everything not immediately tangible to his practical political life. The cowherd might give a most eloquent disquisition on the legal defects of a proposed reform act aimed at remedying the abuse of colonial offices, "but he would be hard put to explain whether the earth revolved around the sun or the other way around, and totally incapable of recognizing that gypsum and marl could be employed as fertilizers or that the recent and abrupt deterioration of the alpine landscape was the product of natural causes. His head was in fact stuffed with superstitions. Every comet, every earthquake, every meteor adumbrated great calamities. This hearty man, so bold in other things, could hardly take a walk in the night woods without trembling at the call of an owl; and the sight of a baby owl near his house would dispose him to make out his last will and testament. His belief in ghosts and in magic was no less firm than his belief in holy scripture."[39]

How is the citizen to rule himself if, steeped in political prudence and practical wisdom, he nonetheless remains ignorant of the natural world in which politics and policies manifest themselves? To work collectively for progress means little if progress is measured either by the burning of

[38] Sprecher draws a stunning picture, from which these remarks are drawn, in *Kulturgeschichte*, p. 374.

[39] *Ibid.*, p. 375.

witches or by the stubbornness with which foreign science is spurned. A woman was tried and tortured as a witch as late as 1780 in Oberhalbstein, and superstitions related to the "walking dead" (*Totenvolk*) were taken seriously well into the second half of the nineteenth century.[40] All too often superstition and ignorance allied with pride and a sense of independence to isolate Raetia completely from economic innovation and rational agricultural planning. Telling a stubbornly democratic people that their autonomous judgment is damaging to their own interests is like telling a semideaf drummer that his art is bad for his ears. Certain Raetian intellectuals, imbued with Enlightenment notions of education and progress, established a popular journal called *Der Sammler* in the eighteenth century in hopes of educating their fellow citizens. The futility of their efforts to expose the costs of such ancient collective practices as common grazing, which made the development of a rational agriculture nearly impossible, can be gauged from some of the charming but devastating stories published in *Der Sammler*. One describes approvingly the constructive remarks of a foreigner who, traveling the main road, comes upon a local cowherd running his cows nonchalantly through a freshly plowed field right next to the road. The foreigner remonstrates gently, pointing out the wanton and unnecessary damage being done to the field and suggesting use of the road. But the Bündner cowherd, with all the force of a thousand-year tradition of common grazing behind him, retorts, "And what business is it of yours? We are not in your country now! We are a free people, and we do exactly what we want to do!"[41] The tone is

---

[40] G. Fient recalls a childhood filled with superstition, *Das Prättigau* (Davos, 1897), pp. 43–45. On the prevalence of witchcraft superstitions in eighteenth century Graubünden see Ferdinand Sprecher, "Der letzte Hexenprozess in Graubünden," *Bündner Monatsblatt*, September 1936.

[41] From *Der Sammler* 1780.

disapproving, but the average Raetian reading the story would be more likely to swell with pride at his brother's fettle than to blush with shame for his mindless obstinance.

There are certain preconceptions, however, involved in our account of the apparent conservatism of a democracy that functions in a climate of ignorance. We have used terms like progress and science and development with that unwarranted complacency so characteristic of American social science. Yet our goal here is precisely to evaluate the Raetian political experience in its own terms in order to develop standards by which the more familiar ideals of Anglo-American political experience can be judged. Ignorance is clearly a cardinal sin in democracies of any kind and is particularly dangerous in a direct democracy. But that an antipathy to economic progress, to modernization, and to the forces which the latter brings in its train is *prima facie* also a sin appears to be much less certain. Indeed, the final chapters of this exploration of the Raetian experience will have to deal frontally with the critical problem of progress and modernization as they interact with political values and traditional beliefs in a direct democratic system; we can already anticipate a conclusion more ambivalent than the simplistic attitudes evident in *Der Sammler* might suggest. For the only lesson worth drawing from this survey of the aspirations and realities of Raetia's experience with direct democracy seems to be that political ideals have inexorable costs—that the very factors contributing to the health of a pure democracy contain the seeds of pathologies inimical to its operation.

We have watched the Bündner mountainman defend his traditional collective values over a millennium—defend them first only instinctively, before they had taken a conscious form in his as yet undeveloped political psyche, then defend them more knowingly against foreign enemies and domestic tyrants; finally, we watched him ward off the threats that seemed to come out of democracy itself, until he could no longer maintain his independent state. The loss of independence for Raetia, however, did not bring his long struggle to an end. On the contrary, it brought him to the most crucial phase of that struggle where he had not merely to battle enemies of freedom but to choose between his peculiar kind of freedom and the multifarious benefits of a modernity that struck most Western men as the best and the only way for all of mankind. The difficulty of his choice was compounded by the undeniable fact that his democratic aspirations had never been approximated by the realities of his political life, and that this had happened in part because of the very nature of direct democracy and collective autonomy.

# PART IV: Modern Graubünden and the Conservation of Freedom

Free Peoples, be mindful of this maxim: Liberty may
be gained, but can never be recovered.
                    —Jean-Jacques Rousseau

Forgive me, Freedom! O forgive those dreams!
  I hear thy voice, I hear thy loud lament,
  From bleak Helvetia's caverns sent—
            —Samuel Taylor Coleridge

## GESPRÄCHE UNTER EIDGENOSSEN

«Das isch e prächtegi Gäget — da chönnt me grad
vier Sächsfamiliehüser ufschtelle.»

From the Swiss satirical review *Nebelspalter*

"What a delightful locale! Why we ought to be
able to build at least four high-rises right here."

# CHAPTER VIII

# Communal Autonomy and Swiss Federalism

MANY years ago a tiny commune with only sixty-five active citizens rebuked the canton's overbearing administration bent on intervention in the commune's affairs in the following startling manner: "This commune existed long before there ever was a canton: it is a sovereign Bündner commune and it denies to the canton any right whatsoever to decide questions concerning its ultimate existence or justification."[1] The commune in Graubünden was in truth heir to an associational tradition with roots in the tribal common association, the canton was but a contrivance of the recent past, more imposed upon than chosen by the Raetian people. It was thus quite natural that the people of Graubünden, in entering the last phase of their history as a Swiss canton, should feel that any vestige of their self-sufficiency, their participatory democracy, and their communal freedom that survived unification and modernity, would do so only in the traditional setting of the commune. The same neighborhood collectivities that had warded off the constitutional innovations of the Carolingians, thwarted the domestic ambitions of the Churraetian bishopric and maintained the independence of their republic against foreign predators now found themselves confronting enemies still more implacable: a cantonal and federal regime that abrogated its rights in its own name, economic conditions that rendered autarky and isolationism grossly inefficient, and a political climate that lacked the patience and understanding to preserve the old values of direct democracy. In

[1] Cited by Peter Liver, "Die Bündner Gemeinde," *Bündner Monatsblatt,* January 1941, p. 2.

207

the Bündner commune, then, the long history of Raetian freedom reaches its climax in a contest for survival with cantonal and federal authorities—a contest that was in theory moderated by the device of federalism but that in fact could only result in the total victory of centralism and bureaucracy.

"Empires come and empires go," writes a thoughtful Swiss historian, "but the communes remain—the most durable of all social bodies."[2] In Graubünden, the "classical land of communal freedom,"[3] they were to be the final redoubt of traditional notions of both freedom and democracy. Even during the days of the republic, the leagues had been of minimal significance in the everyday life of Raetian man; when they lost their jurisdictional competences with the Constitution of 1815, they ceased to matter, albeit they survived on paper until 1851. The large jurisdictional communes (*Gerichtsgemeinden*) and higher jurisdictions (*Hochgerichte*) that had been crucial to both the referendum and the administration of criminal and civil justice during the republic continued to function in the first half of the nineteenth century, but were transformed following 1848 in accordance with the aims of the new Swiss Constitution of the same year. The new Cantonal Constitution of 1854 completed the reform, replacing the higher jurisdictions with fourteen Districts (*Bezirke*) and the jurisdictional com-

[2] Rudolf Jenny, *Einbürgerungen: 1801-1960*, 2 vols. (Chur, 1965), vol. 1, p. 50.

[3] A. Meuli, "Die Entstehung der autonomen Gemeinden in Oberengadin," *Jahresbericht der Historisch-Antiquarischen Gesellschaft Graubündens*, 1901, p. 5.

Marc Bridel notes that the commune is the basic "cell" of the Swiss federal body, and suggests that only in that cell is "Swiss democracy perfectly realized in both its direct and indirect forms," *La democratie directe dans les communes suisse* (Zürich, 1952), p. 7. Nowhere, however, "are the communes so independent in Switzerland as in Graubünden." A. Cahannes, *Bürgergemeinde und politische Gemeinde in Graubünden* (Disentis, 1930), p. 4.

munes with thirty-nine circuits *(Kreise)*,[4] none of which could be viewed as independent of the cantonal administration. On the other hand, the 233 communes recognized by the new constitution, which have today dwindled to 220, emerged from the reform period with their traditional neighborhood autonomy enhanced and their role as "vital nuclei of democracy" confirmed.[5] The shape of the struggle, then, was clear by the middle of the century: village communities with ties to the prefeudal common association were to be pitted against the forces of bureaucratic centralism represented by the canton and the Swiss federal government in a contest to determine the nature of the Swiss future. Parochial neighborliness confronted centralist efficiency, direct democracy confronted rational expertise, and

[4] The succession of Federal and Cantonal constitutions under which the changes we are considering here took place was not quite so confusing as it may seem. Following the rapid turnover of constitutions in 1800 (the Helvetic Constitution), in 1803 (the Mediation Constitution), in 1815 (the Restoration Period Constitution), and in 1830 (the Regeneration Period Constitution), only two federal constitutions were adopted: one in 1848 founding the modern Federal Republic of Switzerland, and the other in 1874 that remains operative. The Cantonal Constitution of 1854 embodied the cantonal operationalization of the federal document of 1848, while the cantonal reform of 1880 responded to the federal innovations of 1874. A total revision of the cantonal constitution in 1892 codified subsequent developments, and remains in force today.

There is a good deal of sentiment for a total revision of the federal constitution today, but many believe it would lead to the kind of chaos envisioned by critics of the proposal for an American constitutional convention.

Edgar Bonjour's *Die Gründung des Schweizerischen Bundesstaates* (Basel, 1948) gives a complete account of the Federal Constitution of 1848, while subsequent constitutional developments can be assessed in the perspective of Gottfried Guggenbühl, *Geschichte der Schweizerischen Eidgenossenschaft* (Zürich, 1948); Z. Giacometti, *Neubearbeitung von F. Fleiner's Schweizerisches Bundesrecht* (Zürich, 1965); and Erwin Ruck, *Schweizerisches Staatsrecht* (Zürich, 1957).

[5] Z. Giacometti, "Die Rechtliche Stellung der Gemeinden in der Schweiz," in Marc Bridel, ed., *La democratie*, p. 41.

limited autarky confronted economic reality. The entire Raetian past embodying traditions of local autonomy and face-to-face collaboration confronted the coming Swiss future that promised material progress, economic well-being, and a depersonalized collaboration among all Swiss and between Switzerland and an industrialized Europe. We want now to look at some representative moments of that struggle, knowing from the outset that it was a contest the communes could never hope in the long run to win. For they were pitted against forces that were successfully remaking not Raetia alone, but the whole Western world.

## THE CANTON AND THE COMMUNES: INITIAL SKIRMISHES

Those entrusted with the administration of the canton of Graubünden under the new federal structure introduced by the Federal Constitution of 1848 were naturally inclined to view communal sovereignty as a parochial obstacle to their program of rationalization, integration, and social progress for the region. Almost before the place of the old neighborhood in the new cantonal structure had been confirmed, measures were being proposed to strip the communes of their special status, and through a uniform communal code (*Gemeindegesetz*) turn them into subordinate organs of the cantonal administration. But, like every effort at promulgation of a communal code right into the 1970's, this early attempt failed. The communes were in the happy position of arguing simultaneously in favor of liberty and self-government and in favor of the past. Those wishing to abrogate local self-government were cast as "progressive reformers" with an antidemocratic and thus reactionary program, a peculiar combination that did little to attract support. Back in the 1830's, reformers elsewhere in Switzerland had used the French Revolution of 1830 to inspire a revolt against aristocratic leadership in the towns;

210

but in Graubünden the "reformers" were futilely trying to steal from the communes popular rights and privileges that they had enjoyed for centuries—a strange revolution indeed. The canton was further obstructed in its efforts at centralist uniformity by the legitimacy implicit in the commune's longevity. How could the canton pretend to a mastery over communes that predated it by a millennium and that had in effect created it?

Having failed to suborn the communes by such direct means as the communal code, the canton turned to subtler forms of indirect warfare. If its own indisputable sovereignty could not be operationalized in daily affairs, it could at least be underscored on paper and celebrated in legal documents. In the Cantonal Constitution of 1854, a small victory for the canton came with the removal of the cantonal referendum from the communal majority in favor of a simple popular majority. This effectively eliminated the special status of the communes in the referendum, which they had enjoyed since 1524, and turned the majoritarian principle enunciated in the constitution into a weapon against communal sovereignty.[6] But for the rest, the canton had to resort to a war of words, to an ongoing intrigue of interpolations and interpretations designed to demonstrate its sovereign preeminence over the communes. Advocates of cantonal hegemony are still at pains to refer to the communes with phrases suggesting they are mere "tools for the objectives of the canton"[7] or "associations wholly subordinate to the state that possess exclusively

[6] Friedrich Pieth gives an account of this singular cantonal success in *Bündnergeschichte* (Chur, 1945), p. 440; see also Peter Liver, *Die Graubündner Kantonsverfassung des Jahres 1854* (Chur, 1954), and Robert Schwarz, "Die Gerichtsorganisation des Kantons Graubünden von 1803 bis zur Gegenwart," *77. Jahresbericht der Historisch-Antiquarischen Gesellschaft Graubündens*, 1947, p. 149f.

[7] A. Gengel, *Die Selbstverwaltungskörper des Kantons Graubündens* (Chur, 1902), p. 41.

delegated prerogatives."[8] Not that these locutions are at variance with positive law: whatever the ancestry and traditions of the commune, their modern legal status is founded entirely on provisions of the cantonal constitution. Article 40 of the present Cantonal Constitution of 1892, although it cedes rights of autonomous administration to the communes, specifies that their very existence stems from the recognition of the canton, and requires that their statutes and ordinances be in full accord with "federal and cantonal laws and with the property rights of third parties."[9] Article 35 even gives the Lesser Council (*Kleiner Rat*) of the canton rights of general surveillance (*Oberaufsicht*) and, under emergency circumstances, the power to take over completely administration within the communes (*Kuratel*). But these provisions had little impact on public attitudes, and the communes in fact continued to enjoy a special status that set them apart from the circuits and districts, whose subservience to the canton had robbed them of whatever minimal autonomy they once had,[10] for

[8] Cited by G. Olgiati, *Die bündnerische Gemeindeautonomie* (Zürich, 1948), p. 47; Olgiati cites the phrase as an opponent not a friend of centralist reforms.

[9] The constitution defines the resident communes as "public corporations which are legally recognized [i.e., by the canton, thus implying its legal preeminence] as having territorial jurisdiction within a determined region." *Verfassung für den Kanton Graubünden von 2. Oktober, 1892* (Chur, n.d.). The laws and decrees leading up to the 1892 formulation can be found in the invaluable itemization of Graubünden's legislative history *Bündner Rechtsbuch: Bereinigte Gesetzessammlung des Kantons Graubündens* (Chur, 1957).

[10] Today, the circuits are electoral regions for the cantonal Grand Council (*Grosser Rat*), and the seat of a lower court with primarily civil jurisdiction and of an arbitrator (*Vermittler*) with narrow, regional competences. The districts serve exclusively as jurisdictional regions for the higher civil court. Neither the circuit nor the district retain the significance of their predecessors—the jurisdictions (*Gerichtsgemeinden*) and higher jurisdictions (*Hochgerichte*)—and neither is viewed, in the language of Swiss public law, as a "self-governing body" (*Selsbtverwaltungskörper*) in the manner of the commune.

the commune and the smaller parish-style fractions into which geography has divided it retained for the long-term resident an "almost sacred meaning and value."[11] As in the prefeudal era and in the period of the republic, the village community remained the locus of all significant face-to-face encounters: the starting point of all political activity and the environment within which men were born, went to school, worked, married, bore children, and died. Paper assaults on its vitality left it unmarked. Unable to challenge the commune's antimodernizing localism by outside pressure, the canton turned to a different and more subtle kind of attack: erosion of the concept of communal citizenship.

## The Erosion of Citizenship

During the republic, citizenship was a simple matter. Whoever was a citizen of a particular commune with all the rights and privileges that communal citizenship brought with it was by definition a citizen of the league and the republic. Communal passports were usually carried, and citizenship was thought of as a natural expression of the commune's sovereignty. But with the unification of Graubünden and Switzerland, the issue of citizenship became far more complicated. Indeed, it became a central problem in the contest between the forces of communal traditionalism and those of cantonal centralism. The Federal Constitution of 1848 had created for the first time a national citizenship that guaranteed citizens basic human rights, including the right to political participation and to settlement anywhere in Switzerland. The communes of Graubünden had responded in 1853 with a Statue Concerning the Settlement of Swiss Citizens that audaciously barred Swiss citizens who "crashed" the commune under the federal mandate from enjoying any of the prerogatives of communal citizenship. Through this device, the communes in effect created two

11 Jenny, *Einbürgerungen*, p. 50.

213

classes of citizenship, only one of which could be exercised *within* the commune. The Cantonal Constitution of 1854 confirmed this peculiar dualism, making of Swiss citizens residing in Bündner communes without the advantages of communal citizenship virtual second-class citizens.[12] Only citizens of the so-called citizen commune (*Bürgergemeinde*) were members of the corporation that owned communal property, fixed communal taxes, profited from communal profits, and regulated communal affairs; all other Swiss citizens belonged only to the resident commune (*Einwohnergemeinde*) that was little more than an electoral district for cantonal and federal elections. Since by the middle of the nineteenth century up to 30 to 40 percent of Graubünden's population lived in communes where they did not hold communal citizenship, this peculiar dualism created widespread inequities in the canton. Many men found themselves paying heavy taxes to and being governed in many details of their life by corporations over which they could exercise not the slightest control. Thus, advocates of cantonal centralism were able to seize on the issue of dual citizenship with a reformist vigor that they could not bring to other legal efforts.

To the egalitarian reformer, reform was a matter of overcoming the inequities of a confusion that made some men second-class citizens; to the cantonal authorities it was also a matter of striking a blow at the source of the commune's real power: its status as an intergral, self-governing corporation with a privileged, self-appointing membership (i.e., the citizen commune). The authorities thus welcomed the

[12] The constitution stipulates that "relations between the citizen commune and the resident commune will be established by law," thus simultaneously recognizing two discrete bodies and calling for a communal code to regulate them. As we will see, however, all subsequent efforts at legislating a Code have ended in failure—the last as recently as 1966. The Constitution of 1854 is reproduced in Liver, *Die Graubündner Kantonsverfassung.*

creation in the 1860's of a reform movement under the leadership of Andreas von Planta devoted to the establishment of a unitary citizenship that would in effect eliminate the obstreperous citizen communes and transfer their functions to the resident communes. By 1874 the movement had succeeded in pushing through a settlement law (*Niederlassungsgesetz*) which ostensibly remedied the inequities of the law of 1853 and, at least in the intentions of its framers, provided the framework for a unified commune.[13]

The intentions of the lawmakers, however, were not especially evident in the legislation that was eventually enacted. The law did transfer a number of significant prerogatives from the citizen to the resident commune, but it left the citizen commune with the right (1) to continue to elect its own members (leaving it self-perpetuating within the commune); (2) to administer the communal social security fund (*Armengut*) in which many of the commune's resources were concentrated; (3) to administer and exclusively use vestigial common land that had been parceled out to individual citizens (so-called *Gemeindelöser*); (4) to sell or otherwise dispose of common property; and (5) to fix usage fees (*Nutzungstaxen*) for communal pastureland. This compromise left the critical issues in doubt and gave to both sides additional rationalizations for their positions. Centralists naturally insisted that the new law had created a single commune of Swiss citizens. Thus, the canton's executive body, the Lesser Council (*Kleiner Rat*), declared that "by extending membership in the communal body to residents the law of 1874 has effectively transformed the citizen commune into the resident commune."[14] The

[13] The commission established to draft the law insisted it had worked to create "the most unitarily organized commune possible." Cited in *Rekurspraxis des Kleinen und Grossen Rates von Graubünden*, vol. 6, no. 5378, p. 72.

[14] *Rekurspraxis*, p. 76. The council's view is supported by G. Pedotti, *Beiträge zur rechtsgeschichtlichen Entwicklung der Gemeinde, der*

citizen commune was thought of as surviving merely as a subordinate, special corporation within the resident commune. Traditionalists countered with their own interpretations: "The viewpoint that the citizen commune is merely an organ of the resident commune is completely untenable: we cannot find any grounds whatsoever in which this conception might be anchored."[15] Rather, the new law had only turned over certain specified functions to the new resident communes, but otherwise permitted the citizen communes to retain their legal character as autonomous, self-governing bodies. The monolithic construction advanced by the Lesser Council was a contemptible "fiction" designed to confuse the citizenry.

The nub of the controversy was a debate about ownership and usage that could be traced back to the feudal period. Traditionalists knowing that ownership carried with it a warrant of existential legitimacy tried to convert the clear rights of usage delegated to the citizen commune by the law of 1874 into a brief for ownership.[16] Centralists, noting that a fundamental split between citizen and resident commune would defy the cantonal constitution and underscoring the legal preeminence of the resident commune in the law of 1874, retorted that real proprietorship of all communal resources had to rest with the resident commune because it was in fact *the* commune. The rights of usage enjoyed by the subordinate citizen commune were a delega-

---

Gemeindeaufgaben und des Gemeindevermögens im Kanton Graubünden (Zürich, 1936), but vigorously opposed by P. Jörimann, *Die Stellung der Bürgergemeinde nach dem Entwurf für ein Gemeindegesetz des Kantons Graubünden* (Chur, 1943) and *Die historische Entwicklung und rechtliche Stellung der Bündner Gemeinde* (Chur, 1961).

[15] A. Cahannes, *Bürgergemeinde*, p. 31. Also see Note 14.

[16] This is exemplified in Olgiati, *Die bündnerische Gemeindeautonomie*, p. 79f.

tion of authority that carried with it no rights of ownership at all.[17]

Because the law of 1874 spoke to this controversy only indirectly, the matter could not be immediately resolved. From the point of view of the cantonal government, including its judicial bodies, there could be no debate; but the people of Graubünden seemed more in tune with the thinking of the traditionalists, for they have defeated every legislative attempt to codify the canton's unitary position that has been made in the last one hundred years. Communal codes that had a great deal to recommend themselves were turned down by referendum as recently as 1944 and 1966, in no small part because they were perceived by the public as an attack on communal sovereignty by way of an assault on the citizen commune.

The canton's strategy of assailing communal sovereignty by undermining the legal status of the citizen commune had in fact backfired. The issue of autonomy that the government would compromise in the name of a legalistic unitarianism in defining the commune mattered far more to the people than the government's legalisms. They could live with the confusion of dual citizenship and competing jurisdictions; they could not live with cantonal intercession in what they regarded as their sovereign rights of local self-government. It now seems likely that the entire controversy will die of attrition and old age before it is decisively settled

[17] The centralist position has been almost universally favored by cantonal authorities since the latter part of the nineteenth century. The Lesser Council has naturally championed the centralist cause, but support has also come from the Grand Council, supposedly more susceptible to the traditionalist sentiments of the people, and from the cantonal court, a decision of which in 1885 is typical of its stance ever since: "the bifurcation of the commune into a resident and a citizen commune is completely at odds with the sense and spirit of the cantonal constitution, which clearly recognizes only *one* commune, namely the resident commune. . . ." *Rekurspraxis*, p. 95.

217

by legislation, for in recent decades other more volatile issues, which are the focus of the next chapter, have become entangled with this one. At the same time, the citizen commune has simply been disappearing as its membership dwindles, its resources decline, and its prerogatives become irrelevant to the awesome challenges of rural survival in an industrial world.

Perhaps most vexing of all has been the complicating presence of confessional antagonisms in recent manifestations of the old debate. Since the Reformation Graubünden had maintained a confessional parity that was rare in Europe. Nonetheless, the slight Protestant majority had lived in continual anxiety. Graubünden's non-Swiss neighbors were all Catholic, and where they had once been in a position to subvert Graubünden's parity by open intervention, as Austria had done in the Prättigau valley in the 1620's, they were in the nineteenth and twentieth centuries in a position, if only inadvertently, to destabilize the balance through immigration and burgeoning birth rates. "At every indication of a renewed flood of immigration," writes one observer about Switzerland generally, "Protestants not unnaturally become apprehensive."[18] Communes threatened with loss of parity regarded the openness of the resident commune as an invitation to destabilization. Pursuing this reasoning, it seemed evident that the citizen commune, the exclusivity of which barred admission of Catholic residents who had settled from other parts of Switzerland, was the only defensible redoubt for Protestants hoping to maintain parity—maintain, that is, their slender majority. By the same logic, Catholics who might otherwise have been ardent supporters of communal autonomy found themselves sup-

[18] Robert C. Brooks, *Civic Training in Switzerland: A Study of Democratic Life* (Chicago, 1930), p. 220. Brooks even suggests that a wariness of Catholicism was a major factor in Switzerland's refusal to accept the Austrian province of Vorarlberg into the Confederation following World War I.

porting reform legislation that would strengthen the resident communes at the expense of the citizen communes simply because they could vote in and hope to control the former while they were excluded from the latter. In this manner, an old political quarrel took on ominous new religious overtones. Although the Swiss prudently refrain from discussing this dimension of the controversy, demographic statistics speak for themselves: the important town of Ilanz in the old Gray League is as a resident commune two-thirds Catholic; but its closed citizen commune remains entirely Protestant. This peculiar situation is repeated again and again in the towns of modern Graubünden, and is reflected in the larger picture of foreign immigration into Switzerland. The fervent and not very pretty controversy that has surrounded what the Swiss have called the "over-foreignization" (*Überfremdung*) problem has contained within it the same confessional divisions.[19] Supersaturated with needed foreign workers from mostly Catholic neighboring states, Switzerland during the 1960's seemed on the verge of renewed *Kulturkampf* on the model of the 1870 battle against the Jesuits, this time with racial overtones.

Had it not been infected with these confessional anxieties, it seems likely that the contest between citizen and resident communes would have abated in contemporary Graubünden, for, while the canton had failed to extinguish the tradition of communal autonomy fostered in the citizen communes, the tradition had been atrophying from within. Today, fundamental economic and political problems threaten the very existence of the commune both as a viable administrative organ within the modern state (the resi-

---

[19] The problem of so-called *Überfremdungs* is reviewed historically and in terms of current pressures in Oskar Reck, *Ist Die Schweiz Überfremdet?"* (Frauenfeld, 1969). Max Frisch summarizes the problem in these unsympathetic terms: "A diminutive master-race sees itself in danger: it calls for foreign manpower-resources, and instead gets living, breathing men." *Tagebuch: 1966-1971* (Frankfurt, 1972), p. 15. See Chapter IX below for elaboration.

dent commune) and as a vehicle of traditional sentiment for autonomy and self-government (the citizen commune). These problems have arisen out of the communes; they have not been foisted upon them by the canton. Perhaps the greatest irony of Graubünden's recent history has been that where the canton failed in a century-long struggle to bring the recalcitrant communes under its firm control, the communes, by their very insistence on their autonomous values and self-perpetuating citizen communes, have brought themselves to the brink of ruin, for they have managed to survive into a world where it now seems impossible for them to function. Less obdurate institutions would have expired long ago with the disappearance of the historical conditions that nurtured them and the coming of newer forces seemingly inimical to them. But the Raetian commune, having contended with "ineluctable" historical forces for a thousand years, persisted in an anachronistic survival—its values ever less suited to the economic realities of modern industrial society, yet at least to residents of the commune, ever more important as symbols of an alternative vision of community existence. Nonetheless, changing conditions have wreaked very real damage.

## The Modern Commune in Crisis: Economic Factors

Initially, the economic and fiscal crisis of the modern Raetian commune may seem little more than a representative manifestation of the more general economic difficulties experienced by local governments throughout the Western world in recent decades. In purely fiscal terms, the problem is quite simply inadequate income to fund rapidly expanding services: too few revenues, too many expenditures. But beneath the increasingly unbalanced budgets lie issues of a more existential nature: are the characteristics of rusticity, demographic modesty, full citizen participation, and far-reaching autonomy that define the classical, self-sufficient

220

Bündner commune compatible with the demands of economic interdependence and efficient political administration? Has not the commune encouraged its own demise by insisting on remaining sovereign in providing services better left to the more ample resources of the canton or federal government? As we look at communal accounts over the last fifty years, and compare declining revenues with expanding aspirations, we cannot help but feel that values rather than figures are the critical issue.

The disparity between income and expenditures is easily demonstrated, especially among the communes of Graubünden where wide differences in the fiscal status of individual villages have added a dimension of inequality to the communal crisis. Four major items have accounted for almost all communal spending in the last one hundred years, two having been extraordinarily demanding in the first half of the period (up to World War I), and two others having become significant more recently. Before World War II, more than a few communes bankrupted themselves trying to convert their primitive trail networks into modern roads suitable to the new transportation technology. The commune of Panix, a village of only several hundred citizens, spent over a million and a half francs between 1908 and 1938 on its roads, and only a small portion of this was paid for from cantonal funds.[20] It was as if a small Massachusetts village like Lenox had been required to fund a short strip of the Massachusetts turnpike. In recent years, federal subventions for highway construction have increased markedly, but the damage done to individual communes by the exorbitant early outlays has in some cases permanently compromised fiscal integrity.

[20] G. Sprecher depicts the plight of several such villages in *Die Bündner Gemeinde* (Bern, 1942). The subvention policy of the canton during earlier decades is reviewed by O. Gieré, *Der Staatshaushalt des Kantons Graubünden seit der Einführung der direkten Steuern bis heute: 1856-1914* (Stuttgart, 1915).

The construction and maintenance of schools have placed a second set of financial burdens on the communes, in what is perhaps the clearest example of the costs of autonomy. The Federal Constitution of Switzerland, like the modern West German one, leaves the administration of education almost completely to the cantons. Graubünden's decentralizing cantonal constitution in turn delegates the full responsibility at least for primary schools to the individual communes (see Articles 40 and 41). This ambivalent tribute to communal autonomy has left the larger, geographically centralized communes unruffled, but most of Graubünden's communes are neither large nor centralized. The average commune has thus suffered dearly for its traditionalist self-sufficiency. Some with fewer than a hundred families have nevertheless been compelled to maintain two or even more elementary schools. The village of Avers had only twenty-two students in the late 1930's, but had to operate two schools in order to reach its scattered pupils. Safien, with sixty children, maintained four schools for a time, and even then some pupils had to walk an hour or more on snow-bound trails to reach the nearest schoolhouse. At the height of this absurd decentralization in 1938, ninety-four communal schools in Graubünden had a total average enrollment of less than fifteen. Among the smallest twenty-three schools, there were forty-eight pupils, a mean of slightly more than two per school. While the teacher-pupil ratio at these favored institutions can only be regarded as remarkable, the costs required to maintain them were an impossible burden on the tiny villages, often resource-poor by virtue of the very altitude and inaccessibility that forced them to build multiple schools and extensive roads. Since World War II, cantonal subventions have increased and an economically desirable trend toward centralized schools, made possible by better roads and transportation, has been increasingly evident.

Yet even as the fiscal pressures of transportation and education are mitigated by the cantonal and the federal governments, other pressures are brought to bear. As recently as 1964 the minuscule commune of Valzeina, which lost nearly 20 percent of its population to the cities in the 1950's and which was deemed by the canton to be one of the "financially needy" communes deserving special treatment, nevertheless laid out more than $50,000 toward the construction of a $150,000 primary school. Moreover, two traditionally minor expenditures have in recent years become major: poor relief and environmental control.

Poor Relief (*Armenwesen*) originally meant little more than alms for the sick, the old, and the indigent who could prove citizenship in the citizen commune. But the more recent law of 1955 made the commune responsible for its resident needy, regardless of their commune of origin. While this is more equitable, it is also much more expensive.[21] Although communes subject to pronounced emigration have been relieved of much of their burden, other communes have had to assume responsibility for the emigrés. Most communes try to maintain a relief fund separate from other accounts, the interest of which covers expenditures; not many succeed in leaving their capital intact, however. Rising costs of living endanger even the most prudently managed funds.

Environmental control in the mountains where nature is an ongoing threat to transportation, commerce, and construction, as well as to life itself, has made heavy demands of the communes. Improved technology has enhanced the efficiency of avalanche and water control measures taken, but has sent costs soaring. Where river corrections, flood controls, avalanche and rockslide guards, and forestation efforts fail, still more expensive restorations and repairs are required to undo the havoc nature still wreaks. On river and stream

[21] The 1955 law superseded the century-old Poor Law of 1857 (cf. *Bündner Rechtsbuch*, pp. 1431–1437) and, with the intercantonal Concordat of 1937, provides security for all Swiss citizens residing in Graubünden.

corrections alone, Graubünden spent 37 million francs from 1840 to 1940. Of this, more than a third came out of the shrinking pockets of the communes, while the canton allowed the federation to pay the lion's portion of its share.[22]

These four items account only for major, ongoing expenditures. Administrative salaries and operating expenses, overhead on communal buildings, and other lesser items crowd into the debit columns as well. To offset these increased budgets, the communes have had only taxes, interest on communal capital, and investments as primary sources of income. Additional revenues are derived from the occasional disposal of woodland and its products, from the exploitation of hydroelectric resources, and from the tourist industry.

Direct taxation has never been a particularly viable instrument of raising revenues in the communes. Indirect taxation is the preferred Swiss approach, and generally speaking the villages that have inadequate taxable assets to make indirect taxation profitable are also saddled with a population whose direct tax-paying capacities are sorely limited.

On the other hand, the communes do possess extensive communal assets that in some cases provide major income. The school fund and poor relief fund sometimes even produce a profit from capital and other investments. Woodland has been of particular value, for Graubünden is second only to Bern in its wooded acreage, and is first in Switzerland in communal ownership of woodland—92 percent of its 161,-571 hectares are held as part of communal property (*Gemeindevermögen*).[23] In recent years, as a result of the quest for electric power, the canton's water resources, which in previous centuries have been only a source of anxiety and defensive spending (antiflood controls, for example), have

22 The figures are from Sprecher, *Die Bündner Gemeinde*, p. 90.

23 *Ibid.*, p. 26. Only 52 percent of Bern's woodland is communally owned.

224

been converted into Graubünden's most valuable natural asset. With over one-quarter of Switzerland's hydroelectric power in their hands, those Bündner communes situated on streams and rivers have discovered that water can be as valuable as the gold it occasionally yields.[24] For once, communal autonomy turns a profit. The water resources law of 1906 specifies that the communes have rights of exclusive exploitation of and control over waterways within their territory.[25] The income raised by taxing the fixed assets of national companies who have contracted with the communes to construct power installations, have made certain lucky communes rich. Others, however, removed from exploitable streams, have been able only to look hungrily on.

Tourism has also spread its fortune around rather inequitably—scenic, main-route villages doing well, closed-in, isolated communes remaining untouched. For the fortunate ones, tourism has meant prospering communally operated facilities (ski tows, cable railways), new taxable corporate assets (hotels, cinemas), and new varieties of tax like the special tourist levy (*Kurorttax*) on vacation residents.

The picture that emerges from these budgetary consider-

[24] The economic potential of water resources was well understood by the 1940's. See for example, Gian 3. Töndury, *Studie zur Volkswirtschaft Graubündens* (Samedan, 1946), Part 2; Otto Wieland, *Die Wasserrechtsverleihung im Kanton Graubünden* (Chur, 1941); and A. Gadient, "Zum Ausbau der Engadiner Kraftwerke," *Bündner Monatsblatt*, June-July 1955.

A dwindling minority has also focused on the ecological costs of water-resource development. See, for example, the Swiss Association for Nature Conservation, *Nationalpark oder Internationales Spölkraftwerk* (Basel, 1947), criticizing projects that have since been completed.

In the most recent years, the development of atomic energy plants (by 1972 there were three in operation in Switzerland) has provided alternative sources of electric power.

[25] The relevant public law, passed in 1906, declares that all water resources are the "property of the communes on whose territory they are found, and must be developed exclusively in accord with the provisions of the individual commune's laws." *Bündner Rechtsbuch*, p. 1018. See Wieland, *Die Wasserrechtsverleihung*, p. 18f.

ations is one of egregious inequality. Certain communes, rich in woodland, water resources, and tourism, grow fat without ever levying a tax on private persons; others, poor in wood, water, and scenic attractiveness, grow lean. Adversity breeds adversity. The young emigrate, tradesmen close up shop, and the disadvantaged communes soon face not merely economic ruin but extinction, for the very factors of inaccessibility and limited population that impair their capacity to raise revenue force them to spend more. The typically poor village will be physically remote with a small population scattered among inaccessible hamlets, too high in elevation to enjoy extensive woodland or exploitable waterfalls; yet by very virtue of these circumstances, it will need several schools, an expensive-to-maintain road network, and a safe avalanche control system. There is no way such a village can balance its budget. It is less and less clear that it can survive.

## THE MODERN COMMUNE IN CRISIS: POLITICAL FACTORS

Survival has become an issue for demographic and political reasons that, although catalyzed in part by economic crisis, have operated independently over the last fifty years. Political participation in citizen communes, the membership of which has been in a constant decline has become increasingly problematical. In Pravtal, St. Peter, and Malans, for example, the citizen commune has become a peculiar fiction with zero population in each village. In other less extreme cases, mere handfuls of citizens have found themselves unable to occupy the half dozen communal offices required to run the citizen commune, and have had to allow the canton to place them under *Kuratel*, an arrangement under which cantonal authorities actually govern the commune. The plight of the resident communes is somewhat less desperate, but political participation has fallen off there as well. Throughout Switzerland, electoral figures have pointed toward growing apathy: 67 percent of qualified voters participated in national referenda in 1938; 60 percent by 1948; under 50 percent by 1963; and less than 40 percent today.[26] Cantonal figures are even more dismal. Between 1923 and 1963 electoral participation in Zürich sank from 73 to 56 percent. Participation in Basel plunged from 64 to 34 percent, and in Bern from 46 to 34 percent.[27] A recent election in Geneva brought 2.83 percent of the electorate to the polls.

Graubünden's record has been somewhat less bleak. Participation varied between 50 and 70 percent for communal assemblies in the years following World War II. But the Lesser Council of the canton reported in 1968 that participation had fallen from a high of nearly 75 percent in 1930 to just over 40 percent in 1968—several percentage points above the national average to be sure, but appalling in an area steeped in the virtues of direct democracy.[28] The reasons for this ongoing decline are manifold. Many of them are related to urban and suburban alienation in an industrializing society, and to the uprooting of men from local soil and parochial traditions. But in Graubünden they also reflect the individual citizen's loss of confidence in the meaningfulness of local politics and the viability of the

[26] The figures are from Jürg Steiner, "Die Beteilung an vier eidgenössische Urengängen," *Neue Züricher Zeitung*, February 11, 1965. We need, however, to keep in mind that voters must go to the polls up to a dozen times a year to participate in a variety of federal, cantonal and local elections and referenda; as a result, Swiss figures are not really comparable with those taken in representative democracies for annual or biennial elections.

[27] These figures are ruefully cited by Max Imboden, *Helvetisches Malaise* (Zürich, 1964) and are confirmed by the more recent Erich Gruner, ed., *Die Schweiz seit 1945* (Bern, 1971), p. 218 and passim.

In 1919, on the other hand, participation in national elections was above 80 percent. See Brooks, *Civic Training in Switzerland*, p. 96f. We will examine this problem carefully in Chapter IX.

[28] Figures from the Lesser Council (*Kleiner Rat*), *Landesbericht Graubünden: 1968* (Chur, 1969), p. 7.

commune, the only salient political body with which he is likely to have had a relationship. The young flee, the old grow weary, and so the communes move inexorably toward death by depopulation. It is always the most vigorous who emigrate, leaving behind only an admixture of stubborn patriots too old to be effective and young complacents too unambitious to care. From 1950 to 1960, 131 communes or more than half of the canton's villages suffered a population decline, some by more than 80 percent.[29] Yet the canton's overall population actually increased during the period. Of the 55 communes requiring emergency cantonal aid in 1961, over 40 suffered demographic attrition in the previous ten years; 92 villages have resident communes of under 200, while 38 have less than 100. Yet many of the smallest are spread out over countless "fractions" and settlements (Höfe) compounding the demands for communal services. Valzeina with a population of 216 has 43 settlements.[30]

Not all who leave, leave by choice to seek the uncertain rewards of a metropolitan existence. The centralization and rationalization of dairy farming has created a situation in which jobs in this critical pastoral sector are available only to one person in six. In 1888 it provided a livelihood for 54 percent of the population. Meanwhile, sheep and goat

[29] From 1950 to 1960 six of fourteen Districts underwent a population decline, while 19 of 39 circuits suffered attrition. Switzerland, *Eidgenössische Volkszählung: 1. Dezember, 1960*, vol. 11, *Kanton Graubünden*. The 1970 census reflects the same development. For a general picture of Switzerland's demography, see Kurt B. Mayer, *The Population of Switzerland* (New York, 1952).

[30] Figures from S. Jenal, "Die Siedlungen der politischen Gemeinden des Kantons Graubünden," *Bündner Monatsblatt*, January-May 1957, p. 6f. Jenal notes that a tiny 6 percent of the population is spread out among 1,148 settlements, while 37 percent lives in 18 large communes with more than 1,000 citizens. (The total population for Graubünden in 1970 was 162,100 out of an entire Swiss population of 6,269,200.)

farming are in a permanent decline. The end of common grazing and the unavailability of personnel willing to spend months of solitude with their animals in summer pasture have made them uneconomic. A faltering economy, a diminishing population, and a changed Swiss environment combine to rob the ancient commune of its natural force and make it ever more vulnerable to the creeping cosmopolitanism that is everywhere expunging parochial vestiges of local patriotism, self-sufficiency, and autonomy. The situation has become critical enough for the canton, which once might have conceived of itself as having a vested interest in the bankruptcy of autonomous communes, to move vigorously toward communal reforms, many of which are directed less at placing the communes under cantonal controls than in restoring them to their earlier position of self-sufficiency. These reforms, which we will now have occasion to review, have been only partially successful, however. The problems run too deep to respond decisively to the anxious ministrations of a single cantonal government.

### The Modern Commune in Crisis: Reform Efforts

As we have seen, nineteenth-century attempts by the canton to bring the recalcitrant communes under their full control were mostly futile, despite the canton's constitutional sovereignty. However, the financial crisis of the communes in more recent decades has given the canton more leverage. Its recommendations have been heeded more conscientiously by communes on the edge of bankruptcy. Unfortunately, by the time many communes were willing to listen and to adjust their statutes to the model communal code (*Musterverordnung*) that had been developed by the canton, their difficulties were beyond simple remedy. In the last seventy-five years more than two dozen communes have had to be placed under the direct governance of the canton (under *Kuratel*).[31] This is less a tribute to reform than a symptom of decay, for *Kuratel* is an extreme measure, precipitated by disasters like bankruptcy or a pathological apathy that leaves communal offices unfilled and the commune ungoverned. By abrogating communal autonomy, *Kuratel* tends to breed and nurture the very complacency that generates the crises leading to its imposition.

Recognizing the debilitating consequences of *Kuratel*, the canton has moved in this century, through a series of decrees and ordinances culminating in the Lesser Council's Decree On Cantonal Take-over of Communal Debts of 1936, to head off communal crisis at an earlier stage.[32] The original decree and the Finance Equalization Plan that superseded it in 1956, which we will evaluate in its proper place below, was designed to buy an advisory voice for the canton in communal affairs by offering to take over communal debts in return for the commune's promise to reform its tax structure and permit cantonal intercession in its governance. Because it treated symptoms rather than causes, however, this approach did little to stem the rising tide of crises. The number of financially unstable communes rose steadily—from 12 with a total deficit of 18,000 francs in 1905, to 22 with a deficit of almost 150,000 francs in 1930, to 36 with a combined deficit of over 300,000 francs

[31] Article 40, Paragraph 7 of the Constitution of 1892 provides that "communes with illegal or inadequate administration (*ordnungswidrig Verwaltung*) may be ordered 'under Kuratel' by the Lesser Council, in critical cases." The cantonal government has employed this power only reluctantly however, and at present (1972) there are no Bündner communes under Lesser Council administration.

[32] The original decree providing for the take-over by the canton of debts incurred by financially deficient communes was adopted in 1936; it was superseded by the Financial Equalization Plan of 1956, discussed below. For a full discussion, see A. Lardelli, *Die Steuerhoheit der Selbstverwaltungskörper im Kanton Graubünden* (Affoltern am Albis, 1951), pp. 181–182ff., and Olgiati, *Die Gemeindeautonomie*, pp. 138–139ff., and Sprecher, *Die Bündner Gemeinde*, pp. 197–198ff.

in 1938.[33] In 1972, although not a single commune stands under *Kuratel*, 57 are regarded as financially needy by the canton. In 1968, a typical year, the needy communes received almost 1.4 million francs in special payments from the financial equalization fund.[34]

In fact, the Finance Equalization Plan (*Interkommunalen Finanzausgleich*) introduced in 1956 has done more than any other reform to ease the plight of depressed villages.[35] Based on a redistribution of revenues that has been successfully utilized in Bern and other cantons, the plan calls for the canton to assume communal powers of taxation on corporate persons; using the revenues gained from these taxes, primarily derived from hydroelectric capital assets, to create a special fund, the canton is then able to make major capital contributions to financially needy communes. In effect, the canton takes from wealthy communes fortunate enough to require no aid and gives to those that despite maximum exploitation of potential revenue sources are too poor to maintain themselves. The worst abuses of the inordinate inequality between communes with water-power potential and those without are thus ameliorated. Incentives have not been unduly dampened, because the plan reduces but does not eliminate communal revenue differentials. Moreover, recipients must demonstrate that they have exhausted all normal sources of taxation within the commune before being eligible, and can employ funds received exclusively for the purpose of major capital improvements (school construction, waterway improvement, etc.) or of mainte-

[33] Sprecher, *Die Bündner Gemeinde*, p. 204.

[34] Lesser Council (*Kleiner Rat*), *Landesbericht Graubünden: 1968* (Chur, 1969), p. 15.

[35] The text of the law is given in the *Bündner Rechtsbuch*, p. 1223f. The possibilities and the inequalities that came with hydroelectric power provoked the Equalization Plan. When a single commune (e.g., Tschappina) could derive as much revenue from a tax on a single power pylon as from all its other tax sources in combination, the arguments for some kind of intercommunal compensation became overwhelming.

nance of basic services (school fund or poor relief fund).[36]

The entire program is forced to operate within the context of communal sovereignty over water rights, however. The canton thus can neither profit directly from the new importance of hydroelectric installations nor remedy in full the inequities that the plan permits it to ameliorate. Even today, communal autonomy stands in the way of rational egalitarianism in communal fiscal affairs. "I would like to see," says a recent observer, "the cantonal assemblyman who would dare come before the Assembly with a proposal to transfer from the commune to the canton sovereign rights over water resources! Yet to do so would be to ask for no more than what is already the case in just about every other Swiss canton!"[37]

An even more creative, if largely symbolic, approach has been taken by a national private organization known as the Swiss Association of Sponsors for Depressed Communes

[36] The Equalization Plan rewards poor but fastidious communes in two ways. It levies a tax on corporate persons in all communes but returns to each an amount determined by the tax rate set by the individual communes on natural persons (i.e., its citizenry). A rich commune will probably not tax its citizens at all, and thus receive no refund from the canton; a poor commune may tax its citizens at the same rate (100 percent) as or even more (120 percent) than the cantonal rate. In the latter case, it will receive back all of or more than all of its payments to the canton. But in addition, communes that qualify as "financially weak" and have demonstrated their good will by exhausting their own resources, may receive large subventions that can be used for school construction or social security funds or other specified projects. It is through these latter payments that the canton achieves some real balance among the rich and the poor communes. Since the law was passed in 1956, over fifty communes have qualified each year as financially weak: in 1968, fifty-seven communes received almost 1,400,000 francs in special subventions, *Landesbericht.*

[37] Liver, "Die Bündner Gemeinde," p. 4. The canton does levy an insignificant "water tax" (*Wasserzins*), but otherwise derived no benefit at all from its natural resources until the introduction of the Equalization Plan.

(*Schweizerische Patenschaft für bedrängte Gemeinden*).[38] Operating throughout Switzerland, the association has persuaded large, affluent city communes to "sponsor" impoverished "sister communes" in depressed rural areas like Graubünden. Over 90 communes have benefited from the association since its establishment in 1940, not a few of them in Graubünden. Marmorera, for example, has enjoyed the patronage of Switzerland's largest city, Zürich. The commune gives the citizens of that metropolis a link with the Swiss rural past and receives important financial aid and administrative guidance in return. The mutual and collaborative character of the relationship is intended to dispel the charitable and patronizing atmosphere that usually enshrouds such philanthropic enterprises, but the association can touch only a tiny proportion of needy communes and its benevolence cannot help but gloss over the basic inequalities and structural deficiencies of the modern rural commune.

Recognizing the need for more basic reform, the canton has in the last three decades renewed its interest in a communal code that would rationalize and standardize relations between the resident communes and both the canton and the controversial citizen communes. In 1943 a code was drafted by the Lesser Council (*Kleiner Rat*) which, it promised, would "in no manner act to constrict the freedom and autonomy of the communes."[39] Traditionalists remained ardently unconvinced. Their leader, President Jörimann of the cantonal supreme court, argued that the new law would "strip the citizen commune of its defining prerogatives right by right, until only a shadow and then finally nothing at all remained of it."[40] It was true that Article 121 of the

[38] See G. Brosi, "25 Jahre Schweizerische Patenschaft für bedrängte Gemeinden," *Neue Bündner Zeitung*, November 13, 1965.

[39] Graubünden, *Botschaften des Kleinen Rates an den Grossen Rat*, vol. 1, 1943, p. 21.

[40] Jörimann, *Die Stellung*, pp. 21–22.

proposed code would compel the citizen commune to admit all qualified Swiss residents to citizenship, while Article 42 resolved the ongoing dispute over which of the two communes had real proprietorship over communal holdings in favor of the resident commune, referring to the citizen commune as a mere "personal association" (*Personalverband*) within the resident commune.

These provisions, however much improvement the balance of the code promised, proved decisively odious. In April 1944 the people of Graubünden once again went to the polls to defeat what they understood to be an assault on communal autonomy. The code was voted down 13,946 to 9,057.

In 1962 the Grand Council (*Grosser Rat*) moved to invite the Lesser Council to draft a new communal code, suggesting that further deterioration of conditions in the communes now made it imperative for the canton finally to have the code anticipated in the 1892 constitution and desperately needed ever since.[41] The Lesser Council responded with a draft that was moderate in its language and prudently respectful of the citizen commune in its provisions. The draft commission even included Dr. Jörimann, the leader of the opposition to the code of 1944. But popular sensibilities concerning communal codes had apparently been too conditioned over the years to be cajoled into placidity at this late day. In April 1966 a slim majority (8,576 to 8,029) buried for another twenty years all hopes for reforms by legislation. We can imagine that by 1984 a well-drafted law will finally secure majority support, but we can feel doubtful that such a law will any longer make a difference.

Graubünden, then, has accomplished a certain amount in its efforts at reform. A relative equalization among disadvantaged and prosperous communes has been achieved through the Finance Equalization Plan, and the most stag-

---

[41] Graubünden, *Grosserrats Protokoll*, 1962, p. 162.

gering economic burdens have been removed from communal shoulders through cantonal and federal intervention. The purely economic problems that remain are part of a much larger economic picture over which neither the communes nor the canton can have much influence. Graubünden is a part of Switzerland's rural southeast which, like Appalachia in the United States, is viewed by the Swiss as a depressed region and a national headache. Its problems derive from its rural character, its unsuitability to heavy industry (although light industries have been assiduously promoted with some success in the region),[42] and its exclusion from new trade and transportation routes. Only the Swiss federal government can begin to deal with these problems on a scale that matters. A new rail route through the southeast to Italy,[43] massive federal subventions, an explicit policy of industrialization—these kinds of reforms would begin to alleviate Graubünden's economic plight. But the federal government has more serious and pressing business: the

[42] Walter Lüthi depicts many of the problems connected with the development of light industry in the mountains in his "Industrialisierung der Bergtäler," *Bündner Monatsblatt*, March-April 1955. Typical successes have been a chemical plant in Ems, paper mills in Landquart, a cement factory in Untervaz, and beer and chocolate factories in Chur; but these are often controlled by extracantonal Swiss interests or even by the West Germans, who have also been speculating heavily in Swiss real estate until a recent federal decree terminated all foreign land speculation.

[43] Eastern Switzerland has long had to compete with central Switzerland for federal rail and road routes. The nineteenth-century origins of the competition are carefully and partisanly presented in Peter C. Planta, *Der 30 Jährige Kampf um eine rhätische Alpenbahn* (Chur, 1885). More recently, the contest has turned on the construction of so-called basis tunnels that provide direct rail and road routes through tunnels ten to twenty miles long. Many argue that the future of eastern Switzerland depends on the development of new tunnels and transportation routes through the Raetian mountains. See, for example, O. Martin, "Die Splügenlinie," *Neue Bündner Zeitung*, December 19, 1964; or "Die Ostalpbahnfrage," *Neue Bündner Zeitung*, March 30, 1965; or Rudolf Jenny, *Ostschweizer Transitbahn Splügen/Basistunnel* (Chur, 1963).

economic status of Switzerland in Europe, its role in the Common Market, its nuclear status in a multipolar world. Help on the scale required thus seems unlikely.

Yet the very magnitude of the solutions demanded point to a more profound dimension of the crisis, for the approach suggested by massive federal intervention, as well as by the several efforts at reform within the canton, is one that in effect rescues the commune from disaster by annihilating its defining autonomy and self-sufficiency. If the commune is to survive it must surrender the qualities that alone justify its survival; if it refuses to pay this price, and clings to its traditional values (as it has in the last two referenda on a communal code), it cannot survive, and its values perish anyway.

Thus, the real dilemma of the commune is a dilemma of values, a study in the incompatibility of what appears to be modernity with traditions of autonomy that have been fought for and maintained for more than a thousand years. In its simplest form, the dilemma poses for us the decisive question: "Is life in small, self-governing relatively autonomous rural communes possible in the Western industrial world in the 1970's?"

# CHAPTER IX

# The Confrontation with Modernity

THERE are still 220 communes in Graubünden and over 3,000 in Switzerland, but more and more the rural village community appears as an anachronism in an age with no tolerance for throwbacks. The self-conscious Swiss government, still cringing at Karl Barth's 1963 remark suggesting that Switzerland was fast becoming "the village idiot of Europe,"[1] and trying ardently to prove that theirs is not "the most archaic governmental system in the West,"[2] seems willing to reconsider the entire political past. Traditions that do not meet the test of centralist aspirations and of bureaucratic efficiency become immediate targets of official propaganda. Talk of a total revision of the Federal Constitution has filled the airwaves and newspapers for over ten years, although (despite the preparatory work of the so-called Wahlen Commission on Total Revision) the Swiss people will probably not be ready for this drastic measure for a decade or more.

While the government tries to demonstrate its modernity, critics within and outside Switzerland decry the provincialism and conservatism that makes Switzerland's direct democracy so peculiarly obstructive and inefficient. Odious comparisons are offered constrasting the progressive heterogeneity of centralized political systems controlling large pluralistic societies, and Switzerland's decentralized confederation of parochial cantons where localism is a reactionary little king. Germany's leading liberal newsweekly *Der Spiegel* thus complains that "century-long negligence, intoler-

---

[1] Cited in "Die Schweiz—Vorbild von Gestern," *Der Spiegel*, August 2, 1971.

[2] Attributed to Herbert Luethy, *Der Spiegel, ibid.*

ance and complacency have made of one of the richest countries in the world what can only be regarded—in a higher
sense—as an underdeveloped land."[3] Somewhat more detached but no less critical *The Economist* notes that "the
Swiss are fond of saying that they are willing to pay a bit
more for things, and take longer over them, for the sake of
keeping the cantonal spirit alive. One wonders whether they
will keep on saying it as the bills of a technological society
roll in."[4] Yet in the rush to accommodate the "progressive"
critics, the Swiss seem in greater danger of ignoring the costs
of wholesale change and the dismantling of traditions than
of miscalculating the price of refusing to change, and abid-
ing by petrified customs. Too often, it is made to appear that
Switzerland's plight and thus the precarious situation of the
village community are simply a matter of overcoming the
rigidities of reactionary traditionalists; that the choices are
between close-minded pig-headedness and common sense, between complacency and public-spiritedness, between the unthought dogmas of a bygone era and the flexible realism
of an unavoidable present. In the competition to be flexible
and forward-looking, the possibility that something more
than mere obstinacy may be at stake in traditionalist attitudes is overlooked. Lip service is frequently paid to communal values, for example, but they are never permitted
to mute the reformer's plea for greater centralization of
administration or efficiency of planning. One reformer thus
calls for both the preservation of communal autonomy *and*
accelerated economic modernization through extensive state

3 *Ibid.*

4 B. Beedham and G. Lee, "Even in Paradise: Switzerland—A Survey," *The Economist*, February 22, 1969, p. viii. These critical stric-
tures need to be treated with a certain skepticism, for Switzerland
like other small, neutral countries, has been generally assailed with
an undeserved venom by foreign observers. Critics from large, quasi-
imperial countries have been particularly self-righteous and unfriendly, and have given the genre a bad name. See, for example, J. C.
Herold, *The Swiss Without Halos* (New York, 1948).

intervention.[5] Another insists on the need to enhance the power of political authorities without seeming to perceive the dampening effect of centralized power on political participation, the decline of which he also rues.[6]

Yet as we watch the rural mountain communes of Switzerland edging into a reluctant modernity that their autonomy cannot hope to survive, the profundity of the choices they are being compelled to make becomes ever more striking. Over a century ago, a Raetian patriot had implored his countrymen to recognize the incompatibility of the past they continued to cherish and the future to which they aspired:

> Pure democracy, extensive public liberty, and at the same time unitary and forceful central administration? A lessening, or at least no increase in state obligations, and at the same time economic progress comparable to other states? Spurn diplomacy and at the same time play a role of importance among European nations? Honor the principle of neutrality and at the same time intervene in the foreign affairs of other states? No, these are incompatible things, principles that in cause and in effect are mutually exclusive.[7]

The dilemmas faced by the communes of Graubünden today are the product of a century-long collision between indisputedly vital communal norms and the apparent requisites of national survival in an industrialized, urbanizing world. Progress in this context may mean the surrender of both meaningful personal autonomy and real self-government. Those who are obstinate in the defense of these values are clearly more than merely pig-headed. Indeed, it may be the reformers, enamored still of rational

---

[5] Georg Sprecher, *Die Bündner Gemeinde* (Chur, 1942), p. 81 and passim.

[6] Max Imboden, *Helvetisches Malaise* (Zürich, 1964), pp. 35, 39.

[7] "Von einem geborenen Graubündner," *Die Heutige Zustände in Graubünden* (Chur, 1838), p. 45.

models of spiraling GNP's and costless exploitation of resources, who are truly blind. In societies that have reaped the ambivalent fruits of full abundance and maximum productivity, the radicals are those who plead for conservation and the restoration of community. It is strange, then, to see Swiss radicals like Max Frisch and Max Imboden so captious about their own nation's reluctance to settle into the facile cosmopolitanism of a liberal Europe bound together by common devotion to out-producing and out-marketing the other world economic monoliths. We need not be new Malthusians or swallow uncritically the projections of the Massachusetts Institute of Technology's study (under the auspices of the Club of Rome) of the approaching limits of growth to recognize that the Western growth mania has exacted a severe price,[8] or to acknowledge that the conflicts in the recent history of the alpine village community may reflect an attempt to grapple, if only instinctively, with the consequences of paying the price.

We want, then, in the concluding chapter of this historical investigation of the challenges faced by the alpine village communities of Graubünden, to examine carefully the competing claims of Graubünden's beneficially parochial communal past and its looming Swiss-European future. It appears improbable that the communes will survive in anything like their traditional, face-to-face democratic form in a world that has abdicated such forms elsewhere centuries ago, but it is probably also true that these dying forms contain the promise of an alternative mode of po-

[8] See D. H. Meadows, et al., *The Limits to Growth* (New York, 1972). Malthusian fashions come and come. Thanks to our centuries-old plundering of the earth, we presently appear to be entering a period of maximum concern with ecology and conservation. But the more intriguing question, raised here but mainly ignored by pessimistic observers of man's deteriorating physical environment, is whether growth has cultural and political costs that, even if we could afford its environmental price, make it undesirable.

240

litical life, the importance of which can only increase as the viability of modernity diminishes.

In order to give to these generalities some substance, we need to localize and specify the conflicts that are at their heart. We need first to look at the vestigial face-to-face community as it appears through the eyes of a no longer autonomous citizenry trying to come to terms with an encroaching world of industry, urbanism, pluralism, and pluralistic possibility; then, to evaluate the crisis of the commune's most perfect political expression, direct democracy, as it fails the growth-oriented tests of efficiency, rationalism, and planning. The failures of communalism and direct democracy reveal the inevitability and potency of pluralistic centralism in an industrializing society, but they also reveal its human bankruptcy, for the eclipse of communalism may mean for the Swiss the eclipse of political man as an autonomous participant in the self-governing of his collective life.

### THE FACE-TO-FACE COMMUNITY IN A FACELESS INDUSTRIAL SOCIETY

To walk in the eighth decade of the twentieth century through a small, alpine village in the shadow of mountains that have watched impassively the coming of industrial society is a remarkable experience in contrasts. A massive peasant house built in the sixteenth century stands placidly across from a completely automated milk processing center in which machines now easily undertake a host of functions once carried out by the peasant family across the way. A swaying cable car carries indifferent foreigners up over common land that the village no longer has sufficient numbers to cultivate. A young girl can still be seen haying on the side of an alpine meadow worked by her ancestors, but she is wearing a miniskirt and ribbed sweater, and she knows

her labors will soon terminate in a big city salesgirl appren-
ticeship. Schnapps-drinking grandfathers play whist at the
Post-hotel pub, but for their nostalgic stories to be heard
they must shout across a blaring jukebox installed for the
benefit of their grandchildren, who waste away their adoles-
cence waiting for the army to liberate them from the confines of the village. With their four months of initial service
over, only a handful will return to take up lives in the
mountains.

Even the village profile has taken on a startling new aspect. Not the stolid communal church, built four hundred
years ago and embodying the integral unity of the village,
but a recently thrown up high-rise apartment dominates
the skyline, and it is as detached from the community in
its colorless heterogeneity as the church was integral to it.
The very mountains seem diminished by the cable cars and
powerlines that everywhere mark their face, in gloating
tribute to the emancipation of alpine man from alpine terrors. Villages thus become towns, and towns burgeon into
cities. The cantonal capital of Chur, once defined by the
cathedral and the guildhalls and public places grouped in
the old city around the bishop's court, now centers on the
high-rises and national chain stores that have sprung up
across town outside the old city walls, its population ex-
ploding by 25 percent from 1960 to 1970.

The same transformations can be seen almost anywhere
in Switzerland, a nation which, because it has avoided the
ravages of war and poverty, can only be remodeled by
planned demolition or relocation. The change is particularly obvious in autonomous villages that sit fortuitously
on the doorstep of large cities. Adliswil, a small village
outside of Zürich, has tripled in size in the last twenty
years, adding 10,000 rootless commuters, emigrés from
Zürich, most of whom live in vertical clusters of several
hundred in high-rise apartments that float above rather

Artificial Integration

Natural Isolation

Bern: New City

Bern: Old City

than inhabit the community.[9] The town council happily projects another 15,000 refugees from the city over the next twenty years, which will bring the population by 1990 to over 30,000. Few of these outsiders can be expected to take an interest in the commune or its insular past. In French Switzerland, the suburbanization of the once pastoral commune has been even more pronounced. George A. Codding has written a dry but telling account of the little commune of Veyrier that "has become over the years primarily a 'bedroom town' for the city of Geneva. The overwhelming majority of its occupants now depends for its livelihood on the income of members of the family who work in the city."[10] That such a town can be regarded as a community in any sense at all is very doubtful. Some villages have refused to capitulate to the agreeable blandishments of nearby cities, but their days seem numbered by their proximity. Frauenkappeln near the Swiss capital of Bern, an ancient cloister and relatively prosperous farm community, recently formed a citizens' association to resist encroachments from the spreading federal metropolis. But Bern grows and grows; its need for additional suburbs intensifies; and if not this year, then next; if not next, then the year after. . . .

The significance of these impressionistic observations lies especially in the climate these developments create for the present and future citizenry of the village community. By a number of objective indicators the commune may not seem so badly off. In 1960, 69 percent of Switzerland's population still resided in the canton of their birth, and 42 percent remained in their commune of birth, certainly one of the highest percentages in the industrialized world. Of

---

[9] Figures from Adliswil Council, *Adliswil* (Adliswil/Zürich, 1971). Also see Benjamin R. Barber, "Switzerland: Progress Against the Communes," *Trans-action*, February 1971.

[10] George A. Codding, Jr., *Governing the Commune of Veyrier: Politics in Swiss Local Government* (University of Colorado, 1967), p. 16.

public monies expended, 59 percent flowed from the cantons and communes, only 41 percent from the federal budget, a healthy tribute to the vitality of federalism. Despite the aspirations of the federal government, intercommunal and intercantonal planning remain disastrously minimal, again underscoring the apparent potency of localism. Yet the impression created by these objective facts is belied by the climate we can sense in the rural communes, and by other kinds of statistics that testify to the behavior this climate has engendered.

The simple fact remains that few young people can be found in Graubünden's mountain communes who anticipate spending their lives in the villages where they were born. The brighter and more audacious the youngster, the more likely he or she is to yearn for the opportunities and flexibilities of a more cosmopolitan life. Not only are economic prospects in the village limited, but the jobs for which personnel are most critically needed (e.g., in the pastoral economy) appear least attractive. Why should a young man spend solitary summers with listless herds high in the mountains, when he can clerk in a bank in a large town, leaving him half of his day for leisure activities? His forbearers had no choice and found rewards in the autonomy and partial autarky their arduous labor brought them. But he does have a choice. The bonds that once drew men together into a loyal collectivity are perceived by him as pointless chains. The Beatles or the Stones represent voices he can understand; the echo of communal patriots pleading over the centuries for the maintenance of communal vigilance against feudal or imperial or other conspiratorial foes glance off him unheard. What can the ghost of a Georg Jenatsch or a William Tell say to an international counter-culture of the young promoted and funded by international capitalism? Who is to remind the young of the sacrosanctity of the village assembly when the important decisions have been taken out of its hands and its vaunted traditions made over into tourist attractions? The village community may still live on in cantonal statutes but in those young citizens who alone can guarantee its survival as an ideal it seems entirely moribund.

The opposition to modernization began in Switzerland long ago. The alpine cantons in particular have never been very hospitable to the innovations fostered by their urban counterparts. Graubünden has usually been regarded as the most obstinate of all. In the late eighteenth century, an English observer had already noted that "in these little republics [of Graubünden] a strange prejudice prevails against commerce, and the project of establishing manufactures is opposed by many leading men of the country."[11] At the beginning of this century this same unswerving antipathy to economic modernization produced a most extraordinary law concerning automobiles. A 1911 statute decreed bluntly: "The driving of automobiles of any type, passenger cars, trucks or motorcycles, is forbidden on all roadways in the canton of Graubünden."[12] This remarkable ban was retained for twenty-one years, and finally was revoked in 1932 only as a result of intense pressure from the Swiss federal government.[13] There was to be sure a certain irrationality in Graubünden's stance, and skeptics are quick to point to the hand of the railroad lobby in the affair. But there also seems to have been a prudent caution about the vulnerability of alpine communalism to corruption by external forces. The potency of the village community derived from its rusticity, its limited and stable population,

11 William Coxe, *Travels in Switzerland and in the Country of the Grisons*, 3 vols. (London, 1801), vol. 3, p. 251.

12 Graubünden, *Amtliches Gesetzes-Sammlung*, vol. 6, p. 649. The influence of the railroad industry on the automobile ban is discussed by Rudolf Jenny, *Historisches Exposé—San Bernadino: Graubünden's Passtrassen und ihre volkswirtschaftliche Bedeutung* (Chur, 1963).

13 In 1925 the ban was partially lifted to allow the operation of sanitation, safety and other public service vehicles, but the prohibition on private automobiles remained in force until 1932.

and the refreshingly parochial nature of its common interests. Opening the commune up to progressive interdependence and the modernizing influence of the outside
world might enhance public affluence, but it could also
jeopardize the public weal as measured by these critical
standards. The canton thus turned its back on what was to
become the symbol of twentieth century civilization, and
what more recently has been referred to as "an ideology
on four wheels."

Urban critics naturally spoke derisively of the ban as
a comical idiosyncrasy of a bull-headed people incapable of
prognosticating the requirements of their own economic
welfare. Yet today, when most of the social and political
damage has already been done (not to speak of the environmental damage), villages and towns throughout Switzerland along with cities throughout the world are reconsidering the place of the automobile within their environs.
Wengen, Murren, Braunwald, and Zermatt are only a few
of the fifty-three alpine communities that have recently
barred passenger cars. Inner-town areas of cities like Murten
have also been closed to traffic.[14] The catalyzing factor in
these recent changes has obviously been environmental pollution, but more than a few communes have shown concern
for the quality of the political as well as the physical environment in legislating against the automobile.

Another example of resistance to modernization is provided by the practice of common-grazing (*Gemeinatzung*),
a symbol of collective rights of usage over communal land
since the Middle Ages and a particular nemesis of economic
modernization in recent centuries. This practice, depicted
in some detail above in Chapter V, allows any communal citizen to graze his livestock on all land in the commune, regardless of its status as private property; it is put to use
mainly in herding stock to and from mountain pastures in

[14] See "Switzerland Without Cars," *The New York Times*, Sunday,
June 16, 1968, Section 10, p. 1.

the spring and fall. As early as the eighteenth century it was clear to advocates of a rational agrarian economy that common grazing was incompatible with progress. Yet ancient usages left the individual who held title to land with only a single recourse: to fence off his property at his own cost. In a region where wood was a scarce and treasured economic commodity and land itself parceled out into minuscule widely distributed plots, the problems of fencing in each piece of privately held land against the semiannual depredations of migrating livestock were almost insuperable. But unfenced, a bit of land could be successfully cultivated only by the lucky.

All of this changed, however, with the coming of the electric fence, one more innovation of modern technology that doomed still another aspect of Graubünden's traditional communalism. Electric fences were cheap, lightweight, easy to put up, and still easier to remove: a propertyholder could finally protect his real estate efficiently and economically. Common grazing went into a steep decline that ultimately affected the entire pastoral economy. Goat and sheep herding, depending heavily on open pasture, underwent permanent contraction. Small owners, unable to provide the necessary personnel to supervise herds no longer able to pasture freely, could not survive. The centralization and technologization of the pastoral economy was thus indirectly catalyzed. At the same time, notions of collective usage that had been kept alive for so long through their realization in common grazing, were left to expire as pointless abstractions. Certain remote regions of the Upper Rhine Valley (in the old Gray League) still cling to the ancient usages of common grazing, but elsewhere it is dead —all to the good of the economy, but at what cost to the spirit of the village-community?

Communal insistence on retaining full control of rights over their waterways and fisheries to the detriment of their economy provides a third example of the clash between traditional values and economic modernization. We have already noted in the previous chapter the enormous inequities to which narrowly exercised communal rights over waterpower led, and the reforms these intercommunal inequities eventually precipitated. The damage done to the fisheries by localism is equally revealing. Communal control of fishing rights prevented the canton from establishing a common season, protecting endangered species, or making rational regionwide decisions of any kind about stocking and maintaining the river and stream fisheries. The results were disastrous, and subsequent commentators have not failed to note the connection between the "extensive damage done" and the "traditional democratic autonomy of the communes" that occasioned it.[15]

It would be convenient to treat these cases as examples of a lethargic alpine Ludditism, a kind of Romantic pastorale to the virtues of simplicity against the depersonalizing improvements of technology. Yet there is no particular animus here against the machine, no self-conscious advocacy of Arcadian alternatives. The issue was and remains the political autonomy and economic autarky of the village community, the preservation of traditional rights against the claims not of the machine per se but the kind of society the machine seems inevitably to create. Thus, when an eighteenth-century critic complains that "the mountain man is so proud of his privileges, so content with his condition,

---

[15] F. Manatschal, "Graubünden seit 1815," in Fritz Jecklin, ed., *Bündnergeschichte in Elf Vorträgen* (Chur, 1902), p. 339. Legislative measures might have been taken, but the cantonal government at the turn of the century "knew all too well how the communes would have reacted: their jealous vigilance where their autonomy was at stake was well-known to it." Otto Wieland, *Die Wasserrechtsverleihung im Kanton Graubünden* (Chur, 1941), p. 21. "I would like to see," writes Peter Liver, "the deputy who dared to come before the Grand Council with a proposal to turn over rights over waterways and waterpower to the canton! Even though in nearly every other canton of Switzerland, cantonal control of waterrights is taken for granted!" "Die Bündner Gemeinde," *Bündner Monatsblatt*, February 1941, p. 4.

that he takes his predilection against innovations to the point of superstition and beyond,"[16] it is not so much the antipathy to change as the devotion to the status quo of a privileged autonomy that strikes us. The question for which the citizen of the commune always wanted an answer was not, "is your reform progressive, efficient, rational," but "will it encumber self-sufficiency and infringe upon autonomy?" A centralized cantonal court was defeated in the eighteenth century and a centralized cantonal school system blocked in the nineteenth and twentieth neither out of traditionalist hubris against justice nor reactionary distaste for education, but because the cost of these improvements appeared to be the abandonment of the cherished freedom of the village community. Industry was opposed as early as the eighteenth century because it was thought that "in free states particularly, manufactures tend to enervate the inhabitants, to introduce luxury, to depress the spirit of freedom, and to destroy the general simplicity of manners."[17] The automobile was excluded from the roads of Graubünden more recently less because it was a machine or an innovation than because it brought with it the outside world and threatened to infect stable communities with that automotive individualism that, as America has so poignantly demonstrated, small-town life simply cannot survive. The automobile takes citizens and makes of them mere individuals; it takes children with roots in a family and ties to a common past and makes of them orphaned vagabonds; it takes communards and sets them loose in a homeless society where independence means loneliness and liberation conveys only the sad sense of solitude.

The resistance, all too clearly, has failed. Rusticity by its very nature cannot long impede the inroads of cosmopolitanism; any more than silence can impede noise, or

[16] de Lüc, "Aus Hrn de Lüc Briefen [sic]," *Der Sammler*, 1781, p. 318.

[17] Coxe, *Travels in Switzerland*, vol. 3, p. 252.

placidity, ambition. Moreover, almost from the beginning of the contest cantonal governments and the Swiss federal government have been allies of economic progress—whatever the costs to the communes.

To Switzerland's centralizing bureaucracies the country's radically decentralized confederal system is an extravagance. Traditionalist attitudes that still linger in the public mind are anachronistic. To "reform" the small nation, to bring it into the twentieth century, means to extend central control and central planning, to nourish a national economy, and to rationalize and unify a sprawling confederal apparatus. The pace of reform, of course, must be prudent. An overly ambitious program produced run-away inflation, labor shortages, senseless demolition of landmark buildings and an egregious sell-out of land and corporate interests to foreign investors (primarily German) in the 1960's. Steps have thus been taken recently to freeze demolition, slow construction, outlaw foreign real estate speculation in Swiss land and otherwise modify the pace of change. In a meaningless gesture to the past, a federal plan to dismantle the Military Department's Horse Cavalry was overwhelmingly rejected by the National Council (*Nationalrat,* Lower House of Parliament) in 1972.[18]

But tactical concessions to prudence and moderation will not stem the urbanizing tide that is transforming the face of Swiss life; nor can stubbornness alter the government's intransigent reformist posture. Foreign land investment in scarce Swiss real estate can be reduced, wholesale demolition of old town districts retarded, and sentimental favorites like the horse cavalry kept momentarily alive. But the depopulation of alpine villages and the death by apathy of communitarian politics continues. It is a telling postscript to the horse cavalry story that at the very end of 1972 the Lower House, having paid tribute with its earlier obstinacy to tradition, capitulated completely to a second government

[18] See *The New York Times,* October 2, 1972.

250

initiative: the ponies have been put to pasture and the cavalry is no more.

The futility of essaying to resist forces that are in fact nearly irresistible has led many Swiss into expressions of frustration and cantankerousness that verge on the pathological. The conservative impulse, too often thwarted, becomes reactionary; the healthy instinct to protect a valued past, if consistently frustrated, turns into perverse intransigence. The Separatist Movement in the Jura mountain region (*Rassemblement jurassien*) of the canton of Bern, for example, has become increasingly violent and extremist, as its once modest aims seem less and less likely to succeed. Beginning as a movement representing the typically Swiss impulse to decentralization and regional autonomy (in this case for the French-speaking Jurassien inhabitants of predominately German-speaking Bern), it has ended as a frustrated vehicle of wholly untypical and mostly futile passion —even violence. In 1968 it was responsible for a violent disturbance at a joint session of the national parliament, the likes of which have not been seen in Swiss politics since the Civil War of 1847.[19]

An even more revealing example of the increasingly

[19] In December, 1968, a radical splinter group of the Jurassien movement called the Rams disrupted a meeting of parliament. Although the movement has suffered a series of electoral defeats even in its home districts where it presumably enjoys maximum strength, it has not advocated independence in the manner of the Free Quebec movement; only regional autonomy. For the program of the movement, see Rassemblement jurassien, *Declaration de principe sur la Constitution et sur les lignes directrices de la politique de l'état jurassien* (Délemont, 1954), and Eric Dellenbach, *Violence au pays des grandes joux* (Tramelan, 1966). The more recent views of the movement's leader Roland Béguelin can be found in his news conference *Conference de Presse* (Délemont, 1969).

The more general questions of violence in Swiss politics are discussed by Kenneth D. McRae, *Switzerland: Example of Cultural Coexistence* (Toronto, 1964); and Jürg Steiner, "Non-violent Conflict Resolution in Democratic Systems: Switzerland," *Journal of Conflict Resolution*, vol. 13, no. 3, 1969.

desperate character of the Swiss resistance to modernity can be found in the so-called Schwarzenbach case. During the boom years of the 1960's, Switzerland's economy underwent a rapid expansion that put severe strains on its already overemployed labor force. As a consequence, a stopgap measure that had provided for the importation of foreign workers during the 1950's was converted into a permanent national economic policy. First Italian, then Spanish, Greek, and other Mediterranean workers found their way into Switzerland to contribute to and participate in Switzerland's remarkable prosperity. The Swiss government, its eye on economic statistics and its ear attuned to the encouraging voices of Swiss industry, lent its full support to this international labor traffic, although it did far less than it might have to guarantee civilized working and living conditions for the temporary immigrants. But the Swiss people were perturbed and became ever more intolerant. Propelled not only by fear and by latent national chauvinism tainted with racism but also by a realistic regard for the precarious equilibrium on which their multiethnic nationality rested, they complained with growing bitterness about the dangers of what was openly called "over-foreignization" (*Überfremdung*). By the end of the decade, apparent government unresponsiveness and the intensification of these fears had created a climate conducive to direct action. Under the leadership of James Schwarzenbach, a publisher from Zürich, a constitutional amendment was introduced by petition that would limit the number of foreigners in any given canton (except Geneva) to 10 percent of the population.[20] Because there were already over 990,000 foreign workers domiciled in Switzerland out of a population

[20] Because Geneva is an international center, it is excluded from the quota system. The text of the referendum proposal known as the "Over-foreignization Initiative II" and aimed at modifying Article 69 of the Federal Constitution is given in Oskar Reck, *Ist die Schweiz Überfremdet?* (Frauenfeld, 1969), pp. 54–55.

of nearly six million, the effect of the amendment would be to expel more than 300,000 men.[21] On June 7, 1970, the amendment came to a national vote by referendum, and was narrowly defeated, to the relief of the appalled federal government, which quickly moved to assume a somewhat harsher stance toward foreign immigration to deter future trouble.

The significance of the Schwarzenbach proposal for us, however, lies not in its ultimate defeat but in the extraordinary vitality of its popular backing and in the nature of the controversy that surrounded the campaign preceding its defeat. The forces arrayed against it were formidable: the Federal Council (*Bundesrat*, or seven-man executive department) was implacably opposed to the measure; the National Council, presumably representative of popular opinion, voted 136 to 1 against it (prior to the referendum); the Council of States (*Ständerat*, representing the cantons) rejected it 39 to 0. Manufacturing, trade, and industrial interests were unanimously critical and funded a record-breaking publicity campaign urging defeat of the proposal and defaming its supporters. Schwarzenbach backers were portrayed as Nazis bent on turning the Swiss white cross into a grotesque black swastika. Not a single major political party, not one significant pressure group or voluntary association could be found that was favorable to the amendment. An outside observer would have to conclude that a handful of maniacs under the demented leadership of a hysterical, neo-Nazi reactionary were about to be given the soundest electoral thrashing of Swiss history by a nation wholly united against them. Yet on June 7, no less than 46 percent of a postwar record turnout (over 74 per-

[21] According to Reck, at the end of 1968 there were 933,142 foreigners in Switzerland of whom over two-thirds were laborers. Between 1959 and 1962 alone, over 280,000 foreign workers entered Switzerland: it would be as if within three years ten million temporary workers, few of whom spoke English, took up temporary residence in America. *Ibid.*, p. 17 and p. 28.

cent of the eligible electorate) voted yes on the amendment, while in seven of the twenty-two cantons the proposal actually carried.[22] Four out of nine voters had gone against their government, against their party, against the unions, against the media, and against what might have been regarded as all the smart money in the land. Though the amendment was defeated, the electoral results were a scandal.

Opponents of the proposal naturally suggested that it was the repressed voice of racism that had spoken—too self-conscious to make itself heard openly through the media and normal political channels, but unleashed in the privacy of the ballot booth.

Certainly both anti-Latin and anti-foreign sentiment was involved. For a decade, Swiss newspapers had carried discreet housing advertisements letting rooms to "working gentlemen: must be Swiss," while sneering businessmen spoke about their non-Swiss employees as "Gotthard Chinese" or worse. But charges of racism, appropriate as they may be, fail to explain the widespread and intense support for the Schwarzenbach amendment. The largest majorities against the proposal were put together in the large cities, where the presence of foreign workers was most acutely felt and where racist sentiments were likely to be most pronounced. Conversely, it was in the rural, Catholic inner-Swiss cantons of Luzern, Uri, Schwyz, Obwalden, and Nidwalden where the largest pro-Schwarzenbach majorities were found; yet few foreign workers lived in these regions, and Catholicism represented a common link that should have softened anti-Latin feeling. Moreover, even in the progressive French-speaking cantons of Vaud and Geneva

[22] The popular vote was 557,714 for to 654,588 against; the cantonal vote, seven to fifteen with Bern, Luzern, Uri, Schwyz, Obwalden, Nidwalden, Freiburg, and Solothurn voting affirmatively. In Graubünden 11,318 voted for and 16,705 against, a fairly decisive defeat for a referendum that had widespread rural support. Figures from Jürg Tobler, *Dossier Schweiz: Democratie—Testfall 7.Juni, 1970* (Zürich, 1971), p. 42.

better than one out of three voted for the amendment. In
the Italian-speaking Ticino, although an expected majority
of nearly 27,000 voted against, more than 15,000 voted for,
the measure. Graubünden's more remote villages voted
overwhelmingly for, although the larger towns managed to
assemble a cantonwide majority against Schwarzenbach's
proposal.

This telling distribution of votes lends credence to a
different interpretation of the Schwarzenbach affair that,
while it does not deny nationalist and racist attitudes, suggests the primacy of a more basic socioeconomic and value
struggle in the contest. In its simplest terms, it suggests that
the opponents of Schwarzenbach were not merely tolerant
liberals defending the international civil rights of hard-
working foreigners, but were the combined forces of efficiency, national planning, centralization and economic
progress representing the political and industrial elite of the
Swiss nation. And it suggests that his supporters were not
simply bigoted reactionaries, but advocates of an integral
communal past founded on autonomous self-government.
Beyond the sledge-hammer slogans ("Do you really want,
thanks to foreign-worker masses, to live like sardines?"), a
more interesting and revealing rhetoric could be heard.
"They would pave over our farms with concrete," warns a
Schwarzenbach pamphlet. Schwarzenbach wanted, suggests
an observer, "to save simple human labor from mass industrial labor, wanted to restore rusticity, wanted to rescue
humility from big-city materialism and its arrogance. . . ."
"You cannot take prosperity with you to the grave," he
liked to say.[23]

Big cities, big government, big industry, and big money—
they were clearly on the side of history, pledged to make

[23] *Ibid.*, p. 32. Oskar Reck notes that many critics of the influx of
foreign workers are also critics of the land sell-out to foreign interests
who use the term "spiritual over-foreignization" to suggest that their
discontent is much larger than the foreign worker issue. Reck, *Ist die
Schweiz Überfremdet*, pp. 34–43.

Switzerland a European power with a modern economy. Little men, the values of the past, the sense of a communal identity stood in vociferous but finally impotent protest against this rosy future promised them by their representatives.

Those who lived in the cities, it appeared, were pledged to make Switzerland an efficient, modern, economically competitive nation—however little they cared for Italians. Their vote against Schwarzenbach was not a vote for justice but for prosperity and progress on the terms outlined by the government. Those in the mountains, who saw little of the cities and knew still less of the Italians and their Latin kinsmen around the Mediterranean voted for a stasis which —they already understood—their countrymen had abjured. But to these alpine traditionalists, Switzerland was no American melting pot, no marvel of cultural assimilation that mixed peoples the way Americans mixed drinks. Its precarious equilibrium had rested on keeping peoples judiciously apart, on maintaining delicate balances that made possible long-term accommodation.[24] For them, to vote with Schwarzenbach was to cry out against the suborning of their towns and villages to a mindless prosperity, against a pretended integrationism that destroyed the tolerant regionalism upon which Switzerland's true heterogeneity depended, against a cosmopolitan life-style that surrendered active citizenship for the rewards of a benevolent bureautocracy, against a remunerative internationalism that meant the death of democratic self-government.

Of course, these are idealizations. We are putting words into the mouths of men who may have merely been ex-

[24] Thus, in 1939—despite Germany's monolithic racial policies and Switzerland's own isolation—the Swiss recognized Raeto-romansh as a fourth national culture along with German, French and Italian. Although only 40,000 Raeto-romansh survived, the gesture was understood as symbolic of Switzerland's commitment to unity through diversity.

256

hibiting their obstinacy or their small-mindedness or their racism. We do not want to make of them simple-minded Heidis, strewing rhetorical garlands over Switzerland's bucolic past. On the other hand, those entrusted with the task of modernizing Switzerland and selling it on the world market know that the story-book spirit of Heidi is very much at stake. A recent *New York Times* full-page advertisement for Swissair thus put its tongue well into its cheek and told readers:

> Heidi lied. Switzerland is not a curly-haired-little-girl-with-dimples kind of place. To be sure there are still the cunning little chalets. And the sweet goats. And the smiling, benevolent grandfathers. But now, the cunning little chalet belongs to a famous French actress . . . complete with 40-foot bar and velvet-walled bowling alley in the basements where goats once slept. And the goats are giving up their skins for some of the wildest apres-ski outfits ever concocted by exhilarated mountain minds. And the smiling, benevolent grandfather? He's still smiling and benevolent. He just made 1,000,000 Swiss francs selling his sloping meadow to a resort syndicate.[25]

Behind the fulsome copy is a point of view that has doomed the face-to-face village community. Those who voted for Schwarzenbach's desperate proposal may have had some inkling that their real enemies were not the foreign workers whose hands had helped remake Switzerland, but the Swiss minds who had directed those hands—who had come to see in the children's myth of Heidi and the pastoral values it embodied an obstacle to creating a new Switzerland. The legendary grandfather's one-million-franc sale is in fact

[25] *The New York Times*, March 16, 1970, p. 37. The advertising copy is presumably the product of a New York firm with little interest in either the Swiss past or the Swiss future, but the Swiss executives who bought the ad campaign presumably understood its blithe commercial antitraditionalism very well.

the sellout of the village community—the trade-off of the village *Allmend* and its way of life for stock certificates in Switzerland's future affluence.

It was hardly an accident that the final redoubt of public distrust of government and the nation's future had been the referendum, for in this century, direct democracy has become the common man's only weapon against the forces of modernity. As a result, Switzerland's traditional democracy too has come under a vituperative assault from future-minded reformers.

REACTIONARY DEMOCRACY AND PROGRESSIVE BUREAUCRACY

The critics are fairly unanimous. Erich Bonjour writes that "the farmer not only left his mark on Swiss culture as a whole; he actually created Swiss democracy with that peculiarly conservative tinge which probably exists elsewhere only in Britain."[26] G. A. Chevallaz attests that "referendum democracy is a far more conservative system than parliamentary democracy. . . . Conservatism then, hostility to new intercession by the state and to new fiscal charges assumed by it, this has been the almost constant attitude of direct democracy."[27] Erich Gruner agrees that "in no other democracy in the world is it so difficult to trigger new political movements with new ideas."[28] Max Frisch, a literary figure less prone to circumlocution than these profes-

[26] Erich Bonjour, H. S. Offler, and G. R. Potter, *A Short History of Switzerland* (Oxford, 1962), p. 316. I. B. Richman writes in a similar vein: "A considerable part of the time of the Landsgemeinde (is) taken up in rejecting propositions emanating from the authorities and reformers. . . ." *Appenzell: Pure Democracy and Pastoral Life in Inner-Rhodes* (London, 1895), p. 117.

[27] G. A. Chevallaz, "La Politique Interieure," in Erich Gruner, ed., *Die Schweiz seit 1945* (Bern, 1971), p. 202.

[28] Erich Gruner, *Regierung und Opposition in Schweizerischen Bundesstaat* (Bern, 1969), p. 29.

sorial colleagues already cited, says bluntly "Switzerland is not a democracy, it is a mediocracy."[29]

Nor are these charges unsupported by evidence. It has often been noted that the referendum at the national level in Switzerland has been used to veto public laws introduced by the parliament almost twice as frequently as to confirm them. Often there seems to be a vindictive willfulness in the public's refusal to endorse its representatives' legislative endeavors. Felix Moeschlin recalls a cantonal election in Zürich between the wars in which nearly one-third of the electorate opposed an entirely *pro forma* enactment of certain technical changes in the Federal Copyright Law, apparently with no other justification than "For God's sake, nothing new!"[30] In 1962, federal deputies to the national parliament were denied a raise in their *per diem* pay by a populace quite content to have them the lowest paid representatives in the West. In 1959 the referendum was utilized to deny women the vote (see below); in 1962 it was used to reject a ban on atomic weapons; in 1969 it was employed to defeat a university reform supported by the government but vigorously opposed by vociferous students to whom we might not have expected the public to be attuned.[31] In brief, where the referendum had once rep-

[29] Max Frisch's most recent commentaries on the homeland he often feels moved to disown can be found in *Tagebuch: 1966-1971* (Frankfurt, 1972).

[30] Felix Moeschlin, *Eidgenössische Glossen* (Zürich, 1929), pp. 27-28. Moeschlin was a perspicacious satirist, which may mean the best kind of social scientist.

[31] Tobler summarizes these votes in *Dossier Schweiz*, pp. 54-55. We need, however, to distinguish three forms of the referendum: the initiative, which requires that a proposal be introduced by a petition of 50,000 voters; the obligatory constitutional referendum on all proposed changes in the constitution (which is used with considerable frequency in light of Switzerland's legalistically detailed constitution); and the voluntary facultative referendum which permits 30,000 petitioners to insist on a referendum on any act passed by the federal parliament. In that the great majority of legislative acts become law

resented, in the Republic of the Three Leagues, a creative if grossly inefficient instrument of constructive public participation in government, it seems in the recent history of the Swiss Republic to have degenerated into a reactionary tool of wanton obstructionism, a development which vindicates the harsh judgments made about Swiss democracy by its critics.

How are we to explain this untoward evolution? What significance does it bear for the uneven contest between the traditional face-to-face commune and the coming urban society in Switzerland? Is direct democracy merely conservative, or also reactionary, pig-headed, and cantankerous? These sorts of questions compel us to find an explanation for the peculiar situation of Switzerland's democracy that will make sense in the larger context we have been exploring—the context of the village community and its apparent atrophy.

The two most common explanations for the conservatism of direct democracy have already been shown to be inappropriate to the Swiss case in earlier phases of our study. The neo-Marxist sociological argument, along with its Jungian psychological variation, links conservatism to the "earth-chained" life-style of the peasantry. Marx, like Edward Banfield in *The Moral Basis of a Backward Society*, perceives in the peasant's bondage to the land, his irremediable subjugation to superstition, conservatism, and torpor. In Switzerland, this reasoning suggests, the conservative democratic peasant is backward looking not because he is a democrat but because he is a peasant and, as

without a referendum, suggesting tacit public approval, the referendum may in fact not be quite so conservative as the critics argue, for it only comes into play when legislation is controversial (provoking a referendum), fundamental (falling under constitutional revision) or sectarian (resulting from a popular initiative). For a discussion see George A. Codding, Jr., *The Federal Government of Switzerland* (Boston, 1961), Chapter 4, and Simon de Ploige, *The Referendum in Switzerland* (London, 1898).

Bonjour suggests, because Swiss democracy is a peasant democracy. Jung, with a particularizing eye on his native Switzerland, provides a psychological catalog of analogous traits definitive of the peasant's "bondage to the earth" including "immobility, parochialism, unspirituality, miserliness, stolidity, willfulness, unfriendliness, and mistrustfulness. . . ."[32]

But these arguments, whatever their merits, are beside the point, for while Switzerland as a whole is somewhat more agricultural in its orientation than Graubünden, it simply cannot be depicted as a nation of peasants. Its rural economy, like Graubünden's, is more pastoral than agricultural, and its collective rural character dominated more by rocks and mountains than furrows and earth. If we are to take seriously psychic metaphors of the kind employed by Jung, the moist, root-nourishing earth will have to give way to impenetrable granite. As we have seen, Raetia's past—and Helvetia was not too different in this regard—revealed a people the mountains would not even support, much less tie down. No earth-bound peasant nation could have produced twenty generations of mercenary soldiers; nor could it support a democracy that demanded not only the people's occasional judgment but also their time and their service. The ancient Greeks required slaves to create the leisure time that their active political lives demanded. The Swiss have been afforded like opportunities precisely because they are not peasants—because the earth is austere and the winters long.

[32] Carl G. Jung, "Schweizer Linie im Spektrum Europas," *Neue Schweizer Rundschau*, vol. 21, 1928, p. 475. Some credence is given these views by the fact that only one cantonal constitution has been revised since World War I, while many villages continue to utilize statutes going back to the fifteenth and sixteenth centuries. The Bündner villages of Brusio and Poschiavo were in 1902 still using statutes enacted in 1388. See A. Gengel, *Die Selbstverwaltungskörper des Kantons Graubünden* (Chur, 1902), pp. 56–57ff.

We may speak, then, of a conservatism of placid mountains and endless winters, but not of the "yoke of the land" or the "bent spirit of the toiling peasant." The studied words of the nineteenth-century Bernese novelist Gotthelf evoke a sense of implantedness, but they would strike no response with landed peasants: "We have a rocky land— what takes root here takes root slowly. But once rooted in our ungiving stone, a tree will defy the wildest stormwinds and splinter the axes that seek out its roots."[33] Gotthelf's tree is Swiss man: inflexible but also indomitable, single-minded and stubborn but self-governed, obdurate not despite but because of his liberty. We need a better explanation for the present crisis of Swiss democracy than peasant conservatism.

A second common critical orientation assumes that the conservatism of direct democracy lies in the intrinsic character of its institutional forms—that the referenda made possible by the Swiss Constitution are by definition conservative and obstructionist, institutional checks on public power, the primary aim of which is to contain the ambitions of power-hungry representatives.[34] This interpretation is credible, however, only if direct democracy is viewed as a variation of representative democracy—a way to maintain the sovereignty of the public in a heterogeneous society, the government of which is an untrustworthy and

[33] Cited by Edgar Bonjour, *Werden und Wesen der Schweizerischen Demokratie* (Basel, 1939), p. 55.

[34] This mistaken interpretation of Swiss institutions is standard among American commentators: for example, "Reduced to its lowest terms, the referendum is a device whereby the electorate may veto an act which a legislative body has already passed. . . . The initiative is a device whereby the electorate may enact legislation against the will of the legislature. The referendum has been compared to a shield . . . the initiative to a sword." Robert C. Brooks, *The Government and Politics of Switzerland* (New York, 1918), p. 135. Or, "A basic conservatism in governmental affairs is evident in the manner in which the Swiss voter assumes the responsibility for direct democracy." George A. Codding, Jr., *The Federal Government of Switzerland*, p. 66.

self-propelling bureaucracy unlikely to pay much attention to the electorate that originally sponsored it. Yet in truth, as our careful review of direct democracy in the Republic of the Three Leagues in Chapter VII illustrated, direct democracy at least in Switzerland has been an instrument of public participation in government, not a substitute for it; it has been a tribute to the unity of active citizenship and good government rather than to the alienation of democratic subjects from elected bureaucracies in the style of nominally representative industrial superpowers.

The institutions of direct democracy are inherently neither conservative nor progressive; they can be employed to bring about rapid and even radical change under conditions of consensus and unity of governing and people. They can obstruct reform and paralyze effective government altogether where the people no longer are one with their governors or synonymous with their government. These factors point to an explanation that seems much closer to the realities of the Swiss situation, and that relates the perverse condition of Swiss democracy to the troubled condition of the alpine village community. This explanation is essentially Rousseauean, for it suggests that the tone and color of a direct democracy will depend largely on the nature of the community within which it operates, that good laws and institutions are conditional and flourish only in accord with "the fitness of the people, for which they are destined, to receive them."[35] Democracy in Switzerland appears reactionary because the conditions that justify it have eroded; democracy in the villages of Graubünden is failing because the village communities are themselves moribund. Neither the institutions themselves nor a putative peasant mentality is to blame. The conditions prerequisite to a successful direct democracy have simply ceased to obtain.

[35] Jean-Jacques Rousseau, *The Social Contract*, ed. G.D.H. Cole (London, 1913), Book 2, Chapter 8, p. 35.

What are these conditions? Rousseau enumerates a set that are suggestive of the required constellation:

> First, a very small state, where the people can readily be got together and where each citizen can with ease know all the rest; secondly, great simplicity of manners, to prevent business from multiplying and raising thorny problems; next, a large measure of equality in rank and fortune, without which equality of rights and authority cannot long subsist; lastly, little or no luxury—for luxury either comes of riches or makes them necessary; it corrupts at once rich and poor, the rich by possession and the poor by covetousness; it sells the country to softness and vanity, and takes away from the State all its citizens, to make them slaves one to another, and one and all to public opinion.[36]

From these we can distill certain base conditions without which direct democracy cannot function constructively, and which, in fact, are descriptive of Graubünden's early experience with democracy in the Republic of the Three Leagues (see Chapter VII): a community limited enough in size to make possible a face-to-face political life; a simplicity of life austere enough to guarantee natural consensus through a natural community of interests; an insularity that protects simplicity and facilitates self-sufficiency; an economic equality pervasive enough to make authentic political equality feasible; a devotion to citizenship and the integration of private and public life that immunizes the community to materialism, private greed, and wayward mobility. We may sum these conditions up under the general terms intimacy, simplicity (rusticity), autarky, equality, and public-spiritedness (the politics of virtue versus the politics of interest). The communes of the Raetian Repub-

[36] *Ibid.*, Book 3, Chapter 4, p. 55. There is a striking similarity between this passage and the remarks of William Coxe on luxury in the Grisons as viewed by the inhabitants (cited above).

lic were, in their ideal state, intimate, consensual, self-sufficient, egalitarian, and antiprivatistic; as a result, their democracy was collaborative, constructive, participative, and purposive. Even its perversions were collective travesties rather than private sins. For the individual, community life defined private goals, citizenship gave meaning to personal aims, and work done together and interests held in common took precedence over ambitions nourished in solitude and self-images rendered in privacy. The freedom experienced within and made possible by the rigid boundaries of the community seemed worth the forswearing of a cosmopolitan but lonely prosperity and the anomic emancipation offered by the world beyond those fixed boundaries.

It is not democracy, but the prerequisite conditions that have today transformed Switzerland's tradition of political participation into an uncertain bastion of reaction. We need only to look at the transformations undergone by the mountain villages of Graubünden in trying to accommodate themselves to a rapidly developing, urban society to be persuaded of this.

The physical size of the village community has remained fairly stable, but the erosion of its demographic boundaries by rapid transportation and economic and social mobility have rendered mere numbers unimportant. The village is no longer anything more than the domicile of men who work elsewhere, send children to regional schools, and generally depend for entertainment and social life on proximate towns and cities. The village remains as a collective bedroom, but the community has become the larger region. Its population is far too large to meet the conditions of intimate size required by traditional direct democracy.

The rustic simplicity of village life that enabled small groups of men to determine a common interest around which collective goals could be assembled has been an even more complete casualty of economic progress. Spiraling budgets are one obvious indicator of a change of scale that puts legislative decisions beyond the scope or even ken of simple communities deliberating in isolation. In the last one hundred years the Swiss federal budget has grown from three and one half million francs to over two billion francs. From 1902 to 1962, the cantonal budget increased from two million to over 150 million francs.[37] Short-term increases in recent years have been even more startling. From 1945 to 1965, the Genevan village of Veyrier's income rose from 71,000 to 860,000 francs.[38] In Graubünden cantonal taxes tripled from 1960 to 1970. But scale is only a part of the problem. Issues have diversified, their scope has enlarged, and their character has become complicated and technical; at the same time, the electorate has diversified, even within a small community, into interest groups, parties, and professional associations. The two developments together destroy the possibility of a simple consensus on simple issues. In 1760, a villager in the Bündner community of Churwalden had only to decide with his fellow-citizens how late in the year the Julier pass route to Italy ought to be kept open, whether a piece of common land ought to be sold, or the price to be put on the sale of timber from communal holdings. In the 1960's that same figurative villager was being asked whether to buy the problem-ridden, scandal-plagued French Mirage fighter-bombers for the Swiss air force, whether Switzerland ought to have atomic armaments or not, how to remedy the run-away inflation that Switzerland had acquired from its interdependence with Europe, what to do about the foreign-worker problem in all of its opaque economic, political, and cultural ramifications. Even in those few areas where technological interdependence had not robbed him of some autonomous and straightforward choices he was being asked to surrender his

---

[37] Comparative figures from Graubünden, *Landesbericht*, 1902, 1964.
[38] Codding, Jr., *Governing the Commune*, p. 78.

own community judgment to the requisites of regional planning and national expertise.[39] "Twentieth Century technological society," warns Max Imboden, Switzerland's surrogate J.-J. Sevran-Schreiber, "demands a political approach different from that of our traditional communal democracy. . . . The profound interdependence of all issues of substance has become a fundamental reality, and effective policy-making now presupposes a deeper kind of expert knowledge and a broader consciousness of subtle, difficult to perceive, interconnections."[40] A bureaucracy of experts, trained in a variety of technological specialties, is in a far better position to make important decisions than a community of technologically underprivileged citizens.

"Democracy may," concedes a French-Swiss political expert, "be able with its natural élan to react in the face of general political phenomena, to defend liberty or to protest against injustice: but it cannot formulate, by spontaneous generation, an economic doctrine."[41] No, it cannot. And this also becomes the key to the erosion of communal autarky. Economic doctrines in an international market society must be geared to regional, national and even international conditions. The insular village bent on going its own economic way is a reckless maverick, fated to an early extinction outside the herd. Since 1959 Switzerland has been a member of the European Free Trade Association, a move which has improved its economic posture in Europe but which has removed still one more set of issues from the purview

[39] Thus the lesser (executive) council of Graubünden recently warned the communes: "In our canton with its pronounced communal autonomy, it is hardly surprising that each village thinks to solve its alpine problems alone . . . but in many cases, the refusal to participate in common solutions costs dearly. We believe that thinking and planning concerning the alpine sector necessarily explodes narrow communal borders, requiring a broader regional approach." Kanton Graubünden, *Botschaften des Kleinen Rates an den Grossen Rat*, vol. 9, 1964, p. 303.

[40] Imboden, *Helvetisches Malaise*, p. 25.

[41] Chevallaz, "La politique interieure," p. 220.

of local citizens. At the end of 1972 a free-trade treaty with the newly expanded Common Market was negotiated by the government, ratified by the Parliament and approved overwhelmingly by a popular referendum (1,345,057 to 509,350) that elicited the assent of all twenty-two cantons. Price structures, production quotas, tariff levels, trade and transportation agreements not only become too technical, too complicated for the communal citizen, but cease to fall within the scope of his sovereignty. Full integration into the Common Market, which now seems inevitable, will only compound the impact of this spreading interdependence.

Nor is that simplistic equality founded on a common pastoral austerity likely to survive economic interdependence in an integrated, capitalist Europe. Privilege in its traditional aristocratic forms is gone, but inequalities in income and in economic opportunity multiply with the ongoing concentration of economic power in the hands of international corporate giants. The industrial and commercial interests that supported the federal government's successful campaign against the Schwarzenbach proposal outspent the proposal's backers four or five to one, simultaneously setting a record for funds expended in defeating a national referendum proposal. The village assembly is hardly a match for industrial monoliths like Brown-Boveri (electrical equipment), Nestlé (far more than just chocolate), or Hoffman-La Roche, Geigy, and Ciba (superpowers among Basel's chemical and pharmaceutical firms), and public opinion can only become that agent of conformity dreaded by Rousseau and James Mill when dominated by money and directed by monopolistic private interests.

Yet the spirit of communalism demanded by direct democracy might have survived these blows to simplicity, autarky, and equality if the sense of integral citizenship that is the most precious and most precarious condition of democracy had remained inviolate. But it too has atrophied, and with it have gone vestigial hopes for the future of a civic politics of maximum participation. It was the quality of village life, the villager's experience of a rewarding communality and the group belief in the priority of the public over the private that lent to politics an aura of meaning and virtue mere self-interest could never give. We have seen how easy it was, in the seventeenth and eighteenth centuries for the citizen to regard himself as the soldier, the worker, and the governor without recourse to specialized role identities. The citizen was, quite literally, a well-integrated hybrid of the citizen-soldier, the citizen-worker, and the citizen-governor. The community, a mirror-image of the citizen as a collectivity, existed as the armed village (the so-called *Fähnlein*), the working village (so-called *Gemeinarbeit*), the self-governing village (the village assembly or regional *Landsgemeinde*). Vestiges of each live on, but where they have not altogether lost their meaning, they are under attack as inefficient and obsolescent.

The notion of the citizen-soldier is most firmly rooted in Swiss soil and retains the most vigor. Every citizen over twenty must still serve in the military and retains an obligation to militia duty until he is sixty. Conscientious objectors are regarded with a venom and treated with an intolerance understandable only in the framework of a nation that views military service not as an obligation of but as integral to citizenship.[42] Over 40 percent of the avail-

---

[42] For an account of conscientious objection in Switzerland, see Paul Huber, *Auch Sie Lieben die Heimat* (Zürich, 1960). Huber was trying in 1960 to justify a highly unpopular form of dissent to a skeptical Swiss public. The erosion of the citizen-soldier concept in the last decade is clearly evident in the very different tone of the following remarks: "The army [in Switzerland] is unpopular today in a way it has rarely been . . . conscientious objectors . . . are more numerous, more virulent, and more generally admired than at any other time." J.-F. Aubert, "Histoire constitutionelle," in Gruner, ed., *Die Schweiz seit 1945*, p. 41.

able male population (800,000 men) were called up in 1940, and Switzerland was only deterring *potential* assaults on its neutrality. To this day, the population is armed in a manner scarcely imaginable in any other country of the world, dictatorship or democracy. Every male owns a rifle and fifty rounds of ammunition, which he is required to keep in good working order at home and to practice with every year. Younger men who have undergone basic training in the recent period of weapons modernization have been issued heavy automatic rifles (like the American M-16), which can also be found nestling in houses and apartments throughout Switzerland. Citizens who did not regard themselves as soldiers or soldiers who did not regard themselves as citizens would quickly turn their weapons on their fellow men or on their government. Anarchy or tyranny could be the only outcome.

The federal government appreciates the military value of the citizen-soldier tradition enough to encourage its maintenance. A controversial civil defense pamphlet issued in 1969 gave detailed instructions on the waging of guerrilla warfare against an imagined invader that had successfully occupied the land.[43] But many military experts are convinced that a national militia with small arms, even one that can be mobilized in forty-eight hours as the Military Department envisions, is obsolete in an era of atomic weapons, technological *Blitzkrieg*, and economic interdependence. They argue for a small, specialized, technically trained professional military corps, offering the same appeals to efficiency and expertise used by progressive economists and political planning experts. Moreover, the enfranchisement of women in 1971 has rendered the traditional equa-

---

[43] Published by the Federal Justice and Police Department under the title "Civil Defense" (*Zivilverteitigung*), this alarmist, pocket-size 300-page pamphlet giving detailed instructions on every aspect of survival and waging victory in conventional and atomic wars created a controversy that has not yet entirely abated.

tion of citizenship and military duty invalid. The Germanic tribal belief in the unity of the sword and the vote that informed so much of Switzerland's and Raetia's history is today no more than a hypocritical appeal to a dead past.

Much the same is true of common work (*Gemeinarbeit*), the practice that once gave to civic responsibility the hard reality of common labor in the cause of decisions commonly taken. A vote for a new common building meant building it, just as a vote for war meant waging it. A decision to improve communal roads was a contract entered into by the head to put the body to work with a pickax. Certain thoughtful reformers have suggested the reintroduction of common work in economically underdeveloped communes,[44] but electrical generators and reinforced concrete schools and cantilevered bridges cannot be thrown up by gangs of well-meaning citizens; nor would Switzerland's placid but pervasive unions permit such a thing.

Even within the individual communes, the individual can no longer function as an integrated political-economic being. Until the early nineteenth century, to be the head of a household in an alpine commune meant to provide for all of its economic needs directly without the mediation of functional specialization. The pastoral economy was itself founded on the holistic participation of the individual farmer in every facet of the dairy process—from the herding and grazing of stock, through the growing and harvesting of fodder and the calving of offspring, to the processing of milk. This so-called *Einzelsennerei* gave the individual a sense of organic involvement in work processes and life cycles prohibited to the modern farm worker.[45] Mechaniza-

[44] Peter Liver has been a firm advocate of Common Labor as a resuscitative device in economically underdeveloped communes. See "Die Bündner Gemeinde," *Bündner Monatsblatt*, January 1947.

[45] Richard Weiss details the differences in traditional work processes of both the Romanic and Germanic populations in Graubünden, and modern processes as conditioned by mechanization and transportation: *Das Alpwesen Graubündens*, (Zürich, 1941), pp. 86-87ff.

tion, specialization, and centralization today reduce him, in the typical fashion of modern industrialism, to partial roles in a fragmented process the ends of which he is rarely permitted to see. This fragmentation has contributed to the breakdown of the traditional notion of citizenship and encouraged individuals to focus even more intensely on their private interests. If the economic and political life of the village can offer them only a specialized servitude, they must naturally seek fulfillment in the unleashing of personal ambition and the anticipation of personal gain. Thus, from traditional communal man comes modern economic man, uprooted from his community, turned in upon himself, alienated from his labor, and ready for a solitary life of affluence in the jungle of cities. Materialism in Switzerland seems at least in part to act as a consolation to men who have lost their citizenship. The noisy city crowds in to fill the larger silence left by the dying rustic village. Self-interest tries to imitate the propelling virtue of public participation. And the cry for rights, for a vigorous opposition, for single-minded parties and aggressive pressure groups, a caustic counter-culture and a forced pluralism, seems colored by inflections of loneliness—the desolate voice of men seeking to compensate a loss that could not be avoided and cannot be tolerated. It is the ghost of Peter Laslett's *World We Have Lost*, haunting the world that has replaced it.

The sense of loss can be felt even in progress that is universally applauded. In 1971, after a twenty-year legislative struggle, women in Switzerland finally achieved suffrage in federal elections. They had been rebuffed decisively in a national referendum in 1959 but had gained important cantonal victories in French Switzerland during the 1960's. In 1968 a woman won the mayoralty race in Geneva. By 1971 the issue was decided. The popular vote was almost two to one in favor of female suffrage, and fifteen and a half of twenty-two cantons voting gave their assent.[46] Most

[46] The actual vote was 621,403 to 323,596 in favor of the proposal

observers regarded Switzerland's tardiness on an issue that every other independent state in the world except a handful of Arab monarchies had resolved fifty years earlier as a quaint and anachronistic tribute to reactionary male chauvinism. And no one will want to deny that the enfranchisement of women remedied what, for a putatively democratic system, was a most remarkable inegalitarianism.

And yet, the sense of loss persists. Despite its unmistakable claim on justice and equality, the enfranchisement of women can only accelerate the ongoing erosion of direct democracy's defining conditions. Half of Switzerland's population is finally recognized as having rudimentary human rights, but as a result the expanded electorate participates far less. Village halls become too confined, village assemblies grow unwieldy, and twice as many voters are given the privilege of turning over to elected representatives what half as many once did for themselves. The citizen-soldier ideal, already under attack, loses the vestiges of a justification, while atomistic individualism—each counts for one in utter isolation from human communities—is given official recognition as the guiding principle of an ever more fragmented, interest-oriented life. And so, equality and justice seem to come only at the price of participation and community.

We have, then, an explanation of sorts for the peculiar conservatism of direct democracy in modern Switzerland: the communal conditions that nourished and supported it

---

and thus reversed the two-to-one margin by which an identical suffrage proposal was defeated in 1959. The first federal election held under the new suffrage act (in late 1971) produced ten women deputies for the National Council (*Nationalrat*), and one female senator for the Council of States (*Ständerat*).

Up until 1968 only the three French-speaking cantons and Basel-City had introduced female suffrage at the cantonal level. Graubünden, for example, had rejected it 13,522 to 8,616 in 1968. But by the time of the 1971 referendum, four German-speaking urban cantons had relented as well.

are going or are gone. It is an institutional anachronism living on into a time that cannot maintain it, struggling to utilize its vestigial powers to re-create the environment it requires to survive. And so the people vote down progressive legislation that in bettering their lives would further damage the conditions that alone make their voting meaningful. They bargain futilely to maintain the autonomy of communes, the very existence of which is in question. They blame foreigners for the lost rusticity with which, in fact, they have purchased their own affluence. They try to bar the vote to women because it has lost its meaning for men. They defend their past haplessly, desperately, hopelessly, against an inevitable tide of progressive bureaucracy, all the while sensing that the communal past is already beyond recovery.

Yet their futile resistance is not quite in vain. The long struggle of the alpine communities of Graubünden to retain vital self-government against a succession of enemies that can almost be said to constitute the major forces of European history illuminates a set of values too rarely seen in our modern world. It suggests that freedom need not be incompatible with communal collectivism; that autonomy for the individual can be won through political participation in self-governing communities; that politics need not always be defined by self-interest but can instead itself define public interest; and that citizenship can help give meaning and purpose to human life. And, finally, it hints that if the world produced for us by modernization—an affluent world of privatistic materialism secured by power, guided by competitive self-interest and protected by law— is inhospitable to such values, it may be a world that even at its very best requires radical remaking.

Direct Democracy

Representative Democracy

# Bibliography

Works Cited on Freedom, Community and Democracy

Almond, Gabriel, and Verba, Sidney. *The Civic Culture.* Princeton, N. J., 1963.

Arendt, Hannah. *Between Past and Future.* New York, 1961.

Banfield, Edward C. *The Moral Basis of a Backward Society.* New York, 1958.

Baratz, Morton S. and Bachrach, Peter. "Two Faces of Power," *The American Political Science Review.* Vol. 56. December 1962.

Barber, Benjamin R. *Superman and Common Men: Freedom, Anarchy, and the Revolution.* New York, 1971.

————, Friedrich, Carl J., and Curtis, Michael. *Totalitarianism in Perspective: Three Views.* New York, 1969.

Bay, Christian. *The Structure of Freedom.* New York, 1965.

Berlin, Isaiah, *Two Concepts of Liberty.* Oxford, 1958.

Bloch, Marc. *Feudal Society.* 2 Vols. Translated by L. A. Manyon. London, 1965.

Bosanquet, Bernard. *The Philosophical Theory of the State.* London, 1951.

Burckhardt, Jacob. *The Civilization of the Renaissance in Italy.* 2 Vols. Translated by S.G.C. Middlemore. New York, 1958.

Cranston, Maurice and Peters, Richard S. *Hobbes and Rousseau.* Garden City, N. Y., 1972.

Crick, Bernard. "Freedom as Politics." Peter Laslett and W. G. Runciman, eds. *Philosophy, Politics and Society.* Third Series. Oxford, 1969.

Eckstein, Harry. *Division and Cohesion in Democracy: A Study of Norway.* Princeton, N. J., 1966.

Engels, Frederick. *The Peasant Question in France and Germany.* Marx, K. and Engels, F. *Selected Works.* 2 Vols. Moscow, 1951.

Fromm, Erich. *Escape from Freedom.* New York, 1941.

Gierke, Otto. *Natural Law and the Theory of Society* (a partial translation of vol. 4 of *Das Deutsche Genossenschaftsrecht*). Boston, 1957.

Hampshire, Stuart. *Thought and Action.* New York, 1967.

Handlin, Oscar and Mary. *The Dimensions of Liberty.* New York, 1966.

Hartz, Louis. *The Liberal Tradition in America.* New York, 1955.

———. *The Founding of New Societies.* New York, 1964.

Hobbes, Thomas. *Leviathan.* Edited by Michael Oakeshott. London, 1960.

Huizinga, J. *The Waning of the Middle Ages.* Garden City, N. Y., 1954.

Laird, John. *On Human Freedom.* London, 1947.

Laslett, Peter. "The Face to Face Society." Peter Laslett and W. G. Runciman, eds. *Philosophy, Politics and Society.* First Series. Oxford, 1956.

———. *The World We Have Lost.* London, 1965.

Lenin, V. I. *State and Revolution.* New York, 1932.

Maine, Henry. *Lectures on the Early History of Institutions.* London, 1875.

———. *Village Communities in East and West.* New York, 1876.

Meadows, D. H., et al. *The Limits to Growth.* New York, 1972.

Montesquieu, Baron de. *The Spirit of the Laws.* Translated by Thomas Nugent, New York, 1949.

Neumann, Franz. *The Democratic and Authoritarian State.* Glencoe, Ill., 1957.

276

Pateman, Carole. *Participation and Democratic Theory.* Cambridge, 1970.

Popper, Karl. *The Open Society and Its Enemies.* 2 Vols. London, 1945.

Pye, Lucian. *Aspects of Political Development.* Boston, 1966.

Rousseau, Jean-Jacques. *Letter to D'Alembert on Theater.* Translated by Allan Bloom. Ithaca, N. Y., 1968.

———. *The Social Contract.* Ed. G.D.H. Cole. London, 1913.

Schumpeter, Joseph. *Capitalism, Socialism and Democracy.* London, 1943.

Strayer, Joseph R. *On the Medieval Origins of the Modern State.* Princeton, N. J., 1970.

Talmon, J. L. *The Origins of Totalitarian Democracy.* New York, 1960.

Tönnies, Ferdinand. *Community and Society.* Translated by Charles P. Loomis. East Lansing, Mich., 1957.

Vinogradoff, Paul. "Feudalism." *The Cambridge Medieval History.* Vol. 3. Cambridge, 1924.

Weber, Max. *The Protestant Ethic and the Rise of Capitalism.* Translated by Talcott Parsons. New York, 1958.

ENGLISH SECONDARY SOURCES ON SWITZERLAND

Baker, F. Grenfell. *The Model Republic.* New York, 1895.

Barber, Benjamin R. "Switzerland: Progress Against the Communes." *Trans-action.* February 1971.

Beedham, B. and Lee, G. "Even in Paradise—Switzerland: a Survey." *The Economist.* February 22, 1969.

Bonjour, Edgar. *Swiss Neutrality: Its History and Meaning.* London, 1946.

Bonjour, Erich, Offler, H. S., and Potter, G. R. *A Short History of Switzerland.* Oxford, 1952.

Brooks, Robert C. *Civic Training in Switzerland: A Study of Democratic Life.* Chicago, 1930.

Brooks, Robert C. *The Government and Politics of Switzerland.* New York, 1918.

Bryce, James. *Modern Democracies.* 2 Vols. New York, 1921.

Codding, George A., Jr. *The Federal Government of Switzerland.* Boston, 1961.

———. "The New Swiss Military Capability." *Foreign Affairs.* April 1962.

———. *Politics in Swiss Local Government: Governing the Commune of Veyrier.* University of Colorado, 1967.

Coxe, William. *Travels in Switzerland and in the Country of the Grisons.* 3 Vols. London, 1801.

de Ploige, Simon. *The Referendum in Switzerland.* London, 1898.

Friedrich, Carl J., and Cole, Taylor. *Responsible Bureaucracy: A Study of the Swiss Civil Service.* Cambridge, Mass., 1932.

Ganshof, F. L. *Feudalism.* 3d Eng. ed. London, 1964.

Gilliard, Charles. *A History of Switzerland.* London, 1955.

Herold, J. Christopher. *The Swiss Without Halos.* New York, 1948.

Huber, Hans. *How Switzerland Is Governed.* Zürich, 1946.

Hughes, C. J. *The Federal Constitution of Switzerland.* London, 1954.

———. *The Parliament of Switzerland.* London, 1962.

Kimche, Jon. *Spying for Peace: General Guisan and Swiss Neutrality.* London, 1961.

Kohn, Hans. *Nationalism and Liberty: The Swiss Example.* London, 1956.

Lloyd, H. D. *The Swiss Democracy.* London, 1908.

Lloyd, William B. *Waging Peace: The Swiss Experience.* Washington, D. C., 1958.

Luethy, Herbert. "Has Switzerland a Future? The Dilemma of the Small Nation." *Encounter.* December 1962.

Lunn, A.H.M. *The Swiss and Their Mountains.* New York, 1963.

McRae, Kenneth D. *Switzerland: Example of Cultural Co-existence.* Toronto, 1964.

Mayer, Kurt B. *The Population of Switzerland.* New York, 1952.

Pirenne, Henri. *Medieval Cities.* Princeton, N. J., 1925.

Rappard, William E. *Collective Security in Swiss Experience: 1291–1948.* London, 1948.

————. *The Government of Switzerland.* New York, 1936.

————. *Pennsylvania and Switzerland: The Origins of the Swiss Constitution.* Philadelphia, 1941.

Richman, I. B. *Appenzell: Pure Democracy and Political Life in Inner Rhodes.* London, 1895.

Sauser-Hall, Georges. *The Political Institutions of Switzerland.* Zürich, 1946.

Schwarz, Urs. "Country Problems in Switzerland." *Disarmament and Arms Control.* Winter 1963–1964.

Siegfried, André. *Switzerland: A Democratic Way of Life.* New York, 1950.

Soloveytchik, George. *Switzerland in Perspective.* London, 1954.

Spiro, Herbert J. *Government by Constitution.* New York, 1959.

Steiner, Jürg. "Non-violent Conflict Resolution in Democratic Systems: Switzerland." *Journal of Conflict Resolution.* September 1969.

Tripp, M. L. *The Swiss and United States Federal Constitutional Systems.* Paris, 1940.

Uhlmann, Ernst. "Defense of the Nation and of Freedom." *Yearbook of the New Helvetic Society: 1963.* Bern, 1963.

Wheare, K. C. *Federal Government.* London, 1946.

SWISS SOURCES CONSULTED

Adliswil Council. *Adliswil.* Adliswil/Zürich, 1971.

Anhorn, Bartholomäus. *Pündtner Aufruhr im Jahre 1607* in von Moor, Conradin, ed. *Archiv für die Geschichte der Republik Graubünden.* Vol. 4. Chur, 1862.

Bachmann, A., and Grosjean, G., eds. *Zivilverteidigung.* Aarau, 1969.

Badrutt, P. *Die Entstehung des Oberen Grauen Bundes.* Chur, 1916.

Béguelin, Roland. *Conference de presse.* Délemont, 1969.

Bernegg, Fortunat Sprecher von. *Geschichte der bündnerischen Kriege und Unruhen* in von Moor, Conradin, ed. *Archiv für die Geschichte der Republik Graubünden.* Vol. 3. Chur, 1856.

Birchler, Linus. *Vielfalt der Urschweiz.* Olten, 1969.

Bonjour, Edgar. *Die Gründung der Schweizerischen Bundesstaates.* Basel, 1948.

———. *Werden und Wesen der schweizerischen Demokratie.* Basel, 1939.

Branger, Erich. *Rechtsgeschichte der Freien Walser in der Ostschweiz.* Bern, 1905.

Bridel, Marc, ed. *La democratie directe dans les communes suisse.* Zürich, 1952.

Brosi, G. "25 Jahre Schweizerische Patenschaft für bedrängte Gemeinden." *Neue Bündner Zeitung.* November 13, 1965.

Büchli, A. *Sagen aus Graubünden.* Aarau, n.d.

Bürcher, B., et al. *Helvetische Alternativen.* Zürich, 1971.

Cahannes, A. *Bürgergemeinde und politische Gemeinde in Graubünden.* Disentis, 1930.

Camenisch, E. *Bündner Reformationsgeschichte.* Chur, 1920.

———. "Die Reformation in Graubünden," in Fritz Jecklin, ed. *Bündnergeschichte in Elf Vorträgen.* Chur, 1902.

Campbell, Ulrich. *Zwei Bücher rätischer Geschichte,* in von Mohr, Theodor, ed. *Archiv für die Geschichte der Republik Graubünden.* Vol. 1. Chur, 1853.

Cloetta, G. C. *Bergün-Bravuogn.* 2d ed. Thusis, 1964.

Curschellas, J. M. *Die Gemeinatzung.* Ilanz, 1926.

Dändliker, Karl. *Geschichte der Schweiz.* 3 Vols. Zürich, 1893.

Danuser, J. *Die staatlichen Hoheitsrechte des Kantons Graubünden gegenüber dem Bistum Chur.* Zürich, 1897.

Dellenbach, Eric. *Violence au pays des grandes joux.* Tramelan, 1966.

de Lüc. "Aus Hrn de Lüc Briefen [sic]." *Der Sammler.* 1781.

de Reynold, Gonzague. *Selbstbesinnung der Schweiz.* Zürich, 1939.

de Rohan, Duc. *Mémoires sur la guerre de la Veltline.* Hgg. v. Zurlauben, 1758.

de Rougement, Denis. *La Confédération helvétique.* Monaco, 1953.

――――. *Mission ou demission de la Suisse.* Neuchâtel, 1940.

――――. "Swiss Federalism." *Yearbook of the New Helvetic Society: 1963.* Bern, 1963.

Dieaurer, J. *Geschichte der Schweizerischer Eidgenossenschaft.* 5 Vols. Gotha, 1920–1924.

Dietschi, Urs. *Das Volksveto in der Schweiz.* Olten, 1926.

"Dörfer und schweizerische Demokratie." *Neue Bündner Zeitung.* March 11, 1965.

Dunant, E. *La réunion des Grisons à la Suisse.* Basel, 1899.

Dürrenmatt, Peter. *Schweizer Geschichte.* Zürich, 1963.

Ewald. "Ein Landmann zu einem reichen Städter." *Der Sammler.* No. 51. 1780.

Fient, G. "Die bündnerischen Gemeinde in ihrer staatsrechtlichen Struktur." *Bündner Monatsblatt.* January-February 1902.

――――. *Das Prättigau.* Davos. 1897.

――――. *Wegweiser zur Einführung in Gesetzes- und Verfassungskunde.* Chur, 1909.

Frisch, Max. *Tagebuch: 1966-1971.* Frankfurt, 1972.

Fry, Karl. *Kaspar Decurtins: Der Löwe von Truns.* Zürich, 1949.

Gadient, A. "Zum Ausbau der Engadiner Kraftwerke." *Bündner Monatsblatt.* June-July 1955.

Ganzoni, R. A. *Beiträge zur Kenntnis des bündnerischen Referendums.* Zürich, 1890.

———. "Die Entstehung der bündnerischen Demokratie." Fritz Jecklin, ed. *Bündnergeschichte in Elf Vorträge.* Chur, 1902.

———. *Rechtsgeschichte der Fuhrleite.* Chur, 1897.

Gasser, Adolf. *Bedrängte Südschweiz.* N.p., 1958.

———. *Gemeindefreiheit als Rettung Europas.* Basel, 1943.

Gengel, A. *Die Selbstverwaltungskörper des Kantons Graubünden.* Chur, 1902.

———. *Verfassungsgeschichte von Graubünden. Separatabdruck aus dem Schweizerischen Zentralblatt für Staats- und Gemeindeverwaltung.* n.d.

Giacometti, Z. *Neubearbeitung von F. Fleiner's Schweizerisches Bundesrecht.* Zürich, 1965.

Gieré, O. *Der Staatshaushalt des Kantons Graubünden seit der Einführung der direkten Steuern bis heute (1856–1914).* Berlin, 1915.

Gierke, Otto von. *Das Deutsche Genossensschaftsrecht.* 4 Vols. Berlin, 1868.

Gillardon, P. "Die Bestrebungen zur Schaffung einer bündnerischen Landespolizei und zur Errichtung eines Zuchthaus im 18. Jahrhundert." *Bündner Monatsblatt.* July 1944.

———. "Das Kriminaltribunal gemeiner III Bünde in der zweiten Hälfte des 18. Jahrhundert." *Bündner Monatsblatt.* April 1942.

———. "Ein neu aufgefundener Bundesbrief von 1524 und die Frage nach der ersten Bundesvereinigung gemeiner 3 Bünde." *Bündner Monatsblatt.* August-September 1932.

Goethe, *Briefe aus der Schweiz. Goethe's Sämtliche Werke,* Vol. 27. Berlin and Leipzig, n.d.

Graubünden, Swiss Canton of. *Amtliche Gesetzes-Sammlung.* Vol. 4.

————. "Bericht über Alppersonalfragen." *Botschaften des Kleinen Rates an den Grossen Rat.* Vol. 9. 1964.

————. *Botschaft des Kleinen Rates an den Grossen Rat zum Entwurf des Gemeindegesetzes des Kantons Graubünden.* Vol. 1, 1943.

————. *Bündner Rechtsbuch: Bereinigte Gesetzessammlung des Kantons Graubünden.* 1957.

————. *Grosserrats Protokoll.* 1962.

————. *Landesberichte.* 1902–1971.

————. *Rekurspraxis des Kleinen und Grossen Rates von Graubünden.* Vol. 6. 1931–1950.

————. *Staatsrechnung.* 1964.

————. *Verfassung für den Kanton Graubünden von Oktober 1892.* Chur, 1892.

Gruner, Erich. *Die Parteien in der Schweiz.* Bern, 1969.

————. *Regierung und Opposition in der schweizerischen Eidgenossenschaft.* Bern, 1969.

————. ed. *Année Politique Suisse.* Bern, 1965–

————. ed. *Die Schweiz seit 1945.* Bern, 1971.

Guggenbühl, Gottfried. *Geschichte der Schweizerischen Eidgenossenschaft.* 2 Vols. Zürich, 1948.

Guler, Johann. *Rechtfertigung des Prättigauer Freiheitskampf,* in Moor, Conradin, ed. *Archiv für die Geschichte der Republik Graubünden.* Vol. 10. Chur, 1877.

Häsler, Alfred A. *Das Boot ist Voll: Die Schweiz und die Flüchtlinge—1933–1945.* Zürich, 1967.

Heusler, A. *Schweizerische Verfassungsgeschichte.* Basel, 1920.

*Historisch-Biographisch Lexicon der Schweiz.* 7 Vols. Neuenburg, 1926.

Hofer-Wild, G. *Herrschaft und Hoheitsrechte der Sax im Misox.* Poschiavo, 1949.

Hoppeler, R. "Beiträge zur Rechtsgeschichte der Talschaft Safien im Mittelalter." *Jahresbericht der Historisch-Antiquarischen Gesellschaft von Graubünden.* 1907.

Hosang, G. *Die Kämpfe um den Anschluss Graubündens an die Schweiz.* Chur, 1899.

Huber, Paul. *Auch Sie Lieben die Heimat.* Zürich, 1966.

Imboden, Max. *Helvetisches Malaise.* Zürich, 1964.

Jecklin, Constantin, ed. *Codex Diplomaticus.* Vol. 5. Chur, 1865.

Jecklin, Fritz, ed. *Bündnergeschichte in Elf Vorträgen.* Chur, 1902.

――――. *Materialen zur Standes- und Landesgeschichte gemeiner III Bünde.* 2 Vols. Chur, 1907.

――――. "Die Volksabstimmungen des Kantons Graubünden von 1803–1847." *Bündner Monatsblatt.* May-October 1921.

Jenal, S. "Die Siedlungen der politischen Gemeinden des Kantons Graubünden." *Bündner Monatsblatt.* January-May 1957.

Jenny, Rudolf. *Einbürgerungen: 1801–1960.* 2 Vols. Chur, 1965.

――――. "Graubündens Passtransit und seine volkswirtschaftliche Bedeutung." *Bündner Monatsblatt.* September-October 1954.

――――. *Historisches Exposé—San Bernadino: Graubündens Passstrassen und ihre volkswirtschaftliche Bedeutung in historischer Zeit.* Chur, 1963.

――――. "Wesen und Gehalt der bündnerischen Kultur." *Bündner Monatsblatt.* June 1949.

Keyserling, Hermann. *Das Spectrum Europas.* Heidelberg, 1928.

Kind, Ernst, *Über das Verhältnis der 8 Gerichte zu Österreich.* Weide i. Thür., 1925.

Kläuli, P. ed. *Freiheitsbriefe, Bundesbriefe, Vorkommnisse und Verfassungen: 1231–1815.* Vol. 1, *Quellenhefte zur Schweizergeschichte.* Aarau, 1952.

Kraneck, H. *Burgen und Schlösser Rhätiens.* Chur, 1837.

Kreis, Hans. *Die Walser: Ein Stück Siedlungsgeschichte der Zentralalpen.* 2d ed. Bern, 1966.

Kurz, H. R. *General Henri Guisan*. Zürich, 1965.

Lamprecht, Karl. *Deutsches Wirtschaftsleben im Mittelalter*. 3 Vols. in 4. Leipzig, 1866.

Lardelli, A. *Das Steuerhoheit der Selbstverwaltungskörper im Kanton Graubünden*. Affoltern am Albis, 1951.

Lasserre, David. *Schicksalsstunde des Föderalismus*. Zürich, 1964.

Lehmann, H. L. *Die Republik Graubünden*. Magdeburg, 1797.

Liver, Peter. "Alplandschaft und politische Selbstständigkeit." *Bündner Monatsblatt*. January 1942.

———. "Aus der bündnerischen Strafrechtsgeschichte." *Bündner Monatsblatt*. March-April 1941.

———. "Die Bündner Gemeinde." *Bündner Monatsblatt*. February 1941.

———. *Von Feudalismus zur Demokratie in den graubündnerischen Hinterrheintälern*. Chur, 1929.

———. "Der Geburtstag unseres bündnerischen Gesamtstaates." *Bündner Monatsblatt*. October 1932.

———. *Die Graubündner Kantonsverfassung des Jahres 1854*. Chur, 1954.

———. "Ist Walserrecht Walliser Recht?" *Bündner Monatsblatt*. February 1944.

———. "Rechtsgeschichte der Landschaft Rheinwald." *66. Jahresbericht der Historisch-Antiquarischen Gesellschaft von Graubünden*. 1936.

———. "Die staatliche Entwicklung im alten Graubünden." *Sonderabdruck aus der Zeitschrift für Schweizerische Geschichte*. Vol. 13, no. 1. 1933.

Ludwig, Carl. *Die Flüchtlingspolitik der Schweiz*. Bern, 1966.

Lüthi, Walter. "Industrialisierung der Bergtälern." *Bündner Monatsblatt*. March-April 1955.

Lütscher, Georg. *Geschichte der Gemeinde und Freiherrschaft Haldenstein*. Chur, 1962.

Manatschal, F. "Eigenes aus Bündens öffentlichem Leben

der letzten 50 oder 60 Jahre." *Bündner Monatsblatt.* July-September 1915.

―――. "Graubünden seit 1815." in Jecklin, Fritz, ed. *Bündnergeschichte in Elf Vorträgen.* Chur, 1902.

Mani, B., ed. "Die Volksabstimmungen des Kantons Graubünden von 11. November 1917 bis 9 Mai 1937." *Typed ms. in the Graubündner Kantonsbibliothek.* Chur, n.d.

Marthaler, E. "Untersuchungen zur Verfassungs- und Rechtsgeschichte der Grafschaft Vintschgau im Mittelalter." *Jahresbericht der Historisch-Antiquarischen Gesellschaft von Graubünden.* 1940, 1942.

Martin, O. "Die Ostalpenbahnfrage." *Neue Bündner Zeitung.* March 30, 1965.

―――. "Die Splügenlinie: Dritte schweizerische Alpenbahn." *Neue Bündner Zeitung.* December 19, 1964.

―――. "Die Splügenlinie gewinnt an europäischen Interesse." *Neue Bündner Zeitung.* August 10, 1965.

Meuli, A. "Die Entstehung der autonomen Gemeinden im Oberengadin." *Jahresbericht der Historisch-Antiquarischen Gesellschaft von Graubünden.* 1901.

Meyer, Alice. *Anpassung oder Widerstand: Die Schweiz zur Zeit der deutschen Nationalsozialismus.* Frauenfeld, 1965.

Meyer, Karl. Über die Anfänge der Walserkolonien in Rätien." *Bündner Monatsblatt.* July-September 1925.

Moeschlin, Felix, *Eidgenössische Glossen.* Zürich, 1929.

Mohr, Theodor von, ed. *Codex Diplomaticus.* Vols. 1-3. Chur, 1865.

Moor, Conradin von, ed. *Codex Diplomaticus.* Vol. 4. Chur, 1865.

Moosberger, H. *Die Bündnerische Allmende.* Chur, 1891.

Müller, I. "Die Entstehung des Grauen Bundes." *Bündner Monatsblatt.* May 1941.

Müller, Johannes von. *Die Geschichten Schweizerischer Eidgenossenschaft.* 5 Vols. Leipzig, 1825.

Muoth, Johannes C., ed. *Codex Diplomaticus*. Vol. 6. Chur, 1898.

————. "Alten Besatzungsprotokollen der Gerichtsgemeinde Ilanz-Grub." *Bündner Monatsblatt*. July-September 1897.

————. "Churrätian in der Feudalzeit," in Fritz Jecklin et al., *Bündnergeschichte in Elf Vorträgen*. Chur, 1902.

Mutzner, P. *Beiträge zur Rechtsgeschichte Graubündens im Mittelalter. Separatabdruck aus der Zeitschrift für Schweizerisches Recht*. Neue Folge. Vol. 2.

*Der Neue Sammler*. 1804–1811.

Olgiati, G. *Die bündnerische Gemeindeautonomie*. Zürich, 1948.

Padrutt, Christian. *Staat und Krieg im alten Bünden*. Zürich, 1965.

Pedotti, G. *Beiträge zur rechtsgeschichtlichen Entwicklung der Gemeinde, der Gemeindeaufgaben und des Gemeindevermögens im Kanton Graubünden*. Zürich, 1936.

Pfister, Alexander. *Georg Jenatsch: Sein Leben und Seine Zeit*. Basel, 1939.

————. *Die Patrioten*. Chur, 1904.

Pfister, H. *Das Transportwesen der internationalen Handelswege von Graubünden im Mittelalter und in der Neuzeit*. Chur, 1913.

Pieth, Friedrich. "Das altbündnerische Referendum." *Bündner Monatsblatt*. May 1958.

————. *Bündnergeschichte*. Chur, 1945.

————. "Ein Unikum in der Geschichte des modernen bündnerischen Verfassungsreferendum." *Bündner Monatsblatt*. June-July 1947.

————. "Einteilung des Alten Graubünden in die Bünde, Hochgerichte und Gerichtsgemeinden." *Bündner Monatsblatt*. September 1942.

————. "Der Freistaat der Drei Bünde und seine Aufnahme in die Eidgenossenschaft." *Bündner Monatsblatt*. August 1941.

Pieth, Friedrich. "Der Schwabenkrieg," in Fritz Jecklin, et al. *Bündnergeschichte in Elf Vorträgen.* Chur, 1902.

———. "Zwei kleinere Beiträge zur Bündnergeschichte." *Bündner Monatsblatt.* December 1941.

Planta, Peter von. "Die Entstehung der Leibeigenschaft auf dem Gebiet des heutigen Kantons Graubünden." *Bündner Monatsblatt.* 7 Parts. February-September 1925.

———. *Geschichte von Graubünden.* Bern, 1913.

———. *Mein Lebensgang.* Chur, 1901.

———. "Verfassungsgeschichte der Stadt Chur im Mittelalter." *8. Jahresbericht der Historisch-Antiquarischen Gesellschaft von Graubünden.* 1878.

Plattner, W. *Die Entstehung des Freistaates der Drei Bünde und sein Verhältnis zur alten Eidgenossenschaft.* Davos, 1895.

Poltéra-Lang. C. *Die Kreise und ihre Verwaltung nach bündnerischem Staats- und Verwaltungsrecht.* N.p., 1921.

Purtscher, F. "Der Obere oder Graue Bund." *Bündner Monatsblatt.* April-June 1924.

———. " 'Zu Nanz und in der Grub': Ein Beitrag zur Geschichte ihrer Entstehung," *Bündner Monatsblatt.* April, May, September 1922.

Putzi, Julius. *Die Entwicklung des Bürgerrechts in Graubünden.* Affoltern am Albis, 1951.

Ragaz, Georg. *Die Entstehung der politischen Gemeinden im Schamsertal.* Disentis, 1934.

Ragaz, J. "Die Bündnerwirren," in Fritz Jecklin, et al. *Bündnergeschichte in Elf Vorträgen.* Chur, 1902.

Rappard, William E. *Les conditions de la prospérité helvétique.* Zürich, 1957.

———. *La Constitution fédérale de la Suisse.* Neuchâtel, 1948.

———. *L'Individu et l'état dans l'évolution constitutionelle de la Suisse.* Zürich, 1936.

Rassemblement jurassien. *Declaration de principe sur la Constitution et sur les lignes directrices de la politique de l'état jurassien.* Délemont, 1954.

Reck, Oskar. *Ist die Schweiz Überfremdet?* Frauenfeld, 1969.

Robbi, Jules, ed. "Die Volksabstimmungen des Kantons Graubünden von 1. February 1848 bis und mit 4. März 1917." *Engadiner Post.* St. Moritz, 1917.

Ruck, Erwin. *Schweizerisches Staatsrecht.* Zürich, 1957.

Rufer, Alfred. *Das Ende des Freistaates der Drei Bünde.* Chur, 1965.

————. *Der Freistaat der III Bünde und die Frage des Veltlins.* 2 Vols. Basel, 1916.

————. "Wie der Bundespräsident im Gotteshausbund gewählt wurde." *Bündner Monatsblatt.* September-October 1930.

Salis, J. R. von. *Giuseppe Motta.* Zürich, 1941.

Salis-Seewis, Johann Gaudenz von. *Gesammelte Gedichte.* Chur, 1964.

*Der Sammler: Eine gemeinnützige Wochenschrift für Bündten.* 1779-1784.

Sauser-Hall, Georges. *Guide politique suisse.* Lausanne, 1956.

Saxer, Arnold. *Die soziale Sicherheit in der Schweiz.* 2d ed. Bern, 1967.

Schmid-Ammann, Paul. *Die Wahrheit über den Generalstreik von 1918.* Zürich, 1968.

Schreiber, P. *Die Entwicklung der Volksrechte in Graubünden.* Chur, 1921.

Schwarz, Robert. "Die Gerichtsorganisation des Kantons Graubünden von 1803 bis zur Gegenwart." *77. Jahresbericht der Historisch-Antiquarischen Gesellschaft von Graubünden.* 1947. "Die Schweiz: Vorbild von Gestern." *Der Spiegel.* August 2, 1971.

Schweizerischer Bund für Naturschutz. *Nationalpark oder Internationales Spölkraftwerk: Stimmen zur Erhaltung des Schweizerischen Nationalparkes im Unterengadin.* N.p., n.d.

Siegfried, André. *Die Schweiz: Eine Verwirklichung der Demokratie.* Zürich, 1949.

289

Spitteler, Carl. "Unser Schweizer Standpunkt." *Neue Zürcher Zeitung.* December 16-17, 1916.

Sprecher, Ferdinand. "Der letzte Hexenprozess in Graubünden." *Bündner Monatsblatt.* September 1936.

Sprecher, G. *Die Bündner Gemeinde.* Chur, 1942.

Sprecher, Johannes A. von. *Geschichte der Republik der Drei Bünde.* 2 Vols. Chur, 1872.

———. *Kulturgeschichte der Drei Bünde.* New Edition by Rudolf Jenny. Chur, 1951.

———. "Das Strafgericht und die Landesreform von 1684." *Jahresbericht der Historisch-Antiquarischen Gesellschaft von Graubünden.* 1880.

———. "Über die bündnerischen Portenrechte." *Bündner Monatsblatt.* October-December 1898.

———. "Die Verwaltung der Unterthanenlande Bünden im 18. Jahrhundert." *Bündner Monatsblatt.* December 1860.

———. "Zustand der Bevölkerung des Veltlins zur Zeit der bündnerischen Herrschaft." *Bündner Monatsblatt.* January-March 1860.

Staub, Hans O. *Dossier Schweiz: Massenmedien.* Zürich, 1971.

Steiner, Jürg. "Die Beteilung an vier eidgenössischen Urengängen." *Neue Zürcher Zeitung.* February 11, 1965.

Steiner, Robert. *Der Kanton Rätien zur Zeit der helvetischen Verwaltungskammer.* Zürich, 1936.

Steinmann, Ernst. *Geschichte des schweizerischen Freisinns.* Bern, 1955.

Switzerland. *Eidgenössische Volkszählung: 1960.* Bern, 1964.

———. *Eidgenössische Volkszählung: 1970.* Bern, 1973.

———. *Schweizerische Parteiprogramme.* Bern, 1969.

———. *Staatskalender der schweizerischen Eidgenossenschaft.* Bern, Annually.

———. *Statistisches Jahrbuch der Schweiz.* Bern, Annually.

Tobler, Jürg. *Dossier Schweiz: Demokratie—Testfall: 7. Juni 1970.* Zürich, 1971.

Töndury, Gian A. *Studie zur Volkswirtschaft Graubündens.* Samedan, 1946.

Tschäni, Hans. *Profil der Schweiz.* Zürich, 1969.

Tuor, Peter. *Die Freien von Laax: Ein Beitrag zur Verfassungs- und Standesgeschichte.* Chur, 1903.

Valer, M. "Die Beziehung Graubündens zur alten Eidgenossenschaft," in Fritz Jecklin, et al. *Bündnergeschichte in Elf Vorträgen.* Chur, 1902.

Von ein geborenen Graubündner. *Die Heutigen Zustände in Graubünden.* Chur, 1838.

Vulpius, Jakob Anton. *Historia Raetica.* In Conradin von Moor, ed. *Archiv für die Geschichte der Republik Graubünden.* Vol. 7. Chur, 1866.

Wagner, R., and von Salis, I. *Rechtsquellen des Kantons Graubündens.* Basel, 1887.

Weilenmann, Hermann. *Pax Helvetica: oder Die Demokratie der kleinen Gruppen.* Zürich, 1951.

——. *Die vielsprachige Schweiz.* Leipzig, 1925.

Weiss, Richard. *Das Alpwesen Graubündens.* Zürich, 1941.

——. *Volkskunde der Schweiz.* Zürich, 1946.

Werli, Fritz. *Zur Frage der Markgenossenschaften.* Vol. 3 of *Studien zur mittelalterlichen Verfassungsgeschichte.* Zürich, 1961.

Wieland, Otto. *Die Wasserrechtsverleihung im Kanton Graubünden.* Chur, 1941.

"Wun und Wied." *Bündner Monatsblatt.* December 1901.

Zschokke, Heinrich. *Die drei ewigen Bünde.* Zürich, 1798.

——. *Freie Bündner, verlasst die braven Schweizer nicht!* Chur, 1789.

——. *Geschichte des Freistaates der drei Bünde.* Zurich, 1817.

——. *Notwendiger und letzer Zuruf an biedere nachdenkende Vaterlandsfreunde.* Chur, 1789.

——. *Selbstschau.* N.p., 1842.

——. *Soll Bünden sich an die Vereinte Schweiz schliessen?* Chur, 1789.

"Zwei Deportierten-Lieder." *Bündner Monatsblatt.* September 1859.

# Index

293

**Library of Congress Cataloging in Publication Data**

Barber, Benjamin R        1939-
   The death of communal liberty.

   Bibliography: p.
   1. Grisons—History.   I. Title.
DQ496.B37        309.1'494'7        72-14018
ISBN 0-691-07554-9